TROLL HUNTING

Published in 2019 by Hardie Grant Books,
an imprint of Hardie Grant Publishing

Hardie Grant Books (Melbourne)
Building 1, 658 Church Street
Richmond, Victoria 3121

Hardie Grant Books (London)
5th & 6th Floors
52–54 Southwark StreetLondon SE1 1UN

hardiegrantbooks.com

 A catalogue record for this
book is available from the
National Library of Australia

Troll Hunting
ISBN 978 1 74379 435 7

10 9 8 7 6 5 4 3 2 1

Supported by

Cover design by Laura Thomas
Typeset in 11/15 pt Minion Pro by Cannon Typesetting
Cover image courtesy of Shutterstock
Printed by McPherson's Printing Group, Maryborough, Victoria

 The paper this book is printed on is certified against the
Forest Stewardship Council® Standards. FSC® promotes
environmentally responsible, socially beneficial and
economically viable management of the world's forests.

Ginger Gorman

TROLL HUNTING

Inside the world
of online hate and
its human fallout

Hardie Grant

BOOKS

For my father, Brian,
who taught me to love words.

Hell is empty, and all the devils are here.
William Shakespeare,
The Tempest, Act 1, Scene 2

THIS IS A work of nonfiction, researched and documented to the best of my ability. There were significant security risks in writing this book. I sought expert advice and wrote according to it. Therefore, some of the trolling syndicates mentioned within these pages have been given pseudonyms or go unnamed. Likewise, some of the trolls themselves are discussed only with a pseudonym.

A few of the trolls who spoke to me behind the scenes are not named at all and others are composites or have been segmented. Some readers may be critical of the decision to provide anonymity for people who are hurting others so much. However, sometimes access to information comes at a cost – and, all things being equal, the trolls gave me great access.

By the same token, some predator-troll victims are in physical danger. This is especially true where domestic violence is involved. In those cases, names and other identifying details may have been altered but the facts of the stories are unchanged. I have worked hard to quote all interviewees verbatim, but for the sake of readability have corrected some spelling errors and syntax. When I'm messaging with trolls in the United States, I use Australian spelling and they use American spelling. For authenticity, I've left this as is.

This is a book about the internet and how it bleeds into real life. When quoting links and screenshots, I've aimed for accuracy. However, the internet is not a static beast. Some posts have changed or disappeared in the time since I started writing.

There's something else. Trolls frequently use language that is designed to shock. It can be deeply offensive, as can their actions. This book invites you to look harder and think harder. If words were neutral, people wouldn't use them like this. Words are a weapon – and a gateway to much greater harm.

– Ginger

Contents

Preface

12 December 2017

As a compulsive social media checker, I can't help it: I click on the Twitter notification straight away. Even after all this time, the sight of his name makes my skin prickle. This is 'Mark', the vicious and committed internet troll. He's a member of an international online syndicate that tries to harm people and wreck their lives. They document all their exploits on their website. We've been in contact for a couple of years now.

He'll go quiet for a while and then suddenly there he is again, trying to reel me in. This time he's sent me a link to a CNN story.[1] It's about William Atchison, a 21-year-old man who shot and killed two teenagers – Casey Jordan Marquez and Francisco Fernandez – in a New Mexico school a few days earlier. Atchison died at the scene from a self-inflicted gunshot wound.

'One of my admins was the shooter,' Mark writes. He's involved in running a trolling-related wiki and so, apparently, was Atchison.

A familiar, creeping anxiety sits low in my stomach. According to Mark himself, trolls lie and their game is to hurt you. Staying calm is the only tool I've got; predator trolls like Mark can sense your fear.

With artificial steadiness, I reply, 'Prove it.'

He sends me another link. It contains reams of information about the shooter and his miserable online life. It's encyclopaedic: photos of Atchison as an adult and also as a sweet-faced, freckled kid. In one photo he's with a black-and-white cat and in another he's with a curly haired spaniel. The pet images are dated July 2008. Atchison would have been twelve years old. He liked animals and somehow this makes the slaughter harder to believe.

The link includes the shooter's birthdate, email addresses, his dozens of online usernames and profiles, his IP address and the time and date he last logged on to this forum. His exact location – latitude and longitude – are listed. There are links to his bigoted, hopeless rants and endless 'jokes' and memes about the 1999 Columbine High School massacre.

I'm scanning the links and threads, looking for something. I'm not sure what until I find it; a sketch of his world:

How am I supposed to function in this world? Wherever I go, I see degeneracy. Pointless materialism, hedonism, sexual decay, dirty niggers who do nothing but slowly break down this society etc. it's fucking everywhere. No way to escape it, 99% of people are part of it and whatever I do I am confronted with the death of the West. Go to the store to buy groceries in peace? Nope here's a group of LGBT liberal filth in line with you. And there's a nigger family with 10 kids over there. And a Finn too, but he's overweight as fuck and he's buying alcohol and shit junk food. Fucking fantastic.

I used to think that this was a phase and we'd get over it but I have now come to realise that I was born into a literal dystopia.

I'm fighting off a suffocating sadness. How did this kid come to be so filled with hate? Why didn't anyone help him before he became a killer?

Clicking and scrolling. Clicking and scrolling. Then I'm staring at a photo of one of the victims. Casey Jordan Marquez's floral skirt has caught the wind and she's smiling. She's so young. In his photo, Francisco Fernandez's hands are clasped together and he's smiling too – as if he knows something you don't.[2]

These kids are in the morgue now. Their parents may well be visiting their bodies as Mark and I correspond.

The police seemed unaware of Atchison's plans. Sheriff Ken Christensen from the New Mexico State Police said, 'It's just a shame that he [Atchison] wasn't on our radar. I don't think he had as much as a traffic ticket or anything else here locally … I don't think that we know so far that anyone else knew of his intentions.'[3]

But Mark and his trolling buddies knew. One of the trolls on the forum where Atchison's details are posted writes: 'Maybe we should have actually said something instead of laughing at him about it for years lol.'

The 'laugh out loud' is deftly placed, right at the end of the sentence so that any regret is negated: *No, we shouldn't have done anything, except what we did do – nothing.* The 'lol' means this is for laughs. Or 'lulz', as the trolls like to say.

Another person on the forum writes, 'Rest in piss', and a third poster describes Atchison as 'an hero'. For the unanointed, 'an hero' in trolling culture is anyone who dies by suicide. It sometimes comes with the added implication that the person was somehow incompetent.[4]

In some detail, Mark describes Atchison's obsession with mass shootings. 'His entire life revolved around talking about the Columbine school shooting,' he explains. Then, a few moments later: 'I just saw what he was posting and talking about and knew it was only a matter of time.'

'You wouldn't report that to the police?' I ask, knowing he'd never report something like this.

Predictably, he replies, 'I'm not going to report something like that because it doesn't bother me but if someone had asked me I would have told them that he was a threat.'

The FBI had interviewed Atchison, along with members of his family, in March 2016 after he made some alarming comments on a gaming forum about mass shootings. But as the would-be killer hadn't yet committed a crime, they were obliged to let him go.

During a press conference with New Mexico police, FBI agent Terry Wade recalled: 'We did conduct an interview with him at his home and we talked to him extensively. He was cooperative. At that time he didn't have any guns … he told us that he enjoyed trolling on the internet …'

At this point in our conversation Mark senses an opportunity. 'Tbh [to be honest] I'm disappointed he aimed so high and for so long but only managed 2 [victims].'

Two years earlier, when Mark and I first came into contact, a comment like this would have enraged me to the point of lashing out. He knows this much about me, but perhaps doesn't realise I've changed since then. He's still trying. Still pushing to get a rise. I get up from my study chair and look around, grudgingly catching my reflection in the mirrored cupboard doors. It's just me. An unshowered, slightly overweight woman wearing a bad headband and rocketing headlong into middle age.

My home suddenly seems incredibly suburban. It's a typical Australian dwelling, sitting on a quarter-acre block – a long way from New Mexico and an even longer way from the world Mark inhabits. There are piles of unsorted washing on the sofa and the dishwasher needs stacking. Any minute my husband and two kids will be home for dinner. They'll be tired and hungry. We'll eat, talk about the day and read bedtime stories. Laughably run of the mill.

I turn back and stare at my computer's black screensaver. I consider the darkness encroaching on my family's small universe. *How did I get here?*

The feeble, rhetorical question dissipates as quickly as it forms. The truth is, I know every brick on the road that led me to the trolls.

Part 1

TROLLS

1

The paedophiles, the trolls and the journalist

I NEVER SET OUT to become a cyberhate expert. What happened was so unlikely, and the twists in the story so strange and horrifying, that the narrative is hard to tell, and just as hard to follow. But, as I've since learned, trolling events are like this. The tentacles are long and deep and tangled.

My tiny second daughter was born on a boiling day in the middle of January in 2013. In the following months of endless patting, rocking and all-night feeding that arrive with a precious newborn, I became the subject of an orchestrated online hate campaign.

Three years earlier, back in 2010, I had been ABC Local Radio's Drive presenter in Far North Queensland, based in Cairns. By June of that year I was also heavily pregnant. While waiting for the birth of my daughter, I thought about how easy life was for me. How I had freedoms – like getting married, having a child and generally getting on with life. Sure, life had thrown me a few curve balls. But I'd never been routinely discriminated against. Not like the people I knew who were LGBTIQ+.

The research I read showed that if you were gay, bisexual or transgender, you were more likely to experience all sorts of disadvantages, including depression, violence, homelessness, drug addiction and suicidal thoughts.[1] This seemed to me an important, untold story. So I wrote an open letter to Far North Queensland's gay, lesbian, bisexual and transgender community asking for people to come forward with their stories. The response was powerful, humbling and sometimes shocking.

Mais described being the subject of a violent assault because of his gender identity. The result was a crack to his skull and severe, ongoing pain. Trish was a young mother with three children who was trapped; she loved her husband and children but was really a lesbian. There didn't seem to be a way out. It was hard not to be moved by the pain in these stories.

As part of the interviews I compiled for this project, I found myself on the doorstep of a lovely home at Kewarra Beach, in the northern suburbs of Cairns. I can remember so clearly pulling up outside. It was a modern-style home, painted off-white, with a manicured garden. A child's bike was lying outside. At the door I was met warmly by Peter Truong and Mark Newton.

Newton, an American by birth, was tall and pale with blazing blue eyes, a strong accent and receding sandy hair. Truong, a Vietnamese Australian, had dark hair and eyes and a frame more compact than his partner's. His teeth protruded when he smiled, seeming to take up more space than they ought to.

Newton and Truong introduced me to their gorgeous five-year-old son. His name was written in wooden letters on the wall and his toys were neatly stacked away. He was told to go off and watch a DVD while I sat between his two dads on the couch and set up my audio recorder.

The two men then proceeded to tell me in great detail about how they had longed to become fathers and, after a difficult journey, ended up having their son via a surrogate mother in Russia. Newton was the biological dad.

At length, the men explained to me how hard it was to get their son into Australia. They told me Australian customs quizzed them for hours at the airport. At a later date, police checked whether the couple had suitable equipment to raise a child: a bed, clothes and bottles.

At this point in the interview I was compelled to ask, 'Do you think there was a suspicion that this must be something dodgy? There must be some paedophilic thing going on here?'

Newton replied, 'Absolutely. Absolutely. I'm sure that was completely the concern.' Both Newton and Truong smiled at the absurdity of the idea they might somehow be suspect. 'We're a family just like any other family.'

After the formal interview we went outside with their son. Like any young child, he was shy at first. After a while he opened up. He smiled and chatted and urged me to come and see his baby chickens. This is the moment that plays over and over in my mind like a home movie: the four of us are in the yard, the chicks cheeping loudly and running loose.

We chat about the chicks. Truong and the boy are trying to catch a couple of them, with some trouble. Truong asks his son if he's fed the chicks today. The boy says no. Truong tells him they would surely be very hungry by now. I ask the boy if the particular chicken he has managed to catch has a name. He replies that he hasn't figured out names yet but he might call this one 'Fasty' – presumably because it is hard to catch. Newton agrees that this chick is indeed fast.

In retrospect, the conversation was remarkable because of its ordinariness.

I snap several pictures of the boy holding a baby chick up under his chin. Peter is holding a fluffy chick too. The boy stands between his two fathers. All three of them are beaming.

At the time I thought this photo was so sweet; it featured on the front page of my gender project's web page on the ABC. Now it is the photo news organisations all over the world have published and republished, with the boy's face blurred to protect his identity. This is the image that reminds me that one single day – one decision – can leave your life irrevocably changed.

In February 2012 I learned that Mark Newton and Peter Truong were being investigated by the United States Postal Inspection Service and the Queensland Police as possible members of an international paedophile ring. The United States Postal Inspection Service is like the FBI, but they investigate crimes committed by post.

I knew straight away there must have been serious reasons to suspect these two men. Why would international policing agencies be cooperating on a case like this unless they had strong evidence?

I hoped it wasn't true but suspected it was. Dread encased me.

On Friday, 28 June 2013, Mark Newton was sentenced to forty years in prison in a US court after pleading guilty to conspiring to sexually exploit a child, and for conspiring to possess child pornography. Peter Truong also pleaded guilty for his crimes and was sentenced to thirty years' jail. (Prosecutors claimed their 'son' was actually purchased from his Russian mother for US$8000 and was not biologically related to either of them.)

'Being a father was an honour and a privilege that amounted to the best six years of my life,' Newton reportedly told the court minutes before his sentence was announced.[2]

I felt dizzy with anger. A pure rage that made my face burn. The word 'privilege' lodged itself in my brain as if it had talons. I momentarily wished to stand before Newton and Truong – these men who'd welcomed me so thoroughly into their farce of a home – to say:

> Being a parent is one of the most profound privileges that exists. Your job is to love that child and keep him or her safe. Instead, you systematically perpetrated heinous sex crimes against your child since he was a baby. It is sickening and it is unforgivable. What will become of your child after what you have done? Did you think about that?

You cannot overestimate the horror of the crimes. Media reports stated that the child, now known as Boy1, was abused from when he was just two weeks old. He was also shared around with numerous other paedophiles in other countries while the family was on 'holiday'.

In an email exchange, Detective Inspector Jon Rouse, from Queensland Police's Taskforce Argos, told me: 'Of the thousands of child exploitation cases I've been involved in, this will remain as one of the most horrendous breaches of a child's trust by persons charged with their care and safe upbringing.'

Within seventy-two hours of Mark Newton being sentenced, I started to get scores of hateful tweets, mostly from people in the United States calling themselves conservatives. They were responding to the article I'd written two years earlier, which was still online.

My trolls insisted I should have known what was going on behind closed doors. They wanted me shamed.

> Ginger Gorman (@freshchilli) sang praises of gay men who paid surrogate to birth boy to be used for sex. SHAME HER!

> So, @freshchilli: When are you and your employers going to own up to the horrible thing you have done?

> @freshchilli pedophile collaborator

> @freshchilli You need to add pedophile enabler to your twitter bio. #Justsayin

> @freshchilli maybe she would've picked up on it if she wasn't so blindly driven by her own biases and prejudices.

Many of the tweets conflated the gay 'lifestyle' with paedophilia. Griffith University's Professor Stephen Smallbone, who has been working on child sex abuse prevention for twenty-five years, believes such a conflation is inaccurate: 'There is a lot of variation among offenders, so it's hard to produce a specific reliable figure. But I think it would be reasonable to argue that the proportion of 'homosexual' abusers could be as low as 10 per cent. The terms homosexual (or gay) and heterosexual are actually very problematic when applied to child abuse. A small proportion of abusers will have a strictly exclusive sexual preference for – or experiences with – children. For the rest, the gender of their adult partners may be different from the gender of a child they abuse. Sexual orientation is in a sense irrelevant in sexual abuse. Whether you like men or women, are gay, straight or whatever, it is illegal to have sexual contact with children. The problem is about age and maturity, and about breaking the law, not gender or sexual orientation.'

Other trolls claimed the ABC pulled the article from their website to 'cover up what they did'. The real reason was simply compassion; Queensland Police requested the ABC take the article offline to protect Boy1's identity and the broadcaster immediately complied.

One of the trolls, despite purportedly caring about Boy1's lifetime of suffering and abuse, had no qualms about publicising this tiny victim's name and photograph. Likewise, the right-wing blogger Robert Stacy McCain was happy to link to a post naming the child and sharing it with his millions of readers. Boy1 became a pawn in the game of moral righteousness.

To this day, my grief for Boy1 is deep and abiding. I think about him often and wonder how his life will turn out. US authorities are understandably cagey about what has happened to him since his 'dads' were arrested. I have simply been told he's safe and has ongoing access to specialist psychological help.

Sometimes I imagine talking or writing to Boy1. Although I'm not religious, it's almost like prayer. That's the only way I can describe it. A hope. A wish. A message, which I have no way to send him.

Dear Boy1, you've become a number. Since your case ended up in court, I'm not allowed to identify you. But in my head I say your name. I can see your face, clear as day. I see your sweet, shining eyes and your cheeky smile. Your white teeth. I can even hear your little voice, imploring me to come and see your baby chickens. If I knew then what I know now, I would have done anything to stop the heinous crimes being perpetrated against you. I would have done anything to end your misery. But I didn't know. I had no idea. None of us did. I'm so sorry. Please, somehow, may you be one of the few child abuse victims who make it through and find a path to recovery.

I'm connected to him because of what happened. And then disconnected too, because I'll likely never know the rest of his story. What I can tell you is the rest of my story.

Late one night not long after the trolling began, I read a tweet that said: 'Your life is over.'[3]

My husband Don and I quickly realised that location services were turned on for my Twitter feed and you could just about pinpoint our house on Google Maps. That night we both lay awake in bed wondering if our children were in danger.

Six days after Newton was sentenced in 2013 came the second frightening moment. Don found a photo of our family on the fascist social network Iron March. The now-defunct website carried the slogan 'Gas the kikes' on its homepage.

In the photo posted on Iron March I was pregnant with our second child, and my older daughter, who was two at the time, was sitting on my husband's shoulders. It's a strange feeling to see that photo, taken with love for our family Christmas card, in such a hateful location. Had I, through the course of my work, put my family at risk?

One commenter called me a 'bitch'. 'Look at the fucking beak on it,' another poster wrote.

My mother's parents were Jews who fled the Holocaust. Some of our family members *were* gassed at Auschwitz. Yet despite the clear threat, there was no way to know if these people meant actual harm. We just had to sit and wait.

2

WTF is trolling?

O VER TIME, THINGS look different. After two years the fear
subsided enough for professional curiosity to take hold. Who
were trolls? What did they want? My original aim seemed
straightforward. I sought to shine a light under the dark bridges of the
internet, into its crevices.

Plenty of people speculate about trolls and their motivations. But
I wanted to know definitively. By 2015, I wanted to go directly to the
source and write about what I found.

Australians Mark and Craig were the first two trolls I met in person;
it's hard to imagine two more different people. We'll return to these two
soon, but what struck me about them is that neither of them consider
'trolling' to be the same thing; nor do they even see the other as a
'genuine' troll. Some trolls, like Craig, see trolling as having a political
objective. Others, like Mark, see it as a way of creating their own
entertainment on the internet.

'Having morals in general is being soft,' Mark says. 'I find that
humiliating people is fun but hurting them is hilarious.'

Another troll, who uses the handle Meepsheep and is well known in
his community, explains: 'There's a lot of division in types of trolls.'

Meepsheep makes distinctions between trolls who use the no-
frills, text-based messaging system 'internet relay chat' (IRC) and

others who are gamers or just stick to social media. He sees this latter category of trolls as 'the most sadistic'. According to Meepsheep, trolls who do things such as creating multiple social media accounts 'just to bully the families of dead kids' are using 'social media as an outlet for specific frustrations'. Social media trolls, he says, also 'tend to be less technically competent'.

When I ask Meepsheep what trolling is, he ponders this for a moment and says, 'I guess I just mean finding humour in pranks resulting in confusion.' Then he adds, 'Part of it, I think, is rebelling against social standards.' Finally, he says, 'I'll have to think of a better definition and get back to you.'

Perhaps the world's most well-known troll, weev, sees it differently still.

In a long and ranty interview with me in January 2018, weev questions the intelligence of people who aren't white – and then claims this view is based on 'verified scientific facts'.

I say: 'weev, you call yourself a troll and I've met a lot of trolls, so I know that they say stuff that isn't true, to wind you up.'

'Trolling is not about saying stuff to rile people up,' he replies. 'Trolling is about using rhetoric combatively and I am preparing my people for a war, a physical war … Very classic pogroms. We're going to have blood in the streets and that sort of thing.'

weev is on the record as saying the Greek philosopher Socrates is one of his favourite trolls.[1] This is perhaps unsurprising given trolls tend to view Socrates as 'a famous IRL [in real life] troll of pre-internets Greece credited with inventing the first recorded trolling technique and otherwise laying the foundation of the science of lulz'.[2]

Presumably, the 'science of lulz' refers to the Socratic method. A resource from the University of Chicago's Faculty of Law describes the long-dead philosopher's technique like this:

Socrates engaged in questioning of his students in an unending search for truth. He sought to get to the foundations of his students' and colleagues' views by asking continual questions until a contradiction was exposed, thus proving the fallacy of the initial assumption.

This became known as the Socratic Method, and may be Socrates' most enduring contribution to philosophy.

Whether or not weev actually adheres to this method is questionable. For now though, let's just agree that the trolls can't agree on what trolling actually is.

I check the online Oxford Dictionary. It defines a troll as 'A person who makes a deliberately offensive or provocative online post'.[3] This is the dictionary's second meaning of the word 'troll'. The first – as you might expect – is a reference to seventeenth-century Old Norse, Swedish and Danish languages.

The Scandinavian folklore connection is one many of us would be familiar with from childhood fairytales, such as *Three Billy Goats Gruff*. This particular fable conveys the idea of an argumentative, antisocial but fairly harmless creature who hides under bridges and makes life hard for travellers. But this analogy doesn't ring true: internet trolls are not only real but they also hurt people. Often, they aren't even hiding. As William Atchison's actions plainly show, it's dangerous to fool yourself into believing the online world is 'virtual' and the person behind the keyboard can't inflict real-life harm.

In her book *This Is Why We Can't Have Nice Things*, US academic Whitney Phillips suggests the etymology of online trolling might also come from fishing. '[T]rolling in that sense involves stringing lines of bait behind a fishing boat.' If you see trolls as 'mean spirited or abusive', Phillips writes, you'll likely favour the Scandinavian definition. If, on the other hand, you are sympathetic or ambivalent to trolling, you'll choose the fishing definition.[4]

Even the Wikipedia entry on internet trolling is quick to point out the term is subjective.[5] Moving out into the wide world, the word 'troll' is now so broad that it can be used to refer to anyone who is disruptive in any circumstance – online or offline.

In a rather inane column in the *Daily Telegraph* about the reality TV show *Married at First Sight*, writer Miranda Devine complains about producers pairing up a seemingly unsuited couple: 'Now in its fifth season, it's just trolling.'[6]

In another article, penned by Fairfax journalist Jacqueline Maley, the headline 'It's starting to feel like women are being trolled' leads into an article that informs us, 'If you're a woman, it's starting to look as though 2016 might be actually just one giant bloopers reel, a series of insults so outrageous that they must have been staged as part of an out-takes special for a new series of *Candid Camera*.'[7]

Neither of these articles have anything to do with internet trolling. Here, the word 'troll' is used loosely to refer to a deliberate type of needling.

As a mundane example from my own life, my seven-year-old daughter, Elsa, loves ice cream. (What kid doesn't?) Recently, I bought a new brand. After taking one mouthful from her bowl, Elsa declared, 'I don't like this ice cream.'

Almost in unison, my husband and I chimed back, 'That's okay. We'll never buy ice cream again.'

Don turned to me and smiled. 'We're trolling her.'

Jumping from my kitchen table to the White House, current US President Donald Trump has been labelled a troll by everyone from the *Washington Post* to comedian Dave Chappelle. After Trump fired off a pair of sexist and demeaning tweets attacking a female TV host in 2017, *New Yorker* writer John Cassidy went a step further, describing the president as 'the troll-in-chief'. In his analysis of Trump's erratic and furious behaviour on social media, the journalist notes, 'Trump's default state of mind now is one of thinly controlled rage at the news media.'[8] Self-identified trolls expressed very similar sentiments to me; they admired Trump as an anti-politician who was prepared to take on the establishment with fire. To them, his lies were immaterial.

In stark contrast to Trump's online attacks, and perhaps what many would consider the classic example of trolling, is the popular internet prank known as the 'rickroll'. An oblivious internet user clicks on a link, believing it to be content relevant to them – a scientific article or a document about fiscal policy, say. The hyperlink, it turns out, leads instead to the music video of Rick Astley's 1987 song 'Never Gonna Give You Up'.

At one point it seemed everyone had been rickrolled in one way or another. Even the White House was guilty of using the prank.

Back in 2011 a Twitter user called David Wiggs complained, 'This WH [White House] correspondence briefing isn't nearly as entertaining as yesterday's.'

'Sorry to hear that,' the official Twitter account of Obama's White House shot back, minutes later. 'Fiscal policy is important, but can be dry sometimes. Here's something more fun.' What followed was a link to 'Never Gonna Give You Up'.

Sure, we can high-five the White House for rickrolling millions of its followers, but there's a bigger question. Is this trolling? Is the ice cream comment trolling? The examples in the news articles?

And if all these unrelated activities *do* constitute trolling, what the hell do we call the activities Mark and his cronies get up to? Rickrolling and winding your kid up about ice cream seem to be altogether different from a president ranting and raving in incoherent tweets and self-identified trolls setting out to incite real-life harm against others.

A clue to untangling this bowl of spaghetti may lie in looking at how trolling, and our use of the word, has changed.

'In the late 1980s, Internet users adopted the word "troll" to denote someone who intentionally disrupts online communities,' Mattathias Schwartz writes in the *New York Times*. 'Early trolling was relatively innocuous.'[9]

Zoë Quinn expands on this point in her enlightening book *Crash Override* – and wraps up our problem in a nutshell:

> Trolling is an activity as old as the Internet itself, though the definition has been warped to apply to everything from someone just being a jackass for laughs – starting an argument with an insincere, asinine, or ridiculous statement to see who will take the bait – to outright hate speech and serious threats.[10]

Quinn was the developer at the centre of the Gamergate controversy, starting in 2014. At its heart, Gamergate was a misogynistic witch hunt, triggered by discomfort at women taking up space in the traditionally male gaming world. Quinn – who uses the Twitter handle Unburnt Witch – was the lynch mob's chief target, thanks to a former boyfriend's accusations of infidelity, among other things. Over a couple of years, an anonymous online mob waged a coordinated and ongoing harassment campaign against Quinn and a number of other women. The campaign, mostly organised via platforms like IRC, Reddit and 4chan, included rape and death threats, hacking into Quinn's online accounts, and doxing. (Sometimes this is also spelled 'doxxing', and it involves publishing personal details online – such as a person's home address, place of work, phone number, or their kid's school.)

It's hard to adequately describe how extreme the abuse was (and is, because it continues to this day). According to Quinn, Gamergate had an enormous impact on her ability to live a normal life; she now suffers from PTSD and has difficulty working at times. It's crucial to point out that many trolls disagree that the controversy had anything to do with online harassment and instead insist, just as Mark does, that 'Gamergate was about people using personal opinions and relationships to manipulate a $100 billion industry'. (Did I mention this is a post-truth era we live in?)

Setting aside the extreme nature of Quinn's experiences for a moment, do we call this online abuse? Perhaps technology-enabled abuse. Or stalking, harassment, cyberhate, cyberbullying, cyber violence, image-based abuse, revenge porn or even … trolling? Amid all these words, it seems we still don't have the language we need. Or perhaps it's more accurate to say we don't have a common understanding of what these words mean, despite using them on a daily basis in public and private conversations. This scrambled mess stops us, as a community, from seriously addressing the issue of cyberhate.

Imagine a person, who is receiving credible threats of violence against her, contacting the police and using the word 'troll'. Presumably because online harassment is still widely viewed as a hurtful but fairly harmless verbal activity, this person complaining will likely be dismissed by law enforcement and told, 'Stay off the internet, love.' It's happened to me, and maybe to you, too. Trolling victims are often blamed for their abuse, as Danielle Keats Citron, Professor of Law at the University of Maryland, points out. 'Victims could go offline but it would make their lives worse,' she writes, referring to all the lost opportunities and social connections cyberhate targets forgo when they are forced offline.[11]

A rickroll is neither here nor there. But becoming so unsafe you flee your home and, after years of abuse, end up medicated for PTSD, as Zoë Quinn did, is a different matter altogether. It's time we mapped out the gamut of trolling and understood it as a spectrum of behaviours, with mild pranks at one end and hate crimes at the other. This is why I've started referring to trolls who set out to do real-life harm as 'predator trolls'.

We're at a pivotal moment in the conversation about cyberhate. When I first tried to pitch stories to editors about trolling and social media self-defence, towards the end of 2014, I was often met with a long pause followed by: 'Sorry, *what* is it?'

That's no longer the case. Victims are raising their voices. Editors are saying yes to stories about trolling and the carnage it creates. I'm increasingly asked to speak in public about cyberhate and, in particular, online misogyny. Although it's never easy to tell the story of being a cyberhate target myself, or to share the stories of other victims in front of a crowd, I'm heartened that the conversation is changing. Alongside public discourse, media coverage about trolling and cyberhate is increasing in frequency, complexity and prominence. On occasion – as with the tragic death by suicide of fourteen-year-old Amy 'Dolly' Everett in 2018 – the issue hits the front page and stays there, triggering national soul-searching.

Make no mistake. The cost of cyberhate is not just 'hurt feelings', as trolls love to claim. Predator trolls are wrecking lives and can cause people to harm themselves and lose their jobs. Their behaviour can even contribute to a target's decision to suicide. They may damage a person's reputation so the victim becomes unemployable. As academic Dr Emma Jane notes, it's a type of 'economic vandalism' and, in cases where a person is online for their work, may represent a new form of workplace harassment.[12] The harms are both physical and psychological. They are deliberate, too.

Before writing this book, I'd been labelled a cyberhate expert by the media, and I started using this descriptor too. That was a mistake. Even a year ago, I didn't know what I didn't know. It's only through building strange and enduring relationships with predator trolls – and getting in so deep I sometimes felt unable to get out – that I started to piece together a picture. Predator trolls aren't usually who you expect. They don't necessarily think or feel what you expect. They are often better educated than you expect. They aren't necessarily motivated by what you expect. And yet the damage they do is beyond imagination.

3

Meet the trolls

ONCE I WENT looking, it wasn't very hard to find vicious internet trolls. I did what any decent journalist does – reached out to my network on social media. Within a few days, I had names, email addresses and phone numbers of guys to interview. (Yes, they were all men.)

To begin with, Mark seemed unremarkable in the extreme. He had a full-time job and a girlfriend. And if you happened to pass him on the street or in the supermarket, nothing would grab your attention. You likely wouldn't recall his bad dress sense, short brown hair, pale skin or slightly awkward manner. Outwardly, there was nothing to suggest he was a highly organised, and dangerous, troll.

The first time I hit the button on my digital recorder back in 2015, after he agreed to an interview, naivety reigned. I wasn't even afraid. Before long, though, a deep unease washed over me. Mark was – and is – far more of a threat than I'd imagined a troll could possibly be.

Right from the start Mark was explicit in his desire to hurt other people. He got enjoyment from it and was vicious, organised and committed to this end. During that first interview, he revealed himself to be a member of a powerful international trolling syndicate. Members of the group participate in orchestrated online hate campaigns. They try to get people fired. They take part in swatting – a practice where a hoax call is made in order to trick armed emergency services personnel into attending a particular address. (Deaths and injuries have been recorded as a result of swatting. Family pets are sometimes killed.)[1]

The syndicate also tries to incite vulnerable people to harm themselves. Mark openly admitted to targeting people with autism or mental illnesses. 'Some people should kill themselves because they're generally pieces of shit,' he said.[2]

He told me about trolling rape victims and the Facebook memorial pages of those who had died by suicide. He offered the example of a young girl who was killed by a train. He tried, successfully, to upset her loved ones by calling her a 'train hugger'.

'If it's a page of someone who's died, you're going to get an emotional reaction,' he said.

This apparent contradiction – that Mark understands the emotions of his victims yet feels no compassion for them – is borne out by research conducted by Natalie Sest and Evita March, scholars at Federation University in Victoria. A study published by the pair in 2017 found that trolls have cognitive empathy, but not affective empathy. This means they can predict and recognise 'the emotional suffering of their victims' yet do not actually care or feel guilty about the pain they cause. 'Thus, trolls appear to be master manipulators of both cyber-settings and their victims' emotions,' the researchers write.[3]

Mark made it clear that getting a reaction is key. He talked about it over and over again. He wanted people to feel unsafe online: 'Sometimes I just do it to get them to, like, quit the internet.'

Craig was a different kettle of fish. The first time we talked on the phone – more than three years ago now – he was unfailingly polite. He patiently answered all my questions: *What is doxing? What is swatting? What is Gamergate? What is 4chan?* By that stage, he'd been trolling for nearly a decade. He knew the lingo and cultural norms like the back of his hand. Perhaps these queries seemed ignorant to him. But if that was the case, he didn't let on. He wanted to help. To explain.

Just like Mark, he was young and white with a full-time job and a girlfriend. Previously, Craig told me, he'd also been a member of an international trolling syndicate. But, unlike Mark, he viewed himself as part of the far left and never trolled on the basis of gender. As a rule, his trolling was politically motivated.

'I don't take part in gender-based trolling such as rape or death threats against women but I know plenty of people that do,' Craig said in that first phone call. 'People take part in this kind of abuse because women threaten the dominant white-male paradigm in the online world.'

Even back then he was quick to make a distinction between 'legitimate trolling' and what he described as 'abuse in the guise of trolling'. 'I don't have time for … the violent, sexist, misogynist trolling, the trolling that forces women to leave their homes. The trolling that gets SWAT teams sent to people's houses, the trolling that leaks nude images of people online and ruins their careers and reputations. The thing I would like to ask those trolls is, "If you are so comfortable doing it, why aren't you doing it under your real name?"'

(For his part, Mark views Craig's style of trolling dimly: 'Being a communist doesn't make you a troll, it makes you a retard.')

After that first phone call, we met face to face in a grand old 1920s hotel with an endless garden. He smiled, shook my hand and looked me in the eye. Craig was hip and good-looking in a suit, with blue eyes and well-groomed facial stubble. Although he did troll people on the right, he often attacked people on the left he viewed as 'not far enough left'.

'Both sides have their fools,' he said, and in 2015 his favourite targets were public figures and so-called 'new atheists', like Richard Dawkins. This was despite Craig being an atheist himself. 'I just don't like this new form of atheism, this sort of hyper form of rationality,' he told me.

To trolls it's frequently – but not always – irrelevant whether they actually believe what they're saying. Marshall McLuhan's famous phrase 'the medium is the message' springs to mind. This facet of trolling behaviour makes me wonder if this is why so many US trolls I talk to support President Donald Trump, despite his making approximately 6.5 false or misleading claims per day.[4] To them, saying something untrue doesn't necessarily decrease your standing.

After leaving the trolling syndicate, Craig took to winding people up online alongside a loose gang of about ten other online friends. 'I really do enjoy going at public figures, especially [people] who you might term thought leaders: politicians, columnists, business people.

'One of the biggest things I draw out of trolling public figures is that they are just as dumb and stupid as the rest of us. There's nothing special about them,' he said.

The people who really irritated him were 'keyboard activists' or 'slacktivists'. 'All they do is post internet memes and images and engage in really soft political discourse. Their political commitment basically extends to what they can operate from their computer.' He continued, saying the centre left was 'easy to troll because they are incredibly earnest in their views'.[5]

'Is that me?' I asked.

'It probably is,' he said with a laugh.

#

There has been some research into the correlation of trolling with narcissism, the psychological category encompassing a grandiose sense of self and a desire to be the centre of attention, while having limited empathy for others. For narcissists, relationships are mainly superficial and exist only for personal gain.[6] As I quickly discovered, some trolls, like Mark, self-identify as narcissists. This may be why, without much trouble, Mark had agreed to that initial interview about the havoc he wreaks – why and how he hurts others.

Research from the University of British Columbia and the University of Manitoba has found that internet trolling correlates strongly with three of the four so-called 'dark' personality traits: psychopathy, Machiavellianism and sadism. Sadism – deriving pleasure from inflicting pain and humiliation on others –has the strongest link. Interestingly, however, the Canadian researchers found that 'narcissism, in contrast, was not correlated with trolling enjoyment'.[7]

Mark continually negates this last point. 'Have you ever read some of my stuff on the internet?' he boasts in another interview, conducted by phone, 'I'm one of the biggest narcissists on the planet.'

Meanwhile, Craig has confessed to being a sadist. 'I would actually own up to that. Yes. But I guess maybe this comes from a sense of self-righteousness that what I'm doing is good and right,' he said. 'I have no problem with upsetting racists, and homophobes and sexists.'

He then went a step further, conceding he enjoys 'inflicting that sort of suffering on someone who I think is a bad person'.[8]

When we first spoke, Mark spent up to fourteen hours a week trolling people. Two years later he tells me it's more like thirty hours a week. He claims he is a psychopath and that his psychopathic tendencies are getting worse as he gets older.

We might have a picture in our heads of the troll as a loner in his mum's basement, harassing others online. The truth, though, is that most of them operate in groups. They may be small, loose gangs – like the one Craig was involved in when we initially met – or highly organised syndicates such as the one Mark belongs to.

Australian National University criminologist Dr Clarke Jones is an expert in gang behaviour and radicalisation. He says while individuals may be 'very isolated' and 'not very strong … on their own', in a gang formation it's a different story. The support of the group 'empowers them because they're quite often quite weak characters otherwise'.

Weak or not, over time I come to view Mark as a spider web. I've flown into the trap, the sticky threads glued to my wings; I can't seem to extricate myself. Regardless of whether I want to stay in touch with Mark, he stays in touch with me. For a while there will be blissful silence. It might last a few weeks, or it might last months. Then a message from him will appear. When it does, a corresponding knot forms in my stomach. If I don't reply, he seems to become irritated and threatens to 'fuck up my life'. After two years of intermittent contact, I am only too aware of what 'fuck up my life' could mean.

In 2015 I sought advice from an eminent Australian cybersecurity expert. This man's job means I can't name him. He had dealt with Mark's type before. The expert was frank about the danger that I was in: 'Don't name him and don't name his trolling gang. Because if he doesn't like what you write and you piss him or his gang off, they will come after you.'

There was no longer any demarcation of where the journalism ended and the rest of my life began. My husband bore witness to the anxiety this bizarre cat-and-mouse dance produced. After all the damage trolling had caused our family, he wondered why I needed to keep reporting on the issue. Why did I need to go so far in?

But something unbending within me couldn't let it go. Maybe if I asked enough questions – or asked the right questions – I'd understand this. The truth, though, was far less convenient. Mark was hurting other people, and I couldn't stop him. The more I knew about him, the less I understood.

'Because it's funny,' he said, by way of explanation for the trolling, and it provides him 'entertainment'. 'I don't really have emotions that much. I have emotions but nothing to do with regretting stuff and that field of emotions [including] sadness.'

This compelled me to ask, 'Do you understand why the things that you're doing make people so upset and so angry?'

'I have a really good understanding of it. That's why I do it so well.'

Even though this might have explained his callousness, the notion of 'morals' still hung limply between Mark and me.

'I don't think it's morally okay,' he said. 'Morals don't come into it. I know everything I do is wrong.'

#

In 2018, I got back in touch with Craig. We'd last been in contact at the end of 2016, when he agreed to my request to appear on camera as part of a television series called *Cyberhate*, with author and TV host Tara Moss. During his TV interview, conducted over Skype, Craig wore a latex Richard Nixon mask. He joked with me over text: 'It's the perfect "oblivious villain" trope.' On camera he said he'd given up trolling because of me. Although this particular quote ended up on the cutting room floor, it stayed on my mind.

Craig, now thirty-one, isn't crazy about talking to me again. He's moved on in life and his career is flourishing. He speaks to me out of generosity. I cut to the chase: 'Why did you quit trolling?'

Craig confirms our first interview in 2015 'made me think about what I was doing and why I was doing it'. More specifically, he started to consider whether his own behaviours were consistent with the dark personality traits.

'I drew away from the notion that I had narcissistic or sadistic traits because they are not desirable to have,' he says. 'I realised I couldn't justify trolling.'

He also wondered what the consequences of trolling were. 'I have an employer that wouldn't view trolling behaviour in a positive light and basically as soon as there was any risk from what I post, I'm done,' he says.

When people find out I'm writing a book about trolling – and that I talk to trolls all the time – they always ask: *Why do they do it?* Mark says for the lulz, whereas Craig says boredom. When he was sixteen he got onto 4chan's most popular board – the random board, /b/ – because a mate suggested it 'might be something funny to do'. For most of us, the board is just a weird internet title with too many slashes in it. Trolls, on the other hand, know /b/ to be the home of endless popular culture memes, including 'lolcats' and rickrolling. Others claim it's the birthplace of the infamous international hacking and activist collective Anonymous. The webpage knowyourmeme.com suggests that /b/ is a place to 'lose faith in humanity'.[9]

It's a joke, of course. lol. Except, perhaps not.

'All males around that age are little shits. You know, I was bored, hyperactive, I guess looking for something to do in between needing to study and going to school,' Craig says. 'I slid into trolling.'

Another take on why we're seeing a surge in trolling comes from Jeff Jarvis, a professor at the City University of New York's Graduate School of Journalism, who likens it to 'the release of a pressure valve (or perhaps an explosion) of pent-up speech'. He posits that finally the frustrated masses 'who for so long could not be heard can now speak, revealing their own interests, needs, and frustrations'. Jarvis believes that over time the online ugliness will fade away because 'we will develop norms around civilized discourse'.[10]

For Craig's part, the activities he got involved in as a teenager were certainly a way of venting his political frustrations. In late 2008 the

Australian government proposed mandatory filtering of pornographic and violent websites.[11] Like numerous other trolls, Craig found it prudish and paternalistic. Alongside hacktivist collective Anonymous, Craig engaged with 'denial of service attacks on Australian Government servers' in response.

He's telling me this three years after we first met. We've been in intermittent contact the whole time and the truth is, I like him. He's smart, self-aware and easy to talk to. He's funny. In every fibre there's a resistance to doing my journalistic duty and pushing Craig further. Holding him to account is like grinding an old engine up the hill in second gear; it's discordant and uneasy.

I say, 'You were still part of an organisation that really hurt people and it continues to hurt people today, to the point where it drives people to suicide.'

He replies, 'Yeah.'

'They really do wreck lives. That is very clear to me,' I say.

'Absolutely,' he agrees, 'It's just for a bunch of far-right people to get their kicks, jerking each other off about how they trolled this feminist or this gay person.'

In a later text message, he writes: 'I can't read it [the syndicate's website], it's like reading Nazi propaganda.'

At university, Craig became a communist. And he started to loathe a type of left-wing discourse he describes as 'civility politics'. 'The main-stream left is too liberal. I mean that with a small "L" for the Australian audience,' he says. 'The mainstream left is quite weak and parochial. They've got very minor demands and they've got their own internal rules about what you can and can't say.'

Turning a cold shoulder to the syndicate, Craig discovered Twitter. For him, it was a paradise of fools. He gives the example of the popu-lar ABC TV panel discussion program Q&A. A large and committed Twitter following live-tweets comments every episode. Some of the messages flash up on screen as the show rolls on.

He had a field day. He'd tweet 'something stupid and simple' such as 'The NBN [National Broadband Network] is a waste of money' and then watch people respond in droves to the bait he'd laid. 'I've just basically wasted a whole bunch of people's time for very little of my own time to get a very predictable reaction from them,' he says. 'Knowing that five seconds of your mental effort has just enraged a few hundred people. That was sort of the attraction for me.'

Although he's given up trolling, his appreciation of it remains. So much so, that he still sometimes discusses it in the present tense: 'It's the simplicity, Ginger. It's absolutely the simplicity which I love. We can become so "online" that some people just lose the ability to filter out things which are obviously false or obviously just a shitpost.'

A 'shitpost' is internet slang for a worthless post – either deliberate or otherwise.

I notice his use of the word 'online': adjectivally. He's referring to a perceived state of being where folks behave differently and, often, more stupidly than they would in the offline world.

'It probably is a bit sadistic but I don't see it on the same level as people who target people for their race or their gender identity, their sexuality,' he says. To further distance his previous behaviour from predator trolling, he declares, 'I'm pretty okay with hurting someone like [political commentator] Chris Kenny's feelings by calling him a hypocrite or whatever it might be. The reason I see someone like him as fair game is because he's using the platform to spread his vile shit everywhere. That's very different to basically ruining people's lives or trying to get them to kill themselves or … getting people fired from their jobs. I think that is way worse. I am not a psychopath and they [predator trolls] are. I don't go out to ruin people's lives or hurt people.'

Meeting these two young men is like boarding a plane with a blindfold on. It's nothing like what I expected – and I don't know where it leads. One of the trolls is thoughtful, educated and considered. He's willing to consider differences of opinion and engage in self-reflection. Whether or not we agree, his trolling makes a clear political point and in different circumstances perhaps we'd even be friends.

The other is callous in the extreme, embodying both sadism and narcissism. He's constantly calculating and manipulating, waiting only for another opportunity to injure others. And when he gets that chance, he'll delight in it. No sense of conscience stands in his way.

The starkness of their differences brings to mind something cyber-security journalist Lorraine Murphy says to me months later about the people you meet online: 'Indeed, the internet teaches lots of lessons about jumping to conclusions.'

4

When the flowers grow funny

THE LONGER I know Craig, the more relaxed I am with him. The opposite applies to Mark. I never feel as if I've cracked the code. The same questions remain: *How did he get like this? What's really motivating him? And – damn it – what am I missing?*

Then finally, three years after Mark and I first met, and through a long chain of events, I get as close as I'm going to.

In the media world, editors and directors want trolls on camera. And somehow I've become the golden ticket. With some hesitation, I contact Mark to speak on camera as part of my major investigation into cyberhate for Fairfax newspapers. He agrees. Perhaps because there's a camera present, he's less effusive than normal. He leans back in the chair in an apparent attempt to look relaxed. His answers are short and there's a scratchiness about him. Before the tape starts rolling, out of earshot of the cameraman, he snaps, 'If I'm going to be anonymous, I don't see why you even need to interview me on camera.'

By now, I'm used to his being contrary. Agreeing to something, then inexplicably being disagreeable. It's vaguely possible he's worried about being identified, although usually his disregard for the safety of others also stretches to his own. Under the Australian Commonwealth *Criminal Code Act*, it's illegal to use a carriage service to menace, harass or cause offence to another person.[1] However, Mark is unperturbed by the lawyers who try to sue him and by the notion that the police will eventually find him. 'I'm not afraid of it. I'm expecting it one day,' he says.

Apparently, this is the reason he wants to talk to me, a journalist. I'm just part of his twisted schema. 'This [being interviewed] is for attention for me, really.'

When I suggest so-called 'digilantism' is on the rise – where women fight back online against trolls – Mark is scathing. 'That's not the way to do it. For one, if you react against [trolls] and try to attack them, it's giving them what they want.

'I think that is incredibly bad for their safety. If someone attacks you online and then you just decide you are going to fight back against them without knowing what you are doing, that's when it can go into affecting your real life. That's when your actual safety is at risk,' he says.

Despite posting revenge porn, telling rape victims they 'deserve' it and doxing women, Mark says he's not misogynistic and actually prefers to troll men.

'I knew you were going to get into this,' he says when I press him on the issue. 'You've got an agenda.' Sometimes, Mark says, he examines my social media feeds and reads my published articles. On the attack, he asks me, 'Do you really believe the shit you write?'

And then, a few seconds later: 'You're stuck in your social justice bubble and you can't see the truth. There's a big, big culture of cyberhate against men. Especially white men. Like I have less rights than you because I'm white and male.'

That's right. In all of this mess, Mark sees himself as a victim. As I would go on to learn, he isn't the only troll to claim this.

The video published as part of my five-month trolling investigation for Fairfax was four minutes and forty-six seconds long. Like most journalistic reporting, it was cut from a much longer piece of footage. Turning that unedited video into something for a general audience took blood, sweat and tears. And fear.

We had high-level security advice. We thought about the physical danger my family and I might be in. We thought about ethics. We thought about the viewer's attention span. With the help of my talented friend and sometime colleague Denby Weller, Mark's voice and face were altered. In the end, those few minutes of heavily edited, anonymised footage were eventually posted.

The entire unedited video of Mark is forty-three minutes long. The public will never see it. The raw video remained in its virtual basement gathering dust. And it would have stayed there, except that something changed my mind.

Jon Ronson's gripping book *The Psychopath Test* outlines the Hare Psychopathy Checklist – a psychological assessment tool, developed by Canadian psychologist Robert Hare in the 1970s, to detect psychopathy in individuals. (If you haven't read this book, you should.) In broad brushstrokes, this is how it works. Professional psychologists score individuals on twenty criteria, including items such as having an inflated sense of your own importance, an excess need for stimulation or proneness to boredom, callousness and lack of empathy, a lack of remorse or guilt and a failure to accept responsibility for one's actions. Broadly speaking, items are scored on a three-point scale that runs from 0–2. '0' indicates there is no match, '1' shows a partial match and '2' a good match. The maximum score is 40. In the UK those individuals who score 25 and above on the Hare Psychopathy Checklist meet the criteria for psychopathy, and in the United States the cut-off is 30.[2]

Reading Ronson's book and considering the time and expertise needed to make a complex diagnosis like this, I start to think: *Maybe a seasoned clinician could see things in Mark's video that a layperson, like me, could not. Cannot.*

There's only one way to find out. Look up a friendly psychopath expert and ask them to view the footage. With Mark's blessing, I reach out to a psychologist. And, as it turns out, I'm missing plenty.

For professional and personal reasons, the expert has chosen not to be named. He's also not able to diagnose Mark, since they're not in the sort of professional psycho-legal relationship that would permit him to. But his insights are fascinating. He's been working with people who have 'challenging personality styles' for nearly twenty years. Put bluntly, he's one of the best psychopath experts you'll find (although he's a humble guy and would never say that in a million years).

Dr Williams, as we'll call him, wears a blue shirt with swirling patterns when we talk; he smiles easily and often. His office is crammed with books on shelves, flanked by yet more books in wonky piles. There's a poster on the wall for the cult 1973 film *The Exorcist* and, above it, another poster, for the defunct American rock band Grateful Dead. There's something about his accent – the way he pleasantly squashes his vowels. An unlikely psychopath expert, perhaps.

He watches the video, taking notes. There's pre-interview B-roll of Mark and me, stuffing around. I introduce Mark to the cameraman, Liam. I'm wearing a green jacket with a crab brooch pinned onto it, claws at the ready. My make-up is caked on for the camera.

Liam shows Mark how to clip his lapel microphone onto his blue-and-white checked shirt. Mark is looking away from the camera. He's pale and seems uncomfortable. He's concerned about his pimples. 'Well, no one's going to see you, so don't worry about it,' I snap in response.

He's wriggling. I cough. Individually, we count for Liam's required sound test: One. Two. Three. Four. The mics are working. Then the interview starts in earnest. I ask Mark about so-called RIP trolling. This is the story he told about trolling the loved ones of the girl killed by the train. He says trolling gives him 'Entertainment. Not pleasure.' Mark makes this point twice in the interview – and Dr Williams notices, pointing it out to me as 'an interesting distinction'.

'I suspect that he thinks "pleasure" equates to sexual arousal, which he denies later on,' the psychologist says. (When I press Mark on whether there's sexual satisfaction in there somewhere, he defiantly says: 'I'm not some serial killer masturbating over his victims.') 'This suggests that the behaviour is stimulating but not enjoyable,' Dr Williams says, adding that the troll carefully selects 'emotionally vulnerable victims and this suggests he has sadistic tendencies'.

On tape I ask Mark how he chooses the victims of RIP trolling: Was this anybody who had died or specific people?

'Pretty much, if it came up in the news, we'd have a look to see if there was a [Facebook memorial] page for it,' he replies.

To Dr Williams, the media element of this is significant. 'He seeks out high-profile targets drawn from news stories. The exposure of the news story means there is a ready-made audience, so his behaviour will reach a potentially large number of people and with maximum impact.'

We're only six minutes in and Dr Williams concludes there are 'conspicuous themes' that 'suggest that he sees the world as essentially hostile. So he has to get the first punch in and make it count. Eliciting a negative reaction both thrills him "as an offensive strategy" and also feeds into his need to avenge – a defensive strategy. He wants to play this game with all of the chips on his side, which means that fairness is not a virtue or a courtesy to be extended to others … and may be a reflection of an unresolved life challenge or crises that he struggled with growing up.

'The selection of victims – people who are emotionally vulnerable following a significant trauma or tragedy – is somewhat predatory. But he's not behaving like an apex predator, i.e. fearless and dominant with a robust self-concept. This may indicate that he himself has experiences – directly or vicariously – of victimisation, with little [or] no mercy shown,' Dr Williams says.

There's so much in his feedback, I think about it for a while. As someone who is frequently scared of Mark, this notion is revelatory: perhaps he, too, is – or was – a victim. When it comes to the notion of perpetrators as victims, Dr Williams urges me to look deeper. To think about this harder. It's something that haunts me in the months of writing that follow.

'These folk didn't come from nowhere, and I would challenge the idea that they fell out of the sky as trolls. These are behaviours that were picked up over time, that were learned either through omission or commission, and in many ways people with challenging behaviours are a kind of a mirror of our communities. If the flowers are growing a certain way, what's happening in the soil?'

This question, as it turns out, is one I come back to over and over again. As one angry young white man after another crosses my path, I come to understand the way they've been brought up – or in many cases *not* brought up – lays the foundation for their urge to lash out.

We move on to who Mark targets. Mark points to specific people who react 'more seriously than a normal person … Mainly autistic people, trannies [transvestites] especially'.

Even reading the transcript of this interaction, I find it hard to stay calm.

'He dehumanises others to make it easier to morally disengage with victims or outgroups,' Dr Williams explains. 'This is also why he uses a word like "retards".' As an example, Dr Williams points to war propaganda: 'The more human attributes that have been taken away from somebody and the more they have been demonised and turned into enemies … that will make it easier for us to aggress against or reject or marginalise them.'

In response to Mark's repeated claim that white men are 'the biggest victims of racism on the planet', the psychologist wonders if perhaps he 'also experienced mistreatment, bullying or unfairness by minorities'.

Mark says his behaviour is about 'destroying' his targets and 'just making them want to kill themselves or quit the internet'. 'Once you attack someone in real life, you take away, like, their job, you take away where they're living and stuff like that. And they don't really have anything left in life. No one wants to talk to them.'

I need to know: 'Why would you want to hurt somebody who has less power than you?'

Mark responds with 'Lulz,' and, when I press him, won't say any more.

'He strikes me as avoidant,' Dr Williams says. 'There is a locked room that he doesn't want you to go into.'

About twenty minutes into the interview I'm hammering Mark about posting revenge porn. He's telling me it's not misogynistic: 'That has nothing to do with them being a woman,' and 'If they were a man, I'd be doing the same thing.'

Dr Williams comes back to the same point. 'There's a rationalisation of his behaviour. He's parading as an equal opportunity troll. At this point, he seems to be attempting to manage you in the interview by deflecting confrontational or incriminating issues. There's that locked room again.'

Then he puts forward a fascinating contention: 'There's something around the sort of sexual space, which I think is really threatening for him because … once you started to get much closer to misogyny he was blocking you and trying to get you to move on. Next topic. There seems to be a sense of that.'

The psychologist also wonders if there's 'something kind of delicate' behind the hostile front Mark would like us to buy into. 'He's certainly taken on the rogue kind of idea … He probably puts a lot of stock into that, that he's his own man and he does things his way, but at the same time, he's shit scared because he's got a lot to account for if he gets caught out.'

When I suggest to Mark his actions are not just immoral, they are illegal, he says of his victims, 'I'm not killing them.' The psychologist points to Mark's 'cognitive distortion' – the ways we convince ourselves of things that aren't really accurate – and his 'denial of responsibility'.

A few minutes later, the interview circles back to the devastating impact Mark has on his victims. I tell him he's effectively quashing their free speech. Mark crosses his arms and says, 'I've never stopped anyone from saying anything.' Dr Williams and I both notice that he has taken 'a defensive posture'.

'You are stopping people behaving as they normally would on the internet because you make them afraid,' I say to Mark in the footage. 'How do you not see that?'

He replies, 'Because the way they were behaving on the internet is the original problem. That's where it all starts.'

This is what's known as victim blaming – something trolls delight in. I tell Mark, 'They should be allowed to express themselves … they're not harming or attacking anybody else—'

He cuts me off. 'So I attack paedophiles, or should they express themselves?'

Mark has read plenty about me online. He knows paedophiles led to me and my family being predator trolled. It's possible he's using this against me now. I try to rein it back in: 'I don't think you should be targeting vulnerable people. It's immoral. Vulnerable groups in society, who have less power than you, are your targets.'

He crosses his arms again, mouth slightly open. Looks annoyed. Casts his eyes down and touches his microphone. 'So, I've gotten paedophiles put in prison. Should I not have done that? Is that wrong?'

I snap at him, 'I am asking the questions.'

He laughs at me and shakes his head slightly. 'All right then.'

Dr Williams considers this combative exchange and says, 'He sees himself as an authority and judge of others' behaviour on the internet and blurs distinction of victims by *also* targeting an easily condemned group: paedophiles.

'He's very anxious about being apprehended, hence his guardedness around the interview. However, despite his bravado, he has no inhibitions about outing others. This is perhaps a parallel process indicative of his earlier experiences of being treated unfairly.

'They [trolls] like the behaviour because it does something for them,' Dr Williams continues. 'They don't want to deal with the consequences because it will come into conflict with their behaviour.'

Right from when I first met Mark, he always positively – even happily – identified with the dark tetrad of personality traits. (If you've forgotten them, a reminder: Sadism. Machiavellianism. Narcissism. Psychopathy.) I always accepted this at face value – Mark had insight into his own behaviour.

Dr Williams sees it differently. 'He identifies with these traits with some casualness. He doesn't seek clarification. Perhaps he just likes the way these terms sound [because it] adds to his self-concept as a dangerous person, to be feared and to be respected. If someone believes they're psychopathic ... it could be a self-fulfilling prophecy about permission: "My behaviour is okay because I'm psychopathic." And so, the label becomes justification.'

Mark has always responded with bravado when it came to the notion of being caught by law enforcement. He says there are incidents where the trolling has almost got him killed. And yet he doesn't stop. This is clearly 'quite nihilistic', Dr Williams says, and certainly displays 'risk-taking' behaviour. The catch, though, is that he's still 'anxious to hide behind anonymity'.

I ask Mark about the trolling syndicate he belongs to. How does it operate? Can he give me an analogy? Is it like a bikie gang?

'Yakuza,' Mark says, referring to the Japanese organised crime syndicates. 'Sounds cooler.'

Dr Williams observes, 'He sees himself on a higher level of danger-ousness, with more prestige and sophistication than other street-level trolls, and this is grandiose.'

Mark might see himself as top of the pile, but some of the other trolls tell me his kind of online harassment is 'D-level'. 'He's preying on people who are obviously vulnerable,' one of them says to me on condition of anonymity. 'It's not just morally fucked but too easy. He's not doing anything to actually alter how people think on a mass scale.'

We go back to the tape. The psychologist muses, 'There must be a lot of power there, too. There must be some real seduction.'

This is something Mark denies. Apparently, he's not after status or power. 'It doesn't come into it. That's not something I've gone out to achieve. It's not something I care about.'

Watching the video again – especially in this forensic manner, with piles of transcripts and notes laid in front of me, stopping every few minutes to consider and discuss the complexities – recasts an imprint of that day. The fear. The adrenalin. The rules I made myself: *Hold your nerve. Keep your voice steady. This is the moment. Use all those years of asking questions as a dress rehearsal. Slice this thing open.*

The moment Mark walked away, I was nauseated, sitting on the stage in this giant, reverberant hall. My breath shallow and unduly loud. The blood rushing in my ears. The cameraman was talking to me and he sounded far away.

'Hold on, Liam,' I said to him, raising my damp palm, 'I just need a moment.'

#

When it comes to trolls and the safety threats they pose, I try to make no sudden movements. Dr Williams and I agree: Mark needs to read the psychologist's assessment of the video. In journalism terms, this is highly unusual. Then again, cavorting with online harassers isn't exactly standard procedure either.

And so, the comments go back to Mark; I hold my breath.

The first thing Mark says in response is, 'I feel like he is spot on in some parts but far off the mark in others, but understandably so.' The second thing he says is, 'There's no locked doors, no bad childhood memories and traumas. I understand why he says that though [because] as a psychologist that would be the case in almost all of the people he sees. I'm not angry at him suggesting I'm a victim and I am doing it because I feel victimised. I expected him to say that. I imagine the concept of someone doing this for no real reason is alien to him.'

When I push him on this, he says, 'There's no hidden closeted motive … I honestly just fell into it. [I've] never been a victim, wasn't even bullied at all in school or anything.' Astoundingly, Mark then volunteers, 'I don't even think I am hostile.'

I say, 'Dude. I've known you for years. You are hostile … You see the world as a hostile place, that's what he's saying. That's how you behave. As if you want to attack first. Before someone else does. You think victims deserve it … and that indicates that you don't see the world as a warm and fuzzy place.'

He replies, 'I think everyone deserves to be attacked. How they respond is their own problem. So no, the world is not a safe space.'

Mark also tries to minimise Dr Williams's suggestion there's 'something kind of delicate' behind the hostile front: 'Hmm, I guess in the video it may have been from being uncomfortable in front of the cameras.'

In our conversations, one of Mark's favourite themes is how he's able to manipulate me. And so Dr Williams's comment that he was 'attempting to manage' me during the video interview appears to delight him.

'I always run the conversation,' he boasts. 'Whenever we talk I control the conversation. I let you ask the questions but when I'm not interested in what you're asking, I steer it in my own direction. Funny that he [Dr Williams] sees it but you don't.'

I ask Mark – for the fifth time – which parts of Dr Williams's analysis are 'spot on'.

'Just the avoiding your questions. Though he thinks I was avoiding them for different reasons,' Mark says, so 'it was only half right'.

The longer we talk, the less he's willing to concede is accurate. Out of the blue, though, he confesses to being dishonest about one particular thing.

'Lol. I just realised I completely lied to you about something, and it's a huge one that literally anyone that knows me knows it's a lie. I said I don't care about power and status on the internet, when my position [within the trolling syndicate] revolves around that. I can do what I want to people because of my status.'

After logging off, there's an immoveable image in my mind. It's a small locked attic room. The room has no key.

5

You are literally the enemy

O NE OF THE things that we, the targets of predator trolling, take comfort in is the notion that our attackers are ignorant, uneducated and alone. *He's a nobody. He doesn't matter.*

This imagining serves to diffuse the hate, making us feel less afraid. What happens when we discover none of those things are true and he isn't who we thought?

Like many of the trolls I've investigated, the man who appeared to trigger the storm of predator trolling against my family and me back in 2013 – conservative journalist and blogger Robert Stacy McCain – was not ignorant or uneducated. And, far from quelling his hate and fear of marginalised people, knowledge and education may have made it worse.

After landing on McCain's blog, I found his two posts about me, the first linking directly to my former Twitter handle. It was headlined: 'Neutral Objective Incompetence: How Ginger Gorham [sic] Aided Pedophile Network.'

'Nary a hint nor a shadow of scepticism dimmed the sunshine-and-rainbows narrative Gorham provided for Mark Newton and Peter Truong,' McCain wrote. 'It amounted to free publicity for their criminal enterprise ... Journalists today cannot *report* about homosexuality, they must only *advocate, endorse, praise* and *celebrate* homosexuality. This paradigm reduces reporters to the role of propagandists, whose job is to parrot the publicity of radical gay-rights activists.'[1]

It's taken four years to work up the courage to contact McCain. Although I sit down at my desk with the express task of emailing him, I do everything possible to avoid writing the message.

I read reams of information about him and re-read his 2013 blog posts about me. I eat chocolate and chips and then yoghurt straight out of the tub with a spoon. Then, after running out of ways to waste time, I compose a brief email asking if he would consent to an interview for this book.

What is the protocol for emailing a man who you believe helped to create a tsunami of hate against you and your family, someone who made you feel unsafe? While I wait to see if he replies, I'm clicking and scrolling, scouring through the detritus each of us leaves in cyberspace.

'I am a poor excuse for a Christian,' McCain says in a 2010 interview with another blogger, 'but I really do have a deep faith in God, and I try to be grateful for his blessings ...' One of these blessings, he goes on to say, is his wife, who always believed he'd 'be somebody' one day. 'And to the extent that I've become "somebody," I credit God's promise in Proverbs 22:29: "Seest thou a man diligent in his work? He shall stand before kings."'

McCain claims he's 'interviewed governors and congressmen and senators'. He scorns social justice and socialism and discusses home-schooling his kids. 'Government schools are just another form of welfare slavery. Stop sending your kids to those liberal indoctrination camps,' he tells the interviewer.[2]

McCain has been writing since 1986 and, since then, has put forward all manner of strong viewpoints, including appearing to excuse date rape: 'Listen up, sweetheart: You buy the ticket, you take the ride.'[3] Back in 1996, during a so-called 'Race Debate', McCain suggested 'perfectly rational people' react with 'altogether natural revulsion' to interracial relationships. 'Equality Über Alles' shouts one headline on McCain's blog, harking back to the Nazi era in World War II. The post rails against same-sex marriage, feminism and equality: 'To say that men and women, as such, are different enough that they cannot be made truly equal in a free society is today such a controversial assertion as to seem wildly irresponsible – even though it is demonstrably true.' He goes on to assert, '[T]o those trapped within the egalitarian worldview – inequality is always evidence of injustice.'[4]

It seems inexplicable that McCain hasn't locked down his Facebook page by activating its privacy settings. But he hasn't. All his photos are publicly available. Among the snaps are several depicting McCain and his wife, Lou Ann. They appear to be at several different weddings. He's wearing a tie. She's wearing a corsage. She has curly hair and glasses and looks fresher and less haggard than him. They are smiling and dancing.

McCain's 2007 Christmas album is jammed full of cute grandchildren opening gifts and playing musical instruments. He writes: 'Great thing about having six kids? Christmas morning is WONDERFUL!'

Some of the photos are work related. He's grinning and holding signage for Libertarian presidential candidate Bob Barr in 2008. The following year he's wearing a press pass for the conservative US monthly magazine *The American Spectator*.

It doesn't take long for McCain to email me back. 'This is an interesting proposal, ma'am, and I appreciate the civility of your communication,' he writes. 'Have you ever come to grips – or written publicly – about how (and why) you were so thoroughly bamboozled by Newton and Truong?' He reiterates his view that journalists serve as 'propagandists' for the gay rights movement, and, after rambling about Hillary Clinton's US election loss and Russian hackers, he gets back to the topic at hand:

> Your concern, I suppose, is that you were singled out and demonized for your reporting about Newton and Truong, once their wickedness was exposed … Well, one thing the Internet has done is to allow ordinary people to 'talk back' to the media, and to develop an online counter-balance to these kinds of blatant biases.

McCain returns to lecture me about my perceived failings:

> My point in relating this to you, Ms. Gorman, is to suggest that you consider your 'experiences on the Internet' a lesson learned. And you

ought to think very hard (as I have) about what the lesson actually is … It seems to me that you, like many other journalists, assume that the cause of gay rights is so sacred – a secular crusade – that anyone who criticizes or opposes it must be evil. Thus, you failed to apprehend that there might be bad actors like Newton and Truong using gay rights as a Trojan Horse for their own nefarious purposes. Lesson learned, eh?

The email concludes with McCain suggesting he 'might be available for a Skype interview at some future point, but today I'll be busy babysitting my two-year-old grandson, and on Wednesday I'm flying to Massachusetts for a five-day trip, so we'll have to schedule after I return'. In fact, we never did schedule an interview because McCain stopped replying to my emails altogether.

I realise that as far as the hate stakes go, I'm McCain's perfect match. I'm a feminist; I've been outspoken on the rights of LGBTIQ+ people and have campaigned for marriage equality. I'm also in a mixed-race marriage. (My husband, although now Australian, is Filipino by birth.) My family has Jewish roots. Although McCain hasn't necessarily been an outspoken anti-Semite, an organisation he's been a key part of – the League of the South – certainly has.[5]

Despite understanding this, I still need to know: *Why was he so willing to put my family at risk when he holds his own family so dear? And how could he label me an accomplice to a crime that no one – not even Newton and Truong's friends and neighbours – was aware was happening?*

I'm driven to lay the evidence on the table. The first time Newton and Truong ever came to the attention of authorities was by chance. Local police were investigating another man, Craig Edward Broadley, for sharing child abuse material on the internet. When reviewing his collection police located images of Boy1.

Detective Inspector Jon Rouse, the Australian policeman who worked with US authorities to apprehend the two paedophiles, describes those photos as 'not illegal but concerning'. This was August 2011 – more than a year after I'd interviewed the couple in Cairns. Two months later, on

19 October, the pair were arrested in Los Angeles and then released due to lack of evidence.

Finally, in February the following year, US police again detained the men, but this time they were arrested and charged. Up until that point in time neither Newton nor Truong had a police record. Even now I wring my hands: *I couldn't have known.*

These are the facts, the questions, the damage and the bigotry that remain hanging in the vast gulf between Robert Stacy McCain and me.

#

Like Craig, McCain doesn't fit our stereotypes of who a predator troll might be. He seems educated, articulate and high profile. These traits are so uncomfortable and unexpected, they point in a direction I'm compelled to follow. We like to believe education is the great salve for festering hatred. McCain's background and his behaviour makes me question this popular wisdom.

In the wake of his communication blackout, the person I turn to is Dr Heidi Beirich, director of the Intelligence Project at the Southern Poverty Law Center (SPLC). She heads up a team that monitors 'the activities of the American radical right' on the Hatewatch blog. They also produce two intelligence reports a year.

Our first conversation is aborted. Although it's high summer here, it's deep winter in Alabama. Beirich emails at the last minute to say: 'This crazy storm we have had has meant I had to go to another house I own and winterize it. There's ice on a river here that never ices over.' Winterise, I learn, means to adapt something for cold weather.

Our second attempt to connect fares better – although I stuff up the time difference and appear on Skype looking unkempt and half-asleep. With good humour, Beirich laughs off my apology and dives straight in. She explains her ability to deal with so much hate, every day. 'You're in a mission-driven situation. You're trying to beat down this heinous way of thinking to make the world a better place and that's what gets you through reading all that. Ultimately,' she says, 'the idea of white supremacy is what is behind slavery, colonialism, Jim Crow, apartheid. I could go on and on and on about all the bad things that come from it.'

With her sandpapery voice and straight-talking manner, she's immediately likeable. 'Of course, an occasional beer is helpful,' she adds. 'You need a little bit of a dark sense of humour.'

When she first came to the SPLC back in 1999, one of Beirich's first projects was to investigate a relatively new organisation called the League of the South. 'We ran across Robert Stacy McCain as being affiliated with the League of the South and then found out about his role in the press. And so he was a very early person involved in the hate movement.

'The League of the South is a neo-Confederate hate group. Those are organisations that want to revive the antebellum era. And in the case of the League in particular, although it's gotten much more hardline just in the last few years, they have always been blatantly racist,' Beirich explains.

For those who aren't familiar with the term 'neo-Confederate', it's historical revisionism that glorifies the complex period that triggered the American Civil War during the 1860s. In essence, seven southern states, all of them pro-slavery, wanted to secede from the north because the new Republican president, Abraham Lincoln, was opposed to slavery. A bloody war ensued, resulting in more than 600,000 military deaths.

Without putting too fine a point on it, those modern folk who hold neo-Confederate (and antebellum-era) views are pro–African American slavery and anti-Asian. SPLC's website further states that neo-Confederates pursue Christianity 'and other supposedly fundamental values that modern Americans are seen to have abandoned. Neo-Confederacy also … exhibits an understanding of race that favours segregation and suggests white supremacy.'

As early as 2000, Beirich recalls, the League of the South was already claiming 'slavery was God-ordained and [they had] written about how black people would be at the foot of their new government. In other words, they would make them the least powerful part of a seceded south. And they gave all these positive attributes to white people – in particular white men, because they're also very misogynistic – and negative traits to homosexuals, as they called them, women and minorities.

'Now, in the last five or so years, the racism has become much more bold on the part of the League,' she says. 'Of course, McCain is not as directly involved as he was back then, and the League has become rabidly anti-Semitic, but it was already deeply racist when McCain was hanging out with them.'

Citing the organisation's own written materials, Beirich says: 'There was never any question about his [McCain's] relationship to the League of the South and his membership. This is a guy who was deeply enmeshed in part of America's hate movement, in particular one of the neo-Confederates, and yet was able to, at the same time, maintain a veneer of respectability in the conservative movement.

'He was working for the *Washington Times*, which is a big conservative newspaper here,' she says. 'He was a very good example, at the time, of hate leaching into the mainstream because of that relationship he had with the *Washington Times*.'

Her point here is striking. Not just in the United States, but in Australia, extreme right-wing voices – like that of fascist sympathiser Blair Cottrell when he appeared on Sky TV in August 2018 – have increasingly succeeded in using the mainstream media to spread their messages.[6] Appearing as clean-cut, hardworking and family-oriented men who epitomise conservative values, right-wing trolls like this can appear benign and likeable. The ultimate wolf in sheep's clothing.

Attempting to get underneath that attire, I ask Beirich: 'If I was sitting next to you at a dinner party and we got into a conversation about this and I asked, "Who is he?", what would you say to me?'

'Robert Stacy McCain is actually kind of funny. He has a sense of humour,' she says. 'He can even correspond with a race traitor like me and make jokes and act like we can be friends, but the truth is the empathy isn't there.' He once even joked about doing karaoke with Beirich, and sent her his cell phone number in case she wanted to talk.

While I see the SPLC as an invaluable resource when I'm trying to figure out who's who in the trolling and extremism stakes, trolls themselves view the organisation with scorn. In a strange and out-of-context rant during an interview I conducted with the well-known and extreme troll weev in early 2018, he said: 'The SPLC makes things, a Hate Map.

And you know what? The SPLC's people have actually shot people on that hate map. Our's [sic] send mean comments. The SPLC's people send bullets. They did it to the Family Research Council. The SPLC declared them a hate group.

'They're an anti-abortion group, an anti–gay marriage group and the SPLC's followers went and shot up the Family Research Council office … They're the violent ones.'

For her part, Beirich takes great issue with weev's assessment of this 2012 incident.[7] 'What weev is referring to here is when a deranged guy shot at a security guard at the FRC's headquarters in Washington, DC. He didn't like their anti-LGBT positions and he found out about them from our Hate Map.

'We didn't list an address, just that the group is anti-LGBT. And he had no connection with SPLC at all, regardless of the crazy that weev alleges here,' she says.

Back on the issue of Robert Stacy McCain, when I mention McCain's email to me and his claim of being 'wrongly smeared as a "white supremacist" by various left-wing Internet vigilantes', she points out that he has never sued or threatened to sue the SPLC, or alleged that they have lied about anything he did.

I describe looking at McCain's family photos and learning that he sees himself as a God-loving man. 'It's pretty hard to reconcile that with his hateful output.'

'I think what we'd like to think of somebody who harbours racist views or other forms of ugly bigotry is necessarily sort of an ogre type, or a Klansman in his hood with teeth falling out, but that is not the case for most of the white nationalists that we deal with,' Beirich replies. She points to Yale University graduate Jared Taylor, founder and editor of white supremacist online magazine *American Renaissance*. He's fluent in three languages and usually appears well turned out in a suit and tie. Then there's Richard Spencer, president of the white supremacist think tank the National Policy Institute. 'He's a guy in khakis and a polo shirt and a nice haircut [who] comes from a good family and has a good education, and yet he's as racist as all get-out,' she says.

(If you're wondering why Spencer's name is familiar, he's the bloke who famously got punched in the head by a protester on the day of Donald Trump's inauguration in early 2017.[8] The same year he helped lead members of the far right at the now-infamous rally in Charlottesville, Virginia, where one person died and dozens were injured. We'll get back to Charlottesville.)

'I say this a lot of times to journalists,' Beirich says, 'but a lot of these white nationalists in particular – that's probably where I would put McCain – are probably better read than the average American.'

Many members of the alt-right 'are well schooled in their ideas' and have consistent arguments about their beliefs, she says. 'You can be extremely educated and believe really, really horrible things.'

This sentiment, when it sinks in, makes the foundations shudder. As a journalist, I've always believed my job is to share information and give a voice to those who don't have one. To show up injustice for what it is. Instigate change in society. As Sir Francis Bacon wrote in 1597, 'Knowledge itself is power.' It helps democracy function better. A lofty notion. But what if it doesn't? What if you teach angry young white men about the American Civil War and instead of having compassion for the downtrodden, they start promoting 'peaceful ethnic cleansing' and an 'Aryan homeland'?[9]

Grasping at straws, I go back to McCain's Christmas album. The sweet children. The presents. McCain may 'express these very nice things about his family', Beirich says, but simultaneously shun people outside his immediate circle – viewing them as 'enemies' and 'race traitors' or 'wiggers' (an offensive portmanteau of 'white' and 'nigger'). 'This belief structure is all about lacking empathy towards other people,' she says.

'So, someone like me would be dehumanised in his eyes? I'm not the same as his family,' I say.

'That's exactly right,' she says. Beirich considers my own social and political creed, my ethnicity and mixed-race marriage in direct relation to Robert Stacy McCain. 'The vision of a society that you're talking about, in which all these different groups of people are equal, is not what he wants. He wants *inequality*. You are literally the enemy to his worldview,' she says. 'When he doesn't like what someone stands for or believes or does, he hits back.'

McCain, sadly, isn't a one-off. He's one of many trolls peddling hatred online and using all manner of sophisticated and bigoted arguments – often rooted in historical, social and biblical learnings – to justify their bile. Far from being ill-informed, this is an intelligent cohort who read and retain information, stacking up the facts and twisting them in the service of intolerance and aggression.

Notes in the margins
What the fuck did you expect?

FOUR MONTHS INTO writing the book there were twenty-four hours where the whole thing seemed to be imploding. It wasn't just that I'd become too close to my journalistic sources; it was almost as if the trolls were suffocating me. Pushing me right into the corner.

Let me back up a bit. To understand how this happened, I need to bend your ear about journalism. Just for a minute.

One of the cornerstones of public service journalism has always been impartiality – the notion that media coverage will be objective and unbiased. Therefore, a reporter's relationships with her journalistic sources or interviewees should not become too close.[1] The logic is that this might compromise the reporting.

Like someone questioning their religious faith over many years, I've begun to wonder about the wisdom of slavishly sticking to these values. I'm not the only one asking these questions, by the way. Journalism academics from Cardiff in the UK wrote an academic paper in 2017 positing that supposed 'impartiality' leads to a narrow range of voices being heard on 'the most important issues'.[2]

Here's the rub. Humans are not objective. We're subjective creatures. The pretence that journalists are otherwise is a lie, serving only to lower the public's trust in the media at a time that we can ill afford to do so. Fake news is like a cancer. US President Donald Trump is waging a deliberate campaign to 'weaken an institution [the media] that serves to constrain the abusive exercise of executive authority'.[3]

Right now, journalism's relationship with democracy and the community feels perilous. And if we journalists want to harp on about transparency and holding power to account, we need to be transparent too. This was my thinking when I became a freelancer at the start of 2015. I'd been a journalist and broadcaster for fifteen years. Observing some members of the media behaving like a pack – chasing each other around and plagiarising each other's work – was making me more disillusioned by the day. Meanwhile, my drive to cover untold social-justice stories was stronger than ever.

After all these years of talking to interviewees, something else was clear. Ordinary folk didn't (and don't) even understand how the media works. They often don't understand, for example, that if you're chatting with them at a barbecue you can't and won't quote them. This perpetual bafflement about what journalism is and how it works led me to create an intensive process, in which I collaborate with interviewees – especially those who have suffered trauma – as opposed to reporting *about* them. I build relationships with them over long periods of time, explaining in detail how their quotes will be used and giving them a degree of control over their story.

Some of my journalistic colleagues were, and are, horrified by this, describing my work as 'gonzo journalism' or, perhaps less flatteringly, 'activism journalism'. The implication is that I'm not objective. In essence, I was already bending the rules of the old guard. Incrementally pushing the walls in. The trolls razed the building.

#

The twenty-four hours start when, in response to a question about trolling culture, Mark tells me he's in the shower. That's too much information – TMI – I reply on the messenger app. With trolls you need to lol, even when you're not. This is meant to be a warning shot across the bow. With him I'm trying – and always failing – to set the boundaries.

He replies, 'I'm not even sending you photos yet.'

It's a counter-threat. I send back a GIF of actress Jennifer Aniston rolling her eyes. This tactic usually shuts him up. Not this time. 'I'm reading that as you asking me to,' Mark writes.

I urge him to STAY ON TOPIC.

'It was definitely an invitation,' he writes.

When I don't respond he continues: 'OK, I'm on topic now. Unless of course you do want to see my dick.'

He wants to throw me and he has. Traditionally, journalism interviews take place at a set time and have an end. With trolls they never end, because trolls are always online. Telling you more. Winding you up. Digging in. Messaging all night and day.

The same day, another troll is talking to me about journalism – something the trolls always know more about than you'd expect. We'll call this guy XT. He's involved with a well-known trolling syndicate. Their exploits often make the news. He'll only talk to me if his identity is protected. 'I trust you,' he says to me that day.

I'm thinking: *What did I do wrong that a troll would trust me? Or maybe … right, because I need him to trust me?* I have no idea which is which because this is unmarked territory. *Don't. Don't trust a journalist. Don't tell a reporter everything you're telling me.*

Instead, I say, 'That's weird,' and then quickly add, 'I mean good, I guess. I am trustworthy.'

'I can tell,' he writes back.

Although we've been talking via Skype and messaging on and off for nearly six months now, our communications are not always easy to decipher. He could be playing me. Yet it feels like he's not. That's all I've got to go on right now. The sense of things.

He's coming off the anti-anxiety drug Xanax. It wasn't prescribed by a doctor – he bought it from a dealer on the black market to try to self-medicate his way out of terrible, traumatic things happening in his life. It's night in XT's time zone. Things aren't good. He's telling me about the stresses in his life. Loneliness. The things that are hard. His breakup.

I know Xanax is highly addictive. Doctors don't recommend that people withdraw alone; they need medical assistance because going cold turkey can lead to fatal seizures.

I wasn't too far into writing the book, and I didn't yet know just how tightly interwoven drug-taking is with trolling and hacking culture. Plenty of trolls take numerous hard and soft substances, all the time. Stimulants and psychedelic drugs especially. And later, I can't help wondering what this means – how the constant drug-taking is connected with their mental health struggles. How it affects their interactions with each other and the strangers they attack online.

In this moment though, I'm thinking only about distracting XT from the physical and mental distress he's in. I start talking about the US dating culture and how different it is from Australia. 'We don't date here. We just get drunk and have sex and end up together,' I say. He seems to find this funny and that's good because it is a joke. My only goal now is lol. Strangely – and despite the oceans between us – we're in this trench together.

On a whim, I tell him a story about Detroit. September 2006, in the middle of the months that changed my life. Crisp edges of the forgotten flooding back. In the bar with Sylvia, my Spanish friend, wearing those aqua-green cowboy boots. They inexplicably attract men. This guy, with his curly hair and dark eyes. Approaching me. Standing right next to me. He's so good-looking I can't breathe. He does a trick with an unlit cigarette. Makes it disappear. To make me laugh. But I don't laugh. Men don't behave like this at home. And if they do it seems sleazy.

I tell the troll, 'I literally had no idea what was going on. I just stared at him and he walked away. My friend turned to me and said, "What the fuck is the matter with you?" I had to go back over to this man and say, "Sorry, can we start again?"'

The man told me, 'I just saw you. I thought you were so beautiful. I wanted to make you laugh. That's all.'

A sharp inward breath because no stranger has ever said this to me. Ever. Not even close. My internal dialogue hoses me down. Shoves back against the unease: it's okay. This is America. This is different. With an effort that's almost physical, I override the cultural resistance. I say, 'It was a good trick. I'm just foreign. The men I know back home don't talk to women like that. Like this. But I'm glad you did.'

Hearing my accent clearly this time over the bar's noise, his face breaks open with a smile. His white teeth. He says, 'Come and sit down.'

Hearing this story – or parts of it – XT asks how it worked out.

I say, 'I was only there for a short time but it was fun. We stayed up all night. We went to the jazz festival and went bowling. Ate Greek food.'

The American flag hanging from the ceiling of his loft apartment. His pet ferret roaming the carpet. My grey t-shirt, with a huge red heart emblazoned across the chest, discarded on the floor. Driving in his car. In the liquor store, he says, 'Shit! Don't do that. It's not safe. Put your money away quickly. This is Detroit.'

In the hour before we leave for the airport, he says, 'Stay in this city with me.' I can't, and don't even want to. We're going to California, Louisiana, Washington.

'Come back,' he says, knowing I won't.

XT and I get talking about Detroit and I confess that, back then, I was a lot wilder. 'That's what happens when you breed. You get fat and eat ice cream out of the tub,' I say. Then, after a moment, 'Actually, journalists are notorious for being wild and drinking too much as well.'

'So are internet trolls,' he replies. The laying of common ground between us, where I'm certain there'll be none.

Finally he thinks he can sleep now. He's going to bed. It's such an addictive drug. The withdrawals can be awful. I've got a pang of fear. *Stay out of it. It's none of your business.*

The pull is too strong: *What if he's not safe?* Blood rushing in my ears. The next message I type says, 'Mate, when you wake up can you tell me if you're all right?'

He does message me when he wakes up. He's okay. He's with his friends. The withdrawal symptoms are subsiding. The degree of my relief is a message in itself; this is too personal.

He says, 'Thank you for asking. Thank you for talking to me in the middle of the night.'

As a way to take the edge off this intimacy, I say, 'No worries. I'm a bleeding-heart leftie, remember?'

He's not a leftie; he votes Republican and loves guns. My comment earns me the trolling compliment 'LMAO': laughing my ass off.

If you read texts about trolling and if you ask the trolls themselves, they will tell you it's always for the lulz. They supposedly shun expressions of sentimentality or emotion.[4] Yet from the fire tower, I can see something else. That when you're online you're only the inside of you – your wit (or wits). The things you think and say. You have no house, car, job, appearance or accent to be judged by. The trappings of the offline world fall away. Paradoxically, this might be why the trolls form such close bonds with each other, although often there are vast physical distances between them.

Maybe that's what's happening here, with us, although I can't – or more accurately don't want to – think about that. *How can you, as a journalist, hold someone to account when you've erased the perimeters?*

#

The dick pics. The Xanax. These lost and angry young men. The shadows of Detroit. My shadows. And an overbearing sense of the personal and journalistic boundaries unspooling. Deep anger with myself at destroying an old and venerated journalistic tradition and replacing it with ... *what?*

My need to pull this unbridled beast in. Pull myself up and together. I (temporarily) delete the Messenger app from my phone.

In the daytime, I'm swimming laps of the pool. Then it's dark and the night is laced with the chill of a coming autumn. I'm drinking red wine at my computer, well after everyone in the house is asleep. Typing and typing, trying to outrun the tiny, irritating voice inside my head bleating: *These are trolls. What the fuck did you expect?*

The answer: not this dirty mess or fallibility. Not this crush of humanness.

Part 2

TARGETS

6

She was asking for it

I N AUGUST 2012, Charlotte Dawson was inundated with online hate. The former model and Australian television personality had been the target of trolls for many years, but this time the level of vitriol was different. Some reporters speculated this was spurred by Dawson publicly referring to her home country of New Zealand as 'small, nasty, and vindictive'.[1] Whatever the case, the attacks were out of all proportion. Her harassers started using the hashtag #diecharlotte.

Reading those streams of tweets now – and her endless responses to them – it's hard not to feel despair:

> @Wild14u72: @MsCharlotteD Please go and hang yourself #diecharlotte

> @Anonanonson: Please put your face into a toaster #diecharlotte

Dawson sent two tweets back just after 2 am on Wednesday 29 August. They read:

> You win x

> Hope this ends the misery.

Alongside these messages, she tweeted a photograph of herself holding numerous pills. A news.com.au article from the time reported,

'Just after 3 am, an ambulance arrived at her home and took her to Sydney's St Vincent's Hospital.'[2]

A week later Dawson did an interview with Channel 9's *60 Minutes* program in which she said, 'I've never had death threats of this ferocity. I've never had a campaign of this ferocity.' As well as confirming she was 'very drunk' at the time she took the pills, she told reporter Tara Brown she aimed to die. 'Sometimes, especially if people are wanting you to kill yourself and you're somebody who has previously tried to end your life, it's very easy to feel like that is exactly what you want to do,' she said. 'It just triggered that feeling of helplessness when the trolls got to me. They got the better of me and they won.'[3]

Often, when it comes to public discussion of trolling, there's a false demarcation between the online and offline worlds – as if what happens in cyberspace is virtual and therefore not real. Yet in this interview, so devastating to watch in retrospect, Dawson clearly connects sustained predator trolling and its real-life consequences.

In February 2014, Dawson was found dead in her Woolloomooloo home. Some sections of the media were quick to claim she was 'trolled to death'.[4] However, as with most truths, this question of causality is complex. A sea of grey. Alongside Dawson's depression and a propensity to drink too much – which she talked about openly – there were many other difficult threads weaving through her life. Her adoption. Sexual abuse. An abortion and the grief that remained in its wake. A marriage that collapsed. Her sense of herself as someone 'unloved and unlovable'.[5]

Her long-time friend, journalist and commentator Melissa Hoyer, deftly paints a picture of Dawson's complexities. 'There were very much two Charlottes. There was the Charlotte who was the television persona, who was … this ballsy, strong woman. She'd be on panels and she'd say what she thought. Let's say when she was on *Australia's Next Top Model*, she'd be very strong and powerful,' Hoyer says. 'But then there was that absolute vulnerable, sort of quiet and quite … brooding Charlotte, which is probably, let's face it, the real girl, the real woman.

'I would imagine, when she did take her life, she felt, *Well, what am I to anyone? I'm not in love. I feel as though I can't be loved. I haven't had a child. At this point, I don't have a job. I've got no money. Why am I here?* She [also] had a mental health issue. So, probably, all of those things coupled together, plus the trolling and the hounding that she got from the media, it just got her,' Hoyer says.

Dawson's self-doubt reminds me of my own self-doubt. The insecurities that haunt every one of us. Thinking about this, I try to couple it with the feeling of being a predator-trolling target. How did those inner and outer demons come together for her?

Having reported on suicide and its complexities for many years, I know it is usually caused by many factors, not just the one. Alan Woodward from Lifeline has been working in the field of suicide prevention for fifteen years and describes 'the journey to suicide' as 'a river forming and as the water flows through the catchment, there are various tributaries that contribute to the creation of that river'.[6]

Still, he acknowledges that the combination of mental illness and other life stresses, such as sustained cyberhate, can be dangerous. 'A person experiencing that level of abuse and trauma from bullying may feel that there's no way out and may feel a sense of entrapment. And that is something that can quite often be associated with suicidal behaviour.'

Radio presenter Mel Greig's experience captures that sense of entrapment. She became the object of sustained predator trolling after an on-air prank went wrong in 2012. The incident, which became known as 'the Royal Prank', was linked to the suicide of a British nurse. After the story made international news, the threats against Greig and her then-partner became so extreme that they needed a bodyguard.

The iron grip of depression engulfed Greig. She tells me she became 'very fearful' of people in real life. 'I remember the first time I tried to do the grocery shopping and I had an all-out anxiety and panic attack because I was looking at these people and in my eyes, they were looking back at me. I was picturing them as Michael from Twitter, as Simon from the news.com.au article and I'm like, "What if that's them, you know? Are these the people that have been abusing me online?" When I wasn't well, people became the trolls in real life.'

Alan Woodward reminds me to think about hope, and says that with help and support, 'people who are going through great periods of difficulty' can often find solutions and start to see a future for themselves again.

#

Dawson's family in New Zealand don't respond to any of my attempts to contact them but when I email another one of her close friends, reporter Megan Hustwaite, she writes back straight away: 'What you're doing would mean a lot to Charlotte and I know she'd want me to be involved.'

We meet in a Melbourne cafe, fittingly called Friends of Mine. Hustwaite hugs me and says, 'I feel like I know you already.' She orders a cheese toastie and says of Dawson, 'Her sense of humour drew me to her … We were happy just catching up anywhere. And we'd have fun whether we were in a marquee at the races, or just having a wine together.

'The whole time I knew her, she was having a lot of trouble online with trolls,' Hustwaite says. She was often with Dawson when the former model received predator-trolling messages and got 'sucked into this vortex on Twitter'.

How much does she think trolling contributed to Dawson's death?

'I guess none of us will ever know, and that's always the awful weight of suicide, but I truly believe that trolling hugely contributed to it,' Hustwaite says.

Needless to say, not all of those who were close to Dawson agree about the extent to which trolling affected her. One friend, who asked not to be named, wrote me a short email on the subject:

> I'm of the strong opinion that Charlotte's online interactions did not play a large part in her decision to end her life. Her first attempt was prior to the internet even being a mainstream thing, and her family and I believe that even without the 'trolls' she encountered online, it is likely she would have made the same decision. I'm sure some of the trolling she endured didn't help her feel at her most chipper when she was having bad days, but nor would a myriad other things. Such is the nature of depression.

#

People who choose to speak out about their experiences of being attacked online are commonly labelled 'snowflakes'.[7] The implication is that the impacts on you, as an individual, aren't serious. And instead of whining about people being 'mean', you should toughen up. What I've learned from analysing the stories of so many cyberhate targets – like Charlotte Dawson – is diametrically opposed to this. Far from being petals wilting at the slightest breeze, the targets of predator trolling frequently sustain enormous and sometimes irreversible damage to their lives. These harms are social, physical, mental and economic. For example, a predator-trolling target may lose their job or be forced to move house.

And yet when I went looking for reliable, in-depth data on the incidence of cyberhate in Australia and the associated monetary costs, it was non-existent. This seemed to be a crucial missing piece of the puzzle.

I started calling economists and asking: How hard would it be to model both the incidence and the national cost of cyberhate? Mostly, they muttered something about the impossibility of answering this question without first having the data, and tried to get off the phone.

The good folk at The Australia Institute (TAI) did not say this. Instead they said, 'This seems important. We'll get the data.' The data, it turns out, is revealing (and snowflakes are nowhere to be seen).

TAI's nationally representative survey of 1557 people undertaken in 2018 for the purposes of this book found 44 per cent of women and 39 per cent of men have experienced one or more forms of online harassment.[8] Far from being a unique experience, TAI researcher Tom Swann notes, 'This is equivalent to 8.8 million Australians experiencing harassment online.'[9]

Strikingly similar statistics are reflected in 2017 data from the Pew Center in the United States, which found 'around four-in-ten Americans (41 percent) have been personally subjected to at least one type of online harassment'. Interestingly, this US research found the reverse of our Australian data in regard to gender: 'Overall, men are slightly more likely to experience any form of online harassment (44 percent vs. 37 percent of women).'[10] It would be easy to jump to the conclusion, then, that men and women are attacked more or less the same amount online.

And, that being the case, is gender even an issue here? (This has been raised with me at conferences and on social media.)

As with many complex issues, it's crucial to scratch beneath the surface. To get a handle on it, let's break it into bite-sized pieces. Our research split online abuse into two forms. In the first instance, we wanted to capture all internet harassment being experienced by Australian adults. The most common form of online harassment that individuals experience is abusive language (27 per cent of respondents). About 18 per cent of the survey sample had been sent unwanted sexual messages or pictures. Threats of violence or death were also surprisingly common (8 per cent).

That's everyone. Now let's think about how gender plays into online harassment. Men experience more abusive language about religion and ethnicity than women (8 per cent versus 6 per cent). Aside from this one exception, women report enduring more online abuse in *all other categories* included in the TAI polling commissioned for this book. For instance, 24 per cent of women were sent unwanted sexual messages or nude pictures – more than double the 11 per cent of men. Another example: 32 per cent of women versus 23 per cent of men had abusive language directed at them.

Women were more likely than men to report receiving threats of sexual assault or rape, violence or death, being followed or stalked, and publication of their personal details without permission in order to intimidate them. This reflects the US findings that, among young women especially, rates of sexual harassment and stalking online are higher than among young men. Notably, harassment of young women online is also more sustained.[11] This has parallels with domestic violence, where experts look for patterns of coercive control rather than one-off incidents of violence.[12]

In the second part of our research, we sought to understand what percentage of Australians were suffering more extreme online attacks. We described this type of predator trolling as 'cyberhate' and defined it as 'repeated, sustained threats or attacks on an individual through the use of electronic devices, which result in real-life harm to the target. These harms may be physical and/or psychological. The attacks may be perpetrated by one or more individuals.' Surprisingly, 8 per cent of respondents reported being the targets of cyberhate. More women (9 per cent) than men (6 per cent) told us they'd been victims. According to Swann, 'this is equivalent to 1.3 million Australians having experienced cyberhate'. To put this in context, this is about the same number of Australians who've ever used ice (methamphetamine) or, alternatively, the same amount of Australians who are affected by hearing loss. It's a hell of a lot of us.

Swann goes on to say, 'Respondents were significantly more likely to report cyberhate if they spent more time online.' This may go some way to explaining why younger groups experienced the most cyber-hate – they use the internet more. 'However, even amongst those using the internet least often, more than one in four reported some form of harassment,' Swann explains.

Therefore, when predator-trolling victims are advised to 'stay off the internet' by everyone from friends and family to law enforcement, we can conclude it's stupid advice. Infrequent usage isn't necessarily a protective factor. Your reputation could be ruined online – with reper-cussions like job loss – without you actually being present in cyberspace.

This perspective doesn't tend to hold with trolls, of course, who prefer victim blaming to self-reflection and tend to believe that if you're online at all, you're fair game. Take weev, the world's best-known troll. In a strange and rambling interview with me he said, 'By and large, everybody that I have ever seen who [has] been trolled on the Internet, they've invited this behaviour on themselves. They've made public political statements. They maintain a public personality. If you don't want to be subject to public commentary, don't become a public figure.'

The upshot of all this? Don't be a woman – and certainly don't be a public figure. And if you happen to be both, woe betide you.

#

Someone who deeply understands the toxic mix of depression and trolling is Australian writer and activist Van Badham. Like Charlotte Dawson did, she suffers from depression. And, like Dawson did,

Badham endures relentless online abuse that frequently bleeds into her offline life.

Dawson reached out to Badham not long before she died. According to Badham, the TV personality wanted to give her strength and encouragement because she could see how badly Badham was being trolled. Dawson's kindness 'meant the world' to her, especially given that the pair didn't know each other, and Dawson had a high profile. She'd taken the time to reach out for no other reason than to be kind.

Then, a few weeks later, Badham learned of Dawson's death. 'When somebody said, "Oh my God, Charlotte Dawson's committed suicide because of trolling," literally, my thought was, *Of course she did*. I could understand. I didn't have to query that at all,' Badham tells me.

While online hate alone is unlikely to cause suicide, predator trolling can be a significant stressor in a person's life. The true danger lies in the melding of such trolling with other difficulties an individual may be experiencing. If you have depression, Badham says, 'trolling fuels the worst instincts of your illness'.

She points to the example of trolls telling Dawson to hang herself. 'The voices you've been fighting in your head when you've been really sick are suddenly external to your head and [this] validates the suicidal ideation. It seems to be evidence. And, for me, [I've] been working through a process of not using the internet to supply myself with evidence when I'm ill. That's the reality. I have episodes where things become very dark and I have to fight my way out of what's like a chemical hole of sadness,' she says.

What happens when this coincides with trolling? 'I have to stay off the internet. I've had to adapt or die.'

Badham's seemingly endless journey into the darkness of online abuse began when she started live-tweeting the ABC's panel discussion program *Q&A* in 2012, and her tweets began to be shared widely – and responded to.

'It became really pointed and really nasty ... And the way I was responding to it was not particularly healthy. When you're emotionally vulnerable, that's where you behave in ways that you wouldn't usually. And so I found myself getting into fights with these guys on Twitter because I was angry because my best friend [Van's father] was dying,' she recalls.

Things really escalated when she agreed to go on a Sky TV program hosted by political academic Peter van Onselen in 2013. Mainly, Badham said yes to give her dying father a laugh. 'I wore this fluorescent pink bra and a leopard-print dress. And they don't do hair and makeup at Sky, so I went on, and you can imagine what I looked like.'

Badham says within a couple of days she had hundreds of messages about 'how sexually ridiculous' she was: '"You're fat. You're ugly. You're a big slut, but you need a good root."'

In her typical style, she made a joke of this, tweeting a tongue-in-cheek response:

I reject the Right's criticism of me on #Contrarians that I 'need a good root'. I just want all my roots to know: you were totally great.[13]

Once a few articles reported about this, the trolling was on for young and old. 'The moment that that happened, all of a sudden I was on a whole bunch of different radars,' Badham says, 'and then the trolling started getting really bad because how dare I speak back to them? I was just in this firing line of these far-right lunatics from that moment on.' Badham sends me screenshots from Facebook depicting the kind of communication she's become used to. Sometimes she'll get hundreds of messages within a twenty-four-hour period – almost always from men:

She can't get a dog to please her.

You belong in an oven.

Bend over for some diseased anal before your throat is cut dumbshit, self-loathing hater of your parents.

Since her Sky appearance, Badham's trolling has been relentless – and has become extremely real-world. There was the time someone followed her home from her former job, at the Malthouse Theatre. Badham only knows this because the stranger found a way to look into her apartment – probably from the multistorey car park opposite her house. He tweeted about everything she did, including what she got up to with her boyfriend that evening.

In a separate incident, a package was sent to Badham's house in late 2015. It contained printed material depicting gang rape and genital mutilation. After that, she had to move house because her alarmed boyfriend insisted she wasn't safe.

The attacks against her are not only from the right. They come from the left too – and arguably these have been far more painful. Badham sends me more piles of screenshots and links. Some are tweets from a woman claiming to be a left-wing feminist. There's also a link to a Change.org petition attempting to get her fired from her column at *The Guardian* and a couple of Facebook hate groups created specifically to attack her. Badham believes these trolls – 'supposedly my left-wing comrades' – see her as 'a heretic' for perceived minor divergences from shared political views and therefore 'don't think of themselves as doing anything wrong' when they troll her. I'm reminded of Craig, suggesting that some on the left weren't left enough for his liking.

Badham can't tell the difference between extreme trolls on the left and those on the right. 'They all see themselves as warriors defending ideological purity. Realistically, both represent politically marginal communities.' She goes on to say their resentment about a perceived lack of influence and powerlessness magnifies their hatred.

This is a point reiterated by the right-wing troll Meepsheep. He believes predator trolling comes from all quarters. 'One of the big issues I have is that society treats cyberhate as if Neo-Nazis and the alt-right are the only people doing it. And the only example journalists ever use is Gamergate. To me this is pretty unconstructively biased. It is making the problem worse because you have all these angry young men who already feel like they're not listened to and then they get solely chastised by society for doing something that other groups are also participating in. What about the online hate coming from sjws [social justice warriors] and leftists too?'

What's striking in both Badham's and Dawson's stories is that they have to be online for their work – there's no choice. And yet it's this very 'workplace' where they are most in danger. This is something Dr Emma Jane, a senior research fellow at the University of New South Wales, returns to repeatedly in her work. She has spent nearly twenty years looking into online harassment, including conducting in-depth interviews with fifty-two Australian female cyberhate targets between 2015 and 2017.

Off the back of this huge body of work, she describes the 'range of professional and economic harms' that can result from the receipt of gendered cyberhate as 'an insidious new form of workplace harass-ment'.[14] This 'silences women, and constrains their ability to find jobs, market themselves, network, socialise, engage politically, and partake freely in self-expression and self-representation'.[15]

Jane identifies the 'double bind' cyberhate targets ultimately find themselves in: '[R]etreating from the internet means they cannot per-form the tasks required to do their jobs, yet staying online and enduring abuse and harassment can also hinder their productivity.'[16]

Employment lawyer Josh Bornstein agrees with Jane's assessment that cyberhate can be a workplace health and safety issue: 'While we have clear laws about the duty to maintain a safe workplace that are imposed on employers, who is responsible for maintaining a safe social media space? That's probably not just employers.'

Within her alarming book *Misogyny Online*, Jane notes some trolls systematically seek out victims who are 'known to be struggling with mental illness'. She writes: 'More and more attacks, which begin exclusively online, are spilling into offline domains.'[17]

The parallels with Badham's experiences are clear. In 2014 Badham even ended up in court after tweeting about a pro-refugee rally. A man tweeted back:

When's the demonstration for all the people who've been raped by refugees?

'I checked out this guy's Twitter profile and it was a far-right racist,' Badham says. 'And I wrote back, "When hell freezes over, you racist cunt."'

The next thing she knew, he was attempting to sue her. Bornstein, Badham's lawyer, wrote to the man's lawyers and they dropped him as a client. But the man continued to pursue her. He tweeted obsessively about her and seemed to be aware of the locations of both her home and work. He mentioned keeping notebooks about her and sent a tweet that referred to giving her two black eyes. On the advice of police, Badham attempted to take out an intervention order against him. He contested the order. Bornstein believes the man's attempt to keep Badham in court was an exercise in coercive control. He advised her to drop the order.

'And then, of course, he decided to go after me for costs, which is unheard of in this kind of complaint. And the cost actions meant that I had to go back to court again,' Badham says. 'He was putting in thousand-page depositions to the court about how I was an enemy of all men and part of a feminist movement that was going to destroy the male gender,' she says. 'He put in subpoenas to have my bank account frozen, have my passport cancelled and to gain access to my email.'

Although the magistrate found in favour of Badham, the process took its toll – you can hear it in the anxious, rapid fire of her voice. 'It was a year of my life,' she says. 'There were … six or seven court appearances and I was strung out, exhausted, stressed out of my mind. I'm not a suspicious person by nature, but the ongoing cyberhate has changed my personality. I mourn the person who used to presume that everybody was good and that everybody always had the best of intentions. I hate being in that defensive mindset all the time. I hate it. It's not me. I'm a very, very open person. But at the same time, when people are … [wanting to] target you and to threaten you, and the implicit threats are genuinely terrifying, that does change the way that you relate to people.'

Listening to her talk, it's hard to see how Badham has managed to come through this so far – or how she will manage in the future. As a whole, the pieces of the puzzle are so extreme. As they were with Dawson, Badham's predator trolls are an omnipresent pack of relentless attack dogs, sniffing out perceived vulnerabilities. Just waiting for a chance to rip into her.

Almost to soothe me as much as herself, Badham says, 'I draw strength from my relationship and I take consolation from my faith. I have to pray for those people and that gives me a sense of control.'

#

Things escalated for Badham to a point where the police became involved. On the day of her father's funeral in 2013, a man who'd been harassing her for some time sent her violent and abusive sexual images of women, with captions such as 'This is what your father thought of you' and 'Your father deserved to die. I'd kill myself if you were my daughter.'

'I just couldn't believe it,' she says. 'I was literally putting my father in the ground when this happened.' She remembers thinking, 'Wow, if I can survive this, I can actually survive anything. I called the police … and the police were like, "Well, get off the internet",' she says, echoing the familiar refrain of cyberhate victims. In all of this, Badham wants to make it clear she doesn't blame the police. For her, it's all about context. 'They've always been really kind because they're cops and … they know you're a victim of something and they respond to you appropriately, but they think there's nothing they can do and that's what's really frustrating.

'My relationship with the police these days is a paper trail in case somebody kills me,' she says. 'When it's really bad and when I think that I am genuinely at risk, I log it all with the police, just so it's all there. So, in case one of these people does dehumanise me to the point where I get opportunistically murdered there will be a trail that the police can follow and that's how I have to think of it.'

I'm a little bit deaf, so when Badham first says this to me, I think, *Did I hear that right?* Then when it's clear this is, in fact, what she said, it's such an uncomfortable thought that my next response is to minimise it: *Surely that's overstating the case?*

The truth is, though, she isn't the only one who feels like this. In Amnesty International's major report *Toxic Twitter*, US reproductive rights activist Pamela Merritt told researchers: 'After five years of online harassment coupled with offline harassment, I have basically reconciled with the fact that I'm prepared to die for the work I do. That might happen. If you get 200 death threats, it only takes one person who really wants to kill you.'[18]

Being killed as a result of predator trolling isn't just a fanciful notion made up by 'hysterical' women – as trolls may imply. In May 2018 the United Nations called upon authorities in India to protect 'journalist Rana Ayyub, who has received death threats following an online hate campaign'. Ayyub's work has included investigations into corrupt police officers and government officials. The UN believed that, given another Indian female journalist, Gauri Lankesh, had been murdered the previous year in similar circumstances, Ayyub's life was in grave danger.[19] Like Badham and Dawson, Ayyub speaks her mind.

Upon hearing of Lankesh's death, Ayyub described the killers of her compatriot as both 'cowards' and 'disgusting'. Despite the credible threats against her, she has so far refused to leave India, believing this would be effectively telling her trolls their intimidation tactics were working.[20]

If you are a woman, and your job is to say things online, sometimes strongly, sometimes against the grain, the potential for real violence increases dramatically. Bornstein, who has acted for a number of trolling victims pro bono, has witnessed the trend, and its fallout: 'Badham is a very good example of someone who's outspoken, who's a woman with strong views, and women with strong views on the internet cop an absolute shocking response … the most vile, revolting, threatening, sexualised, nasty responses. The capacity of one person to torment another and cause harm to another is only limited by their imagination.'

#

Taking this notion of human creativity and online harassment to its furthest extreme, you can even use the internet to cyberbully or predator troll yourself. Experts have started calling this 'digital self-harm'. At a glance, it may seem unfathomable as to why someone would predator troll themselves. But if you dig deeper, this complex behaviour continues to tell the story of how impossible it is to separate the harm we can come to online with the harms that we suffer offline.

The first time digital self-harm entered public discourse was when fourteen-year-old Hannah Smith from Leicestershire, England, died by suicide in 2013 after being harassed online for months. Tragically, it turned out she'd sent herself the vicious, bullying messages on an anonymous social networking site called Ask.fm in the weeks leading up to her death.[21] (The website has been implicated in numerous teen suicides.[22])

During an investigation into Smith's death the following year, the South Leicestershire coroner Catherine Mason heard the young woman had been subject to offline bullying at school, especially in relation to her eczema. Smith's internet search history and posts showed she'd been considering ending her own life for a few months prior to her death.

The person who first told me about digital self-harm – and Smith's case – is Dr Justin Patchin from the US Cyberbullying Research Center in Wisconsin. Along with his colleague Dr Sameer Hinduja, Patchin released research in 2017 investigating the incidence of digital self-harm among 5593 middle and high school students. The paper shows a little more than 6 per cent of students 'have anonymously posted something online about themselves that was mean' and boys 'were significantly more likely to report participation' (7.1 per cent) compared with girls (5.3 per cent).[23]

The researchers further found 74 per cent of those who said they digitally self-harmed had been bullied at school in the last thirty days. Students who had been bullied at school were four to five times as likely to have engaged in digital self-harm than those who hadn't. The same paper indicates that more than 41 per cent of students who engaged in self-trolling had depressive symptoms. Students in this category were also far more likely to engage in digital self-harm than those who didn't have depressive symptoms.[24]

Academics use the term 'suicidal ideation' to encompass whether a person has seriously considered, planned or attempted suicide. Patchin explains that while suicidal ideation is not specifically addressed in the research paper, it is also 'significantly correlated with digital self-harm'. 'The suicidal ideation scale ranges from zero to four,' he says, 'with higher numbers meaning more suicidal ideation. Those who reported participating in digital self-harm scored 1.06 on the scale compared to 0.21 for those who had not participated in digital self-harm.'

It's worth noting that in Smith's case, the coroner was unable to draw conclusions about whether the offline bullying directly caused Smith to partake in digital self-harm or contributed to her death. She stated: 'The evidence I have was that on the balance of probabilities they [the cyberhate messages] would all have been at Hannah's own hand. Why she did it, I don't know.'[25]

Talking to me over Skype from his home office in Wisconsin, Patchin tells me about another relevant case of digital self-harm. While he and Hinduja were in the middle of their research project, a police officer sent him some screenshots of online harassment directed at a teenage girl. The messages had been written on yet another anonymous social networking site, and the girl had shown them to her father, who took them to the police:

You should jump off a roof and kill yourself.

You're pathetic and don't deserve to be alive.

If U don't kill yourself tonight, I'll do it for you.[26]

For Patchin, who was spending his days and nights analysing digital self-harm, something just didn't ring true. 'That's just not typically how students cyberbully each other,' he says. 'Just the language used, it didn't add up.' He promptly emailed the police officer: 'That's pretty bad ... but don't be surprised if she sent these messages herself.'

After contacting the social media platform, he learned the abusive messages were, in fact, written by the teenager herself. They'd only been posted privately because the website's moderators stopped them from going live.

Among the students who participated in digital self-harm, the researchers further noted concerning correlations with other issues, including identifying as 'nonheterosexual' and experience of drug use, depressive symptoms, offline school bullying or offline self-harm. Patchin says a child who engages in offline self-harm is 'over twice as likely' to engage in digital self-harm (compared with one who doesn't engage in offline self-harm).

This is a red flag. While some people stigmatise self-harm as an attention-seeking behaviour, it's usually a sign of deep distress. The teens I've interviewed who engaged in self-harm did so in response to terrible life circumstances. One young woman was starved and physically abused by her father. She told me, 'It [self-harm] was my way of saying: "Please I need help. I don't know to ask for it."' Another young woman I spoke to told me she was sexually assaulted as a very young child. The self-harm was her way of living with the acute trauma that resulted from it.

According to Dr Jo Robinson, senior research fellow at Orygen, the National Centre of Excellence in Youth Mental Health in Melbourne, self-harm is a coping mechanism for 'acute, deep distress'. It is also, she says, 'the single biggest predictor of future suicides'.[27] This link is supported by Patchin and Hinduja's findings.[28]

The study of digital self-harm – as opposed to offline self-harm – is extremely new and there is unfortunately no known data regarding its prevalence in adults. But perhaps when we start to measure the real-life consequences of cyberhate, laying out the pieces and stitching them together, we will discover that it is just one patch in a very large quilt. We might also find, as the stories of Badham and Dawson suggest, that once the patches of online and offline harms are sewn neatly together, the stitches are so small as to be almost invisible. There's no demarcation between harm done online and harm done offline – they are one and the same.

#

'I spoke to her the day before she died,' Charlotte Dawson's friend Megan Hustwaite says, 'and I had no idea on that day. I still don't know what state she was in ... she seemed fine. And then the last thing we said was, "Love you." And I wondered [later] did she know that was going to be our last conversation? It was just so final. And even now, I think of things that I'd tell her.'

Although it seems almost impossible to ask in this moment, I'm compelled to push right up to the edge of this conversation. Trolls, I say to Hustwaite, are always claiming, 'It's just words. It's not real life. The internet can't hurt anyone.'

For just a moment, I can see the grief in her face. And a flash of anger too. 'The trolling and cyber abuse that Charlotte copped was IRL. In internet talk, it was in real life. And she's now dead in real life. So she didn't just close down her Twitter account and that stopped the trolling. She's dead.

'Ultimately, she did what so many faceless strangers told her to do, and how do they feel about that? How are they going to live with that for the rest of their lives? You can't take those things back now.'

Hustwaite asks me to see if I can find one of the people who told her friend to die. I spend a long time trying to locate those trolls. Many of their Twitter accounts are suspended. I send tweets and Reddit messages and emails to those harassers I can find. I even message one bloke via a website where his artwork is listed for sale. Perhaps unsurprisingly, none of them respond.

Not wanting to let Hustwaite down, I text her to explain I'm getting the silent treatment.

'I feel like that says so much,' she texts back.

The closest I get is an anonymous, archived comment from 4chan dated August 2014: 'I use [sic] to troll charlotte too but quickly deleted my posts after she actually killed herself.'

Finally, I ask Mark about it. Offhandedly, he says: 'There wasn't any particular group of people with Charlotte, it was just a mass of randoms. Like, everyone just jumped in and started talking shit to her.'

'So what made her a target?' I ask.

'The reaction. That's all it ever is,' he says. 'She was a reactionary, emotional bitch. Asking for it.'

What's striking about this statement is just how similar it is in sentiment to the frequent implications about Dawson from the media. This is what female victims of male violence have endured for all time: *She wouldn't shut up. She was asking for it.*

7

Misogyny on the internet

ON 8 AUGUST 2018 I appeared on Stan Grant's ABC TV program *Matter of Fact*, to discuss free-speech absolutism. A few days earlier far-right nationalist Blair Cottrell had appeared on twenty-four-hour news channel Sky, spruiking his views on immigration. As someone who had previously expressed fervent anti-Jewish, anti-Islam, anti-woman and pro-Nazi views, his appearance on mainstream TV sparked widespread public debate over whether extremists should be legitimised by being given a public platform.[1]

In the process of writing this book, I'd given substantial thought to the hazy perimeters of free speech, so it stood to reason that I had some things to say on the topic. When Grant's show aired, I received a tweet that didn't engage with my arguments, but instead attacked the way my face looked:

You look like an actual hook-nosed goblin.[2]

(Perhaps a young white male offended that a woman had a voice and was using it. I'm not stereotyping – this is what trolling research points to, so call it an educated guess.[3])

I wish this was an anomaly. This happens pretty much every time I go on television. I'm not alone. Julia Baird – who hosts *The Drum* on the ABC – acknowledges the impact of this type of vitriol in a Twitter message to me: 'Some women are so badly trolled when they come on television that they are reluctant to appear at all on shows like *The Drum* and *Q&A*.'

As a case in point, Shen Narayanasamy, Human Rights Campaign Director for the left-wing lobby group GetUp, declared on *The Drum* in July 2018: 'It's just dangerous for me to be on Twitter. I would get so much abuse it would be pointless.'

She went on to say that right then – as the show aired that night – her staff were staying back in GetUp's office to block all the cyberhate as it rolled in. The aim was to sort the problem out then and there so that they didn't have to trawl through reams of abuse at the start of the working day the following morning. Narayanasamy referred to being a person of colour and wearing a headscarf and pointedly asked, 'Why is it that my coming on this panel, and having a voice that's coming out of my mouth, [is] such a threat to so many people?'

Women, she said, were often afraid to say anything publicly because of the harassment they receive: 'We've got to acknowledge, already, that the way public debate is shaping actively silences at least half the population.'[4]

She's right. If you combine gender with being a person of colour, the situation looks grim. A US study of nearly 974 undergraduate students in 2009 found that 'the group that experienced the most cyberstalking victimization was non-white females, with 53.2 percent of this group experiencing some form of cyberstalking during their lives.'

In case you're curious about how this compares with other groups, the paper goes on to say, 'The next most frequently victimized group was white females with 45.4 percent of white females experiencing cyberstalking. Nonwhite males were the next most victimized group at 40 percent, followed by white males at 31 percent.'[5] Make no mistake. Predator trolling in this context is essentially a tool that is used to delegitimise the voices of women and their expertise.

English columnist and author Laurie Penny has written extensively about sexism and the internet. She homes in on the way outspoken women – just like Dawson and Badham and Narayanasamy – are attacked online:

Trashing is insidious. It can damage its subject for life, personally and professionally. Whether or not people sympathize, the damage has been done. It doesn't matter if the attacks have any basis in truth: What matters is that she is difficult. This woman who doesn't have the sense to protect herself from public shaming by piping down, by walking with her eyes lowered … In the 1970s, trashing had to be done with analog tools. Today, it is faster, harder, more savagely intimate.[6]

And it's not just outspoken women, either. In 2017 Amnesty International surveyed 4000 women across eight countries. Nearly a quarter of those women had experienced online abuse or harassment.[7] (The UN Broadband Commission put this figure much higher, stating '[A]lmost three quarters of women online have been exposed to some form of cyber violence.'[8]) From there, Amnesty found that more than 'three quarters (76 percent) of women who experienced abuse or harassment on a social media platform made changes to how they use the platform'. Some of those women who were abused online 'said they'd stopped posting content that expressed their opinion on certain issues'.[9]

When it comes to the chilling effect of cyberhate, some of us are certainly feeling the cold more than others. British research from 2014 found that female journalists and TV presenters receive three times the abuse of their male counterparts.[10]

As female journalists, we often get the sense that we're copping a tsunami of hate. And although we know male colleagues cop hate too, it's hard not to feel they are dealing with a comparative trickle. Well. It turns out this is not just a feeling. It's backed up by data and research. In Amnesty International's major *Toxic Twitter* report, Dunja Mijatović, former Organization for Security and Co-operation in Europe Representative on Freedom of the Media, submits that 'the severity, in terms of both sheer amount and content of abuse, including sexist and misogynistic vitriol, is much more extreme for female journalists'.[11]

Effectively, then, women in the media are frequently operating in unsafe workplaces. While giving evidence at Australian Senate hearings into cyberbullying in 2018, Maurice Blackburn Lawyers argued that for journalists and other employees who are required to be online as part of their work there ought to be 'enforceable sanctions against employers who fail in their duty of care to provide a safe workplace for their employees'.[12]

The way Badham sees it, 'You have generations of men who have grown up with an expectation of advantage who don't have it anymore. And that displacement in status ... has made a lot of ordinary people very angry.'

More specifically, Badham believes men attack her online because of what she's writing about. 'Where trolling got really, really bad for me was obviously when I started writing for *The Guardian*. I wrote about class, I wrote about economics, I wrote about industrial relations, I wrote about politics and I wrote about the tax system.

'The things that I'm interested in talking about are traditionally seen as male preserves. For a lot of men, it's a disconnect to see women articulating on those issues and women having insight and, God help us, expertise. It is terrifying to them, and like any scared animal, they fight with claws and stings.'

A report from the Association for Progressive Communications and developmental aid organisation Hivos underscores Badham's experience: 'Prominent women bloggers, journalists and leaders are regularly subjected to online abuse and violent threats that attack their sexuality and right to express an opinion, especially when it is related to fields where men have traditionally been held as experts, such as gaming, politics and technology.'[13]

Trying to get Badham fired seems to have become an ongoing hobby for her trolls. In 2015 they fabricated a claim that she'd bashed up an old man at a rally. *The Guardian*'s opinion editor, Gabrielle Jackson, recalls the incident – and a number of similar occasions. 'Of course, *The Guardian* investigates these accusations but it was pretty easy to find out that this was a baseless claim,' she tells me. 'The abuse I've seen directed towards Van Badham is obscene and out of all proportion. There are few people I've seen this amount of vitriol directed towards, it's usually women, and, more commonly, women of colour.'

Some social media platforms appear to be working towards solutions. Facebook, to its credit, recognised the stream of abuse being received by female journalists via private messages. Reporters asked the platform if they were able to publicly share the abuse – something that would normally violate Facebook's privacy policies. '[I]n response to feedback that the sharing of these messages could help stop this type of harassment,' Facebook told recent Senate hearings into cyberbullying, 'we made an exception to allow the sharing of screenshots when done to bear witness to the harassment experienced (provided that it was done in a way that was not itself harassing).'[14]

It's not all positive, though. According to Facebook, all posts must comply with their 'Community Standards'. Broadly speaking, these policies govern safety on the platform. So far so good. The issue – when I first started writing this book – was that Facebook's bullying policies, which run alongside the Community Standards, did not apply to public figures. Journalists are considered public figures. Facebook's rationale was that the company wants 'to allow discourse, which often includes critical discussion of people who are featured in the news or who have a large public audience'.[15] This might be a lofty democratic ideal but in the face of disproportionate attacks on female journalists, the policy effectively skewed against women in the media.

Sherele Moody is one of these women. She's a journalist and founder of the Red Heart Campaign, which aims to raise awareness about violence against women and children. This activism makes her the target of relentless misogynistic and homophobic predator trolling from 'people who think I needlessly highlight male violence'. Most of it starts on Facebook – but it does not stay online.

'The trolls often post my photos on their socials, making comments about my looks, my sexuality and my gender,' Moody says. 'One even implied I had sex with my dog … There is a real undercurrent of hating women in it. The attacks are personal and often centred around me being female. For example, the language they use – rape threats or jokes about my appearance – would never be used if they were having this discussion with other guys.'

As a demonstration of this, Moody sends me a screenshot of a meme made by one of her misogynist trolls. Underneath a photo of her pixie-like face the text reads: 'Man hating feminist or teenage boy who works at Coles? You decide!'

Misogynistic abuse is one thing. But what's terrifying in Moody's story is just how far the trolls will go to hurt her. Despite being a silent voter, they know where she lives. And despite the security features installed in her home, they've found their way onto her property. 'About twelve months ago my Great Dane, Reuben, was poisoned with some sort of acid. The chemical melted the flesh on his mouth, tongue and throat. I was extremely lucky not to lose him. I do not know who did it and no one has been charged but I have no doubt it was someone that I've pissed off online.

'On Sunday night my horse, Frank, disappeared from his paddock. On Monday evening an unknown bloke left a message on my message bank saying the horse had been sent to the glue factory. Frank is still missing. He has been reported stolen and I sent photos of him and his brands to the knackery, in the hope that he won't be killed if that is where he is,' she says. 'There is nothing that is off limits to these people. Nothing.'

A few days later Moody tells me that Frank was found dead in thick scrub. She can't make herself believe someone has killed him on purpose: 'We don't know if it was deliberate or accidental. We will bury him this morning in his paddock.'

It's not just her personal life that's affected by predator trolling but her ability to run the Red Heart Campaign. Aside from flat-out abuse and threats, the men's rights trolls employ a particular tactic with Moody that gets her temporarily banned from Facebook over and over again. She tells me this has happened at least fifteen times.

'Basically, a group of people calling themselves anti-feminists encourage people to mass-report my page, personal and public, [including] all the comments I make as well as the comments made by my friends,' she says. 'The aim is to trick Facebook into shutting down myself and people connected to me. In one week I had six bans – and five of them related to me highlighting male violence and one related to homophobia.'

Moody believes trolls are gaming the system: 'The use of the Facebook hate speech reporting process is a really effective way to silence women who speak openly about issues such as gendered violence.'

Although Facebook's media team has talked Moody through their reporting processes and worked with her to get some of the bans overturned, she's still frustrated: 'This has been going on for more than two years, so nothing has actually changed,' she says.

In my seemingly endless email correspondence with Facebook's public relations department, they acknowledge they have been working closely with Moody. The email to me states 'on background' (which means I can use the information but can't attribute it to anyone or quote it directly) that the company makes decisions about whether to remove a piece of content based on its Community Standards and not the number of times it's reported.[16] The email also points me to brand-new bullying policies, posted by Facebook's Global Head of Safety, Antigone Davis, just the day before.[17] '[S]evere attacks that directly engage a public figure will not be allowed under the new policy,' she states.

We'll just have to wait and watch as to how those changes play out and whether they make a real difference to someone like Moody. Perhaps some of us would consider giving up our advocacy after sustaining such damage to our lives as a result of it. Yet for Moody, her fight against gendered violence is personal. She's a survivor of parental abuse. And, quite aside from that horror, her stepfather was also a murderer and a rapist.[18] 'It really distresses me that people put so much hate and vitriol into shutting me down instead of using that anger to shut down violent men.'

For days I can't stop thinking about Moody's dead horse. I write and ask how she's going.

'The man who brought him back to our place and dug his grave made a heart-shaped mound over him. At least he is home,' Moody writes back.

My instinct is to latch on to this show of compassion – from a man to a woman – in the sea of hate. Yet as I read through endless online chatlogs related to trolling, over many months, hope fades.

#

From my research into the notorious troll weev, I have screenshots of IRC chats from December 2011. He seems to be relaying a violent sexual fantasy about sodomising a woman who is crying: 'Her makeup gets all over the blanket.'

What women really want, weev says in this stomach-churning rant, 'is to be pinned down and viciously fucked and raped like the whores they are'.

'Women should be beaten. If a woman gets out of line, hit her til she falls to the floor and kick her in the stomach,' weev writes.

(Bizarrely, in the same IRC session weev repeatedly mentions watching *My Little Ponies* videos. When I try to ask him about this via Skype chat, he ignores me.)

I mention this IRC exchange to Meepsheep, who has known weev for a long time. 'All this stuff about punching and raping women is making me ill,' I write.

He sends back a virtual shrug: 'He says a lot of that kind of stuff. I guess when you're interacting on IRC you just get used to it.'

Not long afterwards, I read an article by *Newsweek* journalist Michael Edison Hayden about the deep-rooted misogyny within the alt-right. 'The alt-right movement – which critics suggest is merely a rebrand of an older white supremacist ideology – has struggled mightily to recruit white women to their cause in part because of the abusive rhetoric and actions of movement leaders, analysts suggest,' Edison Hayden writes.

Referring to an incident where prominent Neo-Nazi Matthew Heimbach was arrested on charges of domestic battery, the journalist continues, 'The alleged incident with Heimbach is not an isolated one – either in terms of his own violence toward women or the way in which women who are close to the movement are treated on the whole.'[19]

And I wonder then about the men who created the internet all those decades ago. How they believed in the great democratisation of knowledge and envisaged a worldwide web that would connect us all and give us a voice.[20] Certainly, they were visionaries. But how far could they actually see? *Did they really understand what it would mean?* That those motivated by hate and fear would effectively be handed megaphones for the endless amplification of their prejudice. That this would create the modern version of the Salem witch trials every day of the week.

8

Deep in the grey

O N THIS CLEAR March day the sun is shining and the sky is cloudless blue. I'm driving off the highway and there are paddocks of crops and small towns stuffed with antique stores. As I often have over these last six months, I'm thinking about the long, strange and damaging process of writing this book. How it has led me to some people and places within driving or flying distance and to others so far away and isolated that only a Skype connection will get me there.

With one hand on the steering wheel and the other resting on my leg, I'm humming to the Cowboy Junkies. The troll hunter is also on my mind. He's a lawyer, journalist and hacker. He hates bullies and, sometimes, when the online attacks become extreme, he'll hunt predator trolls to try to figure out who they are. The troll hunter understands the inside of their world but he's not on their side. This makes him a crucial ally for me. He's the one who told me about Jeffery Richards – the man I'm driving to meet. (For reasons that will become clear, this is not his real name.)

A few weeks earlier, the troll hunter sent me a huge file of screenshots of the online bile directed at Richards and told me this case represents 'the worst trolling I've ever come across'. Having piqued my interest, the troll hunter leaves me to investigate. Although he loosely indicates that Richards' mental health has been severely damaged by cyberhate, he doesn't forewarn me that the threads of this story are so tangled they can't reasonably be straightened. Or that the pivotal question of how much you – and your decision-making – can be damaged by cyberhate will be thrown into stark relief and yet remain perpetually unanswered and unanswerable.

At this early stage, I can't know that Richards' story will bring me face to face with the very demons that led to me and my family being trolled in the first place. And that because of this – and my fear of being hoodwinked again, and hunted online by a lynch mob – I will consider deleting this chapter from the book altogether. His is not an open-and-shut case of extreme cyberhate. It's complicated by issues of mental health, problematic contact with a child and possession of child exploitation material.

Like me, most people don't want things to be in this deep shade of grey – ambiguous and morally confusing. They want black and white. Things are easier if other individuals are either cast as monsters or saints. Either *just like us* or *not like us at all*. The truth for Jeffery Richards, for the trolls themselves, and in fact for most of us, is far blurrier.

I park the car. This isn't an interview. Richards just wants to meet me first. To figure out if he trusts me. He expresses concern that I'm travelling such a distance just to talk.

'Mate,' I tell him, 'this is my job.'

Ours is not a conversation strangers could casually and comfortably overhear. So I've done my research and found a cafe with a garden. When he arrives, I'm already sitting down away from the buzz of customers and the speakers blaring gratingly cheerful music. Always short on time, I'm scribbling in a notepad.

Compared to the photos I've seen of him, he's heavier and more haggard. 'This isn't on the record, is it?' he asks and I place the pen down and push it away.

'No, it's not,' I reply and order us coffee, bringing it back to the table in paper takeaway cups. We talk for nearly two hours. As we're winding down to leave, I ask, 'How would you characterise the effect this has had on your life?'

He's been forced to move house three times, has lost six jobs and more than $270,000 worth of income as a result of being a predator-trolling victim.

He's crying and wipes his face with his shirt. 'Sorry, I'm so labile now.' Finally, he says, 'It's destroyed my life.' (To ease your troubled mind, yes, Richards gave me permission to print this part of our conversation – despite it being ostensibly off the record.)

#

The second time we meet it's in a sprawling workers' club. He talks about having activism in his blood and that when the Cronulla race riots hit the headlines in 2005, everything changed; he couldn't stand the racism. Along with a couple of like-minded friends, Richards started both a blog and a Facebook page against racism. For the purposes of this story, we'll call it NoRacismOz. It quickly developed a large and committed following.

'It just was born out of frustration because Facebook never took down a single racist post that we reported,' he says.

After giving a speech at a major public event in 2011, Richards says, he was photographed and followed home. The trolls got into his mailbox and found his payslip – indicating he was employed as a teacher – and electricity bill. Not long after, details of his home address, his place of work and the names of his mother and brother were posted online.

Among the screenshots of Facebook comments and memes made by his enemies over many years, there are posts referring to plans to 'bring him down' and 'disfigure him'. Their memes and posts repeatedly contain references to him being a paedophile. For a teacher, this was the worst possible way to be smeared. Terrified, he went to the police. A newspaper story from the same year reports that police were looking for the troll (or trolls) who created a fake Facebook profile, pretended to be a teacher and targeted children at the educator's school in order to frame him as a paedophile. The teacher in the article isn't named, but Richards tells me it's him.

One troll posted the Facebook profiles of eleven of Richards' family members with the message, '[T]hese are all Richards' family, we are going to take photos from their accounts then photoshop their pics with filth or pedo stuff or anything sick and degrading … [T]hen send them back to all his family … and hopefully his own family might bash him.'

Richards' family certainly felt the pain of being attacked. His mother's apartment was broken into and photos were stolen. All kinds of things were put into her letterbox – including a dead rat, a dead fish and the doctored photographs implying her son was a paedophile.

The predator trolls – who used more than 300 separate Facebook accounts – also made numerous separate memes about Richards' brother and his beloved late grandmother. He says they took one of his favourite photos of him with his grandmother. 'We were having such a lovely day together. They doctored the Australian paedophile Dennis Ferguson's face onto it and passed that around everywhere. My grandma's face was still fully visible in it and it just broke my heart. There was a lot of that kind of stuff, but that was probably the hardest one.' Richards is visibly upset talking about this.

'I still feel quite strongly that the backlash was my fault,' he says, 'and that I had a chance many years ago when it [the trolling] started, to walk away from activism, and perhaps it might not have escalated.'

By way of explaining why the self-declared 'patriots' responded with such vitriol, he explains, 'There were some people who had lost their jobs as a direct result of having their screenshots reaching a wider audience [on NoRacismOz].'

This theory seems to be backed up by Facebook comments from the trolls themselves. In one post the author writes he missed out on a well-paying job 'because of Jeffery Richards and his … lefty knuckleheads. I'd love to disfigure him big time the filthy rockspider!'

The trolling was already bad. But it was about to get a whole lot worse and damage Richards' life to an unfathomable extent. During the many hours we spend together, it sometimes feels like we're two people sitting, dirty and blinking, in the aftershocks of a nuclear explosion.

Richards loved his job as a schoolteacher and the kids loved him too. He'd get into school at 7 am and often still be there at 6.30 pm. 'I just liked the way you could structure a day so that there was a good mix of fun and educational challenges. Everybody in the school – other teachers, students, parents – knew that I was one of the hardest-working teachers there. Principals would always get letters from parents saying, "I want my kid to be in his class", he tells me.

By 2012 the abuse escalated to the point where a group of trolls made good on their threats to turn up at his school in 'protest'. According to Richards, they did this several times, waving Australian flags and trying to hand out pamphlets to parents. He felt obliged to bring up the harassment with his class. He explained to his students that because of his activism, he was the target of extreme trolling.

'I don't want you to go googling my name,' he told them. 'I'm asking you as a human being just to not do that because it's not healthy and some of the stuff online will be very damaging for you to read.'

Richards tried to alert the authorities: 'Leadership in schools knew about it. The union knew about it. The [education] department knew about it. None of them helped, by the way. None of them gave me any assistance whatsoever.' Neither the union nor the education department responded to my repeated email queries about his case.

On advice from police, Richards always took screenshots of the abuse. The trolls weren't just making memes and writing abusive messages. They were continually making fake 'Jeffery Richards' profiles that spewed out messages purportedly advocating adult sex with children. Some of the trolls were also sending him child abuse material. He'd get videos of naked children playing, for example, alongside offensive messages such as, 'Here's some wank fodder for you, disgusting pedo.' He saved all the evidence to Dropbox and every three or four months, he'd visit the police station and give them the material he'd collected.

Meanwhile, in 2014, he was promoted to assistant principal at a new school. While this should have been a career highlight for a young man in his thirties, he struggled.

'Nobody knew me,' he says. 'I'd ride the day out, feeling pretty empty and lonely and then just sort of looking forward until after school finished. I was pretty emotional all the time and I'd often stupidly pass up the opportunity to ... sit in the staffroom and eat with people.'

Reflecting further on the impact of leaving behind his former school community, Richards says: 'I was definitely very depressed … I just lost a whole bunch of people who really loved me.'

However, according to Richards, his declining mental heath didn't greatly affect his home life. Although sometimes he'd 'have a bit of a private cry', nothing changed between him and his wife. Their relationship was solid.

Much later – after it all started to unravel and Richards made a sequence of choices he couldn't undo – he was diagnosed by a clinical psychologist with chronic adjustment disorder, alongside severe anxiety, severe stress and severe depression.

#

Olive was a child from Richards' former class. According to him, the nine-year-old didn't have a father figure and looked up to him. Although her mother, Sandra, used to flirt, Richards describes their relationship as 'matey'. 'I had no real attraction to her or desire to leave my wife for her, but she was one of those people you can talk to and you kind of get along with jovially,' he explains.

Although Richards had accepted a Facebook friend request from Sandra, he didn't accept requests from students. One evening, after moving schools, his loneliness was getting to him. He missed his former students and decided to accept all the requests that were sitting there – about twenty-five of them. 'I validated it to myself, "Well, I'm not their teacher anymore",' he says. 'I knew that they would say things, like, "I miss you." "You were the best teacher I ever had." "Why can't you come back to the school?" I wanted to see them written down. It's pretty narcissistic, I guess. Would that be the right word? It just gave me a good feeling.'

When I press him – because this doesn't seem like a good enough explanation for communicating with a young child in this way – he says: 'The awkward thing is that when you do something well or you do something that is right and just, like fighting racism or being a good teacher, there's a big part of you that wants to do it because you think it's the good thing to do. But there's also the affirmation that you get out of it.'

It's at this point that I start to wonder how these seemingly disparate parts of his story click together. Was it the impact of moving schools that altered Richards' judgement? Or was the insidious, sustained cyberhate corroding his ability to remain on an even keel – just like it had with Dawson and with Badham?

While I'm unable to state where Richards lives, I can tell you the code of conduct for that state's education department explicitly forbids teachers developing a relationship with a pupil that may be considered personal as opposed to professional. It also states it's unacceptable for teachers to be friends with students on social media platforms.

Out of all the students' requests that Richards accepted, Olive chatted to him the most on Facebook Messenger. He admits to feeling slightly uncomfortable. Richards says he'd ask Olive, 'Can you just make sure your mum knows I'm talking to you?' He never checked whether Sandra actually did know.

'At the more innocent end of inappropriateness, I was saying, "Oh, I really miss you. You were so sweet." And I'd always say things like, "Stop being cute." At the worst end of the inappropriate scale, I was cracking jokes about bums,' Richards says.

According to court documents Richards also sent Olive 'numerous "hugs" and "kisses" using the abbreviation "o" and "x"' and told her 'a number of times' he 'misses' her. Olive and another child had started sending him silly pictures, including one with their clothed backsides pointing at the camera. In response Richards sent Olive a picture of naked toddlers with a comment about their bottoms. Some of his messages used words like 'beautiful' and 'cutie' and referenced nudity. At one stage, he asked for a photo of Olive and the other child's feet.

'I knew they were crossing the line,' Richards says about his messages. 'I can't justify it … I've spent the last four years reflecting on what a fuckwit I was.' He says he was 'giddy on just reconnecting' and wanted to keep the kids 'totally excited about the conversation'. 'Kids always love talking about underwear and kids love talking about [children's author] Andy Griffiths' books about bums,' he says.

'This looks like grooming,' I say.

'My end goal was not "Let's eventually have sex with these kids". My end goal was I want them to continue to be engaged in this conversation because I'm enjoying it,' Richards says. 'I know they're in this room together, laughing their heads off. I know that they just see me as someone completely different to all the other teachers, who just couldn't give a shit.' He tells me he never had any attraction to Olive or, more broadly, to children.

There is no way to know the exact effects of the sustained predator trolling on Jeffery Richards, how it affected his brain chemistry or his later decisions. The insights of a clinical psychologist's report in 2017 are limited; the omissions are glaring. Aside from mentioning several times that Richards was the 'target of racist groups', the psychologist does not unpick how this may (or may not) have affected him. The psychologist does note, however, that 'there is nothing in Mr Richards's psychosexual development to predict aberrant sexual behaviour ... Mr Richards was, in my opinion, in a regressed state during the offending period'. When psychologists use the word 'regressed' they usually mean a person abandons age-appropriate behaviour and instead slips into a more child-like state. This is a coping mechanism.[1]

'In my opinion, Mr Richards was in the throes of significant and severe symptoms of depression and anxiety ... which in turn would have interfered significantly with his judgement and his ability to think rationally,' the report states. The psychologist notes Richards was tearful during his psychological examination, that he has 'moderate difficulties in the area of anger management' and 'has entertained suicidal thoughts with some intent'. This comment refers to the period after Richards was charged.

#

Somehow Sandra, Olive's mother, came across the paedophile memes Richards' trolls had posted – by the dozen – online. One of them featured Richards' image. It suggested he was 'WANTED' and stated:

HE IS STALKING YOUR
CHILDREN AND POSTING
THEIR PICTURES TO HIS
PEADOPHILIC [sic] PORN SITE

Underneath was the graphic and phone number for Crime Stoppers, the service that allows members of the public to anonymously contact the police about criminal activity. In that moment, Richards says, 'My life's battles for more than ten years met at a very awkward position ... I've never blamed that parent. I would have gone to the police straight away as well.'

The police investigated Richards late in 2014. They searched his house and went through all his electronic devices. They took his laptop but, according to Richards, reassured him that although his actions were 'inappropriate' they were not 'indecent'.

'I felt that if I was honest about things, hopefully the picture would piece itself together. There's no point in hiding anything or staying silent. I assumed they'd have the context,' he says, referring to the hundreds of URLs and screenshots he'd supplied to law enforcement over many years.

While police investigations were underway, Richards was put on alternative duties at work. 'They had me ... sitting at a desk, looking at the wall for the whole day. That was demoralising. That was so difficult. But I always believed, if I pass this, I've learned a fucking big lesson about how to behave like a decent person,' he says. 'And then I got the call. It just broke my heart.'

Richards was charged with possession of child abuse material and using the internet to transmit an indecent communication to a person under the age of sixteen. Part of the evidence used against him by police were four videos on his laptop, which Richards claims were stored only for the purposes of documenting the predator trolling. In the Statement of Agreed Facts, police say one of the videos showed 'two young girls in their underwear provocatively prancing around in a bedroom, touching their private parts in front of a video camera'. Another video depicted 'a young Asian boy lying on the ground playing and laughing with another boy'. One boy's pants were undone, 'exposing his penis' and the second child puts 'his mouth around the penis for a short time'.

'The offender stated he was sent links to all of the videos,' the document reads, 'and he saved the videos in order to present them to police. *However, the offender did not report these videos to police* [original emphasis].'

'The videos were less than a week old,' Richards tells me, and were located in an unprotected folder on the desktop marked for saving to USB for reporting. 'I downloaded them from YouTube because when I had provided URLs to officers in the past, the videos were often removed after I reported them and officers either didn't check the URL or when they did, the video no longer remained online. I did not select these videos but instead received them via unsolicited communication,' he says.

As a way of trying to get some perspective on Richards as a person, I phone a good friend of his, Rick (not his real name). They used to teach at the same school. Rick describes Richards as someone who is a 'big talker' and 'easy to get along with' with a 'sarcastic-funny' sense of humour. Once the charges were laid, Rick says all teachers at Richards' former school were told by the state education department not to have contact with him.

'That was pretty poor and … I wasn't really going to listen,' Rick says. He remembers his colleagues would speculate about what Richards had or hadn't done and 'didn't even want to hear his story'. For Rick, this wasn't an option. Even though his friend 'shut down' once the claims against him were made public, going to ground and changing his phone number, he persisted in trying to find him 'to get his side'.

Eventually he succeeded and now the two friends catch up often. Rick tells me he has three children himself, and it has never even crossed his mind to be concerned about Richards having contact with the kids. '[There's] no second-guessing him with me,' Rick says. 'He is a good bloke.'

#

Out of all the screenshots of Richards' trolls' efforts, one sticks out, in its suggestion that trolls were working with the police to collect evidence against the former teacher:

> Have just spoken to the detective in charge of the Jeffery Richards case ... Can ANYONE who has messages or screenshots of Richards' activities please inbox me and I will give you the details of the bloke to contact. He is very keen for anything showing a pattern of Richards' behaviour and of his Internet habits. Please pass this onto others within your circles to contact me.

The man tags more than a dozen people in the post. Despite repeated efforts, the police did not respond to my questions about Richards' case and gave no indication as to whether or not they worked with his predator trolls to gather information to use against him in court.

Nearly two years after police started investigating, Richards was tried before a magistrate. On his lawyer's advice, he pleaded guilty and received a year-long jail term. During the sentencing, the magistrate stated Richards' offending was 'to a great degree' and 'was pre-planned'. He described Richards' contact with Olive and the other child as 'a clear abuse of trust' and 'highly inappropriate' and further suggested the videos 'would be considered indecent by a reasonable member of the community'. The magistrate rejected Richards' claim about the URLs as 'somewhat incongruous', questioning why, if he was indeed sent the material by trolls, 'he did not retain the original emails ... but felt the need to retain the actual videos'.

When I email Richards about this criticism from the magistrate, he tells me 'the four screenshots of Facebook messages relating to the four videos found on my computer were never searched for/located – or they were ignored by forensic officers. They were somewhere on my computer which police had in their possession. When I attempted to remotely access files on my computer, I could not find those four screenshots.' Richards goes on to say he has been informed the laptop has since been destroyed.

In court Richards' lawyer proposed that he was under attack due to his activism. The magistrate responded by saying, '[H]e has placed himself in those positions by his own choices.'

Poring over the transcript of that hearing, I stumble across a peculiar incident. The furious magistrate ejects a member of the public from the court – a man who appears to be one of Richards' online trolls, making his presence felt in real life. 'You have distracted me on three occasions by pulling faces and you're in my direct line of sight. It is inappropriate for you to do so and if you believe that your actions are in any way intimidatory on the defendant, I am asking you to leave the court room now, please, sir,' the magistrate says, before repeating his request for the man to 'Step outside, please, sir.'

He then launches into a tirade against online lynch mobs who take justice into their own hands. 'The material that I have seen that has been presented to me … by members of the community who seem to feel that they can be their own judge and jury, it is outrageous and inappropriate,' the magistrate tells the court, adding that it's for 'the courts [to] deal with it according to the law, not some vigilante mob who feel they have their own rights … And that sort of behaviour should not be allowed in any circumstances. It is disgraceful'.

After reading this part of the transcript – and a Facebook post by one of Richards' trolls, boasting about being in court during his hearing – I go back to Richards and ask about this strange incident. He says, 'I have these trolls sitting next to and behind me every time I am in court. They whisper in my ear and speak about me to each other, looking for a rise. My lawyers have never helped me with this issue, but simply told me to ignore [them].'

When I started my career as a cadet journalist, I reported on the magistrates court as one of my rounds. I saw and heard some very strange things – including a drunk man charged with 'deliberately' farting at a police officer. Yet even so, Jeffery Richards' trolls turning up in real life and mocking him in court seems extraordinary proof of how far they will go to hurt him. It reminds me of Moody's dead horse.

Karen Percy, an ABC journalist who reports on magistrates cases, is 'gobsmacked' that 'the trolls would be so brazen, taunting the defendant and the magistrate in that way'. She's never seen anything like it in thirty-one years of reporting. 'You have to remember that court complexes are full of cops, corrections officers, security guards, so most people get the picture – that if you act up there will be consequences. It takes major chutzpah to go to court and get in the ear of a defendant in this way. We think trolls just hide behind their keyboards but that's obviously not the case,' she says to me.

#

Richards' recollection of his sentencing is vivid – and traumatic. 'I was just numb.' After his lawyers paid bail, he walked out of the court and was greeted by the media. He recalls cameras rolling and journalists shouting questions at him. About 20 metres away his mother and brother waited in a car to collect him – but he was surrounded.

After that day, he remembers being afraid to go out in public to catch the train. 'I didn't want to run into anyone I knew,' he says. 'It was a nauseating feeling. I could feel the heart pumping out of my chest. I had a huge lump in my throat. I thought I was going to throw up and cry at the same time.'

Richards' jail sentence was commuted to an 'intensive corrections order' on appeal in 2017. This means community service, instead of a jail term. He still has a criminal record and will never teach again. In the last two years Richards has lost six full-time jobs – which he puts down to employers googling him. He has also had to move his family four times because the trolls keep hunting him.

'I do feel like I'm a victim,' Richards tells me, 'but the recurring thing is that I still have heaps of regret over the way I behaved.

'I hate the thought of someone thinking I'm telling a story or I'm trying to give my perspective because I want to somehow nullify or diminish what it was that I did. It's not even regret. It's regret times a million.'

If he was principal of a school, Richards says he would have fired a teacher who behaved as he did. Still, he can't help thinking about everything he's lost. 'I've lost my job, I've lost a lot of money, I've lost my privacy, I've lost my reputation, I've lost my mental strength. I've lost a billion and one things and a lot of them can't even be quantified with a figure. I don't deserve that. I honestly don't deserve any of that,' he says.

I ask Richards whether he has to be branded by this for the rest of his life.

'I'm now essentially labelled as a paedophile. I've got a conviction of that nature against my name … and I'm not a paedophile,' he says. 'That bothers me and it will never stop bothering me.

'When I take my child to the park, I am embarrassed to sit there and look at kids because I have a feeling that every person in that park knows who I am, knows what I've been through, knows my label and is therefore judging me,' Richards says, 'and I can't shake that feeling.'

Flicking through a huge file of screenshots the troll hunter gave me, for about the fifth time, and trying to work out if I've missed anything, I stumble on a message written by Richards' troll-in-chief.

The post says, 'I fixed [Jeffery] Richards, [sic] well drove the prick to insanity.'

Another Facebook message posted by the same man reads, 'I stitched him up nicely. These things take time to filter through the system but filter through it shall.'

Eventually, as I often do during the writing process, I go back to the troll hunter. I text: 'After thinking about this for so long, this is still just as unclear to me. Yes, the trolling against Richards was extreme. But also he behaved in a highly unethical way towards that child. So how do we view those things when they are put together?'

The troll hunter's first message says: 'I'm not a psychologist so I can't say they are connected. But what's clear is that the motivation for his being trolled wasn't the offence he was charged with. The motivation was his speaking out and attempting to expose racists.'

Then, after thinking about it for a few more days – and reflecting on how long the cyberhate against Richards continued – he messages again: 'His actions were just words. Words which led the mother of a child to online material which reinforced the inappropriateness of his interaction with the young girl. You have to wonder, if the police had actually acted on his initial complaints, if any of this would ever have happened?'

#

No matter which way I look at Jeffery Richards' case, I can't see the wood for the trees. It's like turning a Rubik's Cube around and around, yet never managing to make the colours line up. There's a deep disquiet within me, and for a few weeks it wakes me up in the middle of the night and I can't get back to sleep.

In the end I telephone Dr Gerard Webster, one of Australia's leading forensic psychologists. He has more than thirty years of experience in treating sex offenders, and he's willing to look at situations in all their complexity. I know from our numerous previous conversations that he'll sit there with you, deep in the grey. I can ask these alarming questions without judgement. *Why am I so confused? Can you be a sex offender and also seem like a nice person? Despite what Richards thinks, is it possible that predator trolling could damage your mental health to the point where you make decisions like he did?*

The first thing Webster wants us to do in Richards' case is be 'very wary of absolutisms'. 'None of us are omniscient. We don't know what's going on inside the mind of a person. We don't even know, unless we were actually there, what they've actually done.'

At the same time, Webster warns that when it comes to sex offenders, there's 'also an ongoing motivation for people to be deceptive' because 'they're frightened, they're trying to get the least severe punishment, or get off if they possibly can'.

Webster makes no bones about it. As a community, we must protect children. However, this doesn't mean we should be simplistic about sex offenders. We prefer to see sex offending as 'a black-and-white idea', he says. 'You're either a sex offender or you're not. We think that a person is like us or they're not like us. That kind of clumping is a gross simplification.'

The truth, of course, is murkier. 'Most people who are sexually offending just move around in the community like everyone else. They don't stand out,' he says. 'There's no telltale sign that any particular person is likely to sexually abuse a child. Estimates vary, but about 25 per cent of men have attraction to prepubertal children – not just teenagers, but prepubertal children,' he says, underscoring this. 'But what they do with that is often shut it down due to the utter disgust that they have with themselves for that experience. So it's not that it's a rare thing to be attracted to children, but it is obviously hugely problematic.'

Still talking statistics, Webster points out 'roughly one in three or four females [and] one in six boys are sexually abused by the time they're eighteen, and most of that abuse is perpetrated by someone close to them'. Boiling it down, he explains that this means the number of people in the community who are prepared to sexually abuse a child is 'huge'.

'If, for argument's sake,' I ask, 'you had a propensity to offend against a child, is it unusual that this might happen in your mid thirties for the first time?'

Webster is unequivocal: it's not unusual at all. 'About 30 per cent of all sexual abuse against children is effectively perpetrated by another child, somebody under the age of eighteen … who is often very, very close to the child [such as] a sibling or a cousin, or a child in the neighbourhood. And then the next peak, which is just as solid, is with people in midlife, around their mid thirties. And so, with the case that we're looking at, he's right on that target.'

Richards' case has been through the court system, Webster reminds me: '[H]e has been assessed according to the highest standard of evidence. Of course, courts can get it wrong, but the court was in the position of listening to all sides of the story. The simplest explanation is probably the most likely to be true.' He poses the rhetorical question, 'What's the likelihood of somebody not having some sexual motive when they're doing something that's completely, clearly sexual?'

He picks this apart further. 'There's grooming with conscious intent. There's grooming with unconscious intent. But there's also the possibility that, with him, he wasn't grooming and that it was just as he said, that there was a desire for affirmation [and] that was what was motivating his behaviour. But the behaviour was sexualised,' Webster reiterates.

The other thing that bothers me is a chicken-or-egg-type question. *How do we explain the idea that the trolls kept saying Richards was a paedophile, seemingly without evidence, and then he ended up pleading guilty to these offences?*

'If we go with his account, he was appalled by it,' the psychologist says of the child-abuse material, 'but he was getting a lot of it. So it might have been that if there was some part of him that was also attracted to kids, he may have been both appalled, but also turned on by these images.'

'This is an individual who has clearly been under an enormous amount of stress,' Webster adds, 'and was perhaps bound to reach breaking point in one way or another.' For some people, this might be excessive alcohol consumption or workaholism. For others, it's sexually offending. He underscores that while stress and isolation may trigger a person with a disposition towards sexual offending to act, 'it's definitely not causal'. 'Trolling is a vile attack on the mind and the reputation of the victim,' he says. 'The perpetrators are breaking the law. They're breaking all sorts of moral codes by their psychological violence. And it is bound to have an impact of causing an otherwise healthy person [to feel] incredibly powerless and frightened.'

But despite the mental health impacts that sustained trolling may have on a victim like Richards, Webster is adamant: 'The troll is not responsible for another person's perpetration of sexual abuse of a child.'

If, as Lifeline's Alan Woodward suggested, the multiple stressors that cause suicide should be viewed as tributaries flowing into a river, and cyberhate could be considered one of those stressors, might it be possible that these tributaries flow to other rivers? After talking to Webster I wonder if, given certain conditions, cyberhate could be a tributary into other devastating life choices – like offending against a child. Not an excuse, because it's inexcusable, but perhaps part of an explanation we've been hitherto unwilling to hear.

9

Your demons are omnipresent

S OMETIMES, AS I WRITE, the myths about predator trolling seem to stack up around me – and I realise they are falling like a house of cards:

Trolling doesn't matter. It's just people being mean online.

You can just pull your big-girl panties up. Don't be so sensitive.

Trolls are just losers sitting alone in their mum's basement attacking strangers online.

Trolls are thoughtless and uneducated.

Trolls can't hurt you in real life. Just block and delete.

Only loud-mouthed white feminists get trolled. (And, frankly, they're asking for it.)

You could be forgiven for believing this last one – we loud-mouthed white feminists tend to discuss our experiences on pre-existing media platforms – but the reality is that cyberhate targets are not necessarily high-profile individuals. Dr Emma Jane suggests that 'arguably any woman who is making use of the 2.0 affordances of the internet is a type of media worker and has a type of public profile'.[1] (This point would realistically apply not just to women but to all people.) Jane further reminds us that some cyberhate targets – such as Canadian-American gamer and media critic Anita Sarkeesian and games developer Zoë Quinn – 'were not widely known until *after* they were subject to large-scale cyber attacks' (my emphasis).[2]

Many of the stories in this book involve predator trolls finding strangers online and systematically ruining their lives. Often though, the trolls are not strangers. For several reasons – mainly related to the way the public conversation is currently framed – it takes me a while to understand this. What it boils down to is this: if a stranger persistently harasses you online, we might label it 'trolling' or 'cyberhate'. If someone who is (or was) intimate with you uses technology to stalk or harass you, we call it 'technology-facilitated abuse'. As a community, we're therefore currently using different language for behaviours that can often constitute the same thing. Both these behaviours may result in real-life harm to the target.

The person who helped me start thinking about predator trolling by current or former partners is Karen Bentley, National Interim Director of the Women's Services Network (WESNET), a national Australian advocacy organisation for women and children experiencing domestic violence (DV). Bentley's expertise lies at the intersection of DV and technology. In one of many conversations, she tells me: 'We know there's almost a complete overlap now. If you're experiencing DV, some of that DV is going to be through technology.'

After that, I go hunting myself and start looking at the evidence in a different way. SmartSafe, a 2015 survey of 546 domestic violence sector workers, found that 98 per cent 'had clients who had experienced technology-facilitated stalking and abuse'.[3] This is consistent with research from the United States, which shows '97 percent of domestic violence programs reported that abusers use technology to stalk, harass, and control victims'.[4]

Like many people who have an interest in technology, I've been aware of the Gamergate controversy since it erupted in 2014. What I didn't know is that Zoë Quinn, the author of *Crash Override* and the person at the centre of the conflict, says the torrent of cyberhate that came her way started in domestic abuse.[5]

Quinn is not alone. Predator trolling and domestic violence are commonly part of the same story. For single mother Justine, the impact of cyberhate and predator trolling by her ex-partner has been 'catastrophic'. 'It made me want to kill myself. I take two medications now and I see a psychologist. I've got PTSD and anxiety and depression,' the 45-year-old says.

Justine met Mitchell nearly twenty years ago. At the time, she was a young single mum suffering from low self-esteem, and her previous partner had been unfaithful. In contrast, Mitchell 'was very attentive', Justine recalls. 'He did spoil me and made me feel very special.'

From the minute they met, the relationship was 'intense'. Almost straight away he told her it was love; he'd never felt this way about anybody before. The pair got engaged. 'The week before we got married was the first time that he got screaming angry at me, to the point that I took my toddler son, Charlie, and went and stayed with a relative for the night because I was frightened of him. He just turned it straight back onto me, so I just felt that it was my fault, that I'd made him like that,' Justine says.

After giving birth to their son, Hunter, eighteen months after the wedding, Justine needed a minor operation. 'Mitchell had to take time off work. And he came up to the hospital and they kept me in for five days and I remember they had to remove him from the hospital because he was screaming at me. He was angry I was not at home looking after Hunter.'

Once she was home, Mitchell's violence escalated. He'd monitor her phone and stop Justine from going out with friends. There was a cycle – he wouldn't talk to her for days: 'Not one word. And then all of a sudden, he would snap. He'd hit me with household items, push his arms up in my neck and hold me so I couldn't breathe. He would keep me awake for three days and he would stomp and get in my face and scream and spit all over me. Every time I'd start to fall asleep, he would wake me up.

'He would make me have sex with him every day. And he would make me have anal sex. It was horrible. After I had Hunter, I had sex with him three days later and I had had a caesarean. I was in agony.'

With the help of some friends, Justine managed to leave Mitchell at the end of 2007. She went back to her home town of Griffith in New

South Wales. Mitchell followed. His harassment escalated to a whole new level once Justine was introduced to Facebook a few years later. As well as stalking her offline, he'd stalk her online and make constant public posts about her. The posts maligned her character and appearance, insistently painting her as a liar who was 'after him for money'.

'It just made me feel like I was being watched all the time,' Justine says. 'I'd go out and then he'd immediately post something about how fat I was.'

People around her brushed the cyberhate aside, telling her to 'Stop looking at it. Don't respond to it. Don't react to it.' But the impact on her was crippling. 'The trolling and incitement for others to pile on became so much part of my life that I stopped going out. It just absolutely consumed every part of me. Everywhere I went in town, I felt shame.'

Justine didn't just suspect local people, many of whom she'd known her whole life, were talking about her. She knew they were; the proof was on social media. Her experience is further reflected in research showing 'that perpetrators would exploit any perceived vulnerabilities that women had, particularly if they were from a small community and the perpetrator could effectively use technology to further isolate them'.[6]

Reflecting on Mitchell's incitement of others against her online, Justine says: 'He manipulates people by making him[self] out to be a victim of me. He says that he's never been violent and he says that he's never done anything wrong to his children ... and people get on the bandwagon because it's easy to hate on a supposedly villainous woman.'

Karen Bentley says 'dog-piling' or 'stalking by proxy', where the perpetrator incites others to harass the victim online, is relatively common. 'We understand domestic and family violence is a power and control issue. What we see is that technology is just a new tool to do that.'

The SmartSafe report states that the phone was the most common vehicle for tech-abusers to harass their victims. Facebook was the second most common mechanism: '[W]omen often had great difficulty in getting support from Facebook to remove these harassing posts.'[7]

This tallied with Justine's experience. She told me none of Mitchell's Facebook posts, which she'd reported to Facebook, had ever been removed.

Like so many cyberhate targets, Justine says it's been impossible to get help. 'I've reported it to police. I've reported it to Facebook. I've reported it to my lawyer and no one's done anything about it,' she says.

After I contacted Facebook on Justine's behalf, a spokesperson (who didn't wish to be named) wrote back to say: 'We have removed any content that was reported to us which was found to be in breach of our Community Standards. We don't want Facebook to be a place for any kind of abuse – including domestic abuse – and our bullying and harassment policies are clear.'

The spokesperson also pointed out that not all content that upsets people actually violates the company's policies. 'There are also situations, however, where people post about personal issues which can be painful for others to see, and yet the content does not violate our policies … One of the most difficult things we do at Facebook is navigate the line between allowing people to express themselves freely and keeping our community safe on the platform.'

Having said this, Facebook is currently testing a number of tools that will allow users to more easily search for and block offensive words from appearing in their comments and news feeds.[8] Users of Instagram, which is owned by Facebook, can already filter out offensive and bullying comments by keyword.[9] In the future this may go some way to shielding DV victims from receiving cyberhate. However, it still doesn't stop someone like Mitchell publicly posting lies about Justine on his own social media accounts or inciting others to pile on.

#

Much like Justine, Eva – who is now forty-one – was a single mother when she met her former partner, Simon. Their relationship also moved fast – they were engaged after three weeks. 'He wanted to commit. He wanted to have kids … [it] just sounded perfect,' she says. 'What I wanted was stability and he was stable.'

At the time, it made sense. Simon, who worked in a high-level role in the information technology sector, was 'very romantic'. He bought her flowers and piles of new clothes. 'I thought that was really nice, but what he was doing was he was changing my wardrobe so I wouldn't show cleavage and I wouldn't wear short skirts.'

As the months went by, he began monitoring Eva's phone and controlling her finances. Increasingly, Simon became more overt about his control over her wardrobe. He suggested her V-neck work tops made her look like 'a skank', and he prevented her from swimming in public. 'He thought it was slutty and that people would look at my breasts,' Eva says. 'I wasn't allowed to wear anything that was above the knee.'

The first time Simon raped her, he used her clothing as an excuse, telling her, 'You know, you asked for it. You keep wearing these provocative clothes. I'm just going to show you what happens.' The rape became a regular part of their relationship and Eva lived in constant fear.

With the help of her workmates, she left Simon in early 2014. Once he realised she wasn't coming back, 'he started to get really nasty'. 'It wasn't until after I left I found out there were cameras all through the house and he'd put tracking on my phone. That's why he always knew where I was,' Eva tells me. 'He uses his ICT [information and communications technology] skills to continue to monitor and harass me. It continues to this day, particularly in my workplace.'

Simon continually hacks into Eva's email and social media accounts. She often gets notifications about attempts to reset her passwords. Compounding the problem is that as a teacher, her work email address follows a strict format, including both her first and last names. She can't change it – and this has aided her troll. He's sent emails to her colleagues full of false, damaging allegations about her personal life.

Simon also makes sure she's flooded with vile spam. 'He'll sign me up for things, which can impact on my career. For example, he'll pose as me and through my work email, I will be getting emails about Russian mail order brides, sex toys, lingerie. Like all workplaces, email and web activity is monitored. So his behaviour puts my employment at risk.

'He has previously logged in as me, and if he did something like downloaded child porn, I'd lose my job and get registered as a sex offender. When he sends me spam, he focuses a lot on anal sex toys because that's how he liked to rape me. You come to work and you'll have eleven-plus emails the first thing in the morning when you sign in.

And so the first thing you think about when you start work is him and what he's done to you, and that stays with you,' she says. 'It's like having a scab that never heals.'

Fortunately, IT staff at her school helped to filter out the most damaging spam emails. These days they've slowed to a trickle. Although she has a new partner and things are looking much brighter for Eva, the effects of the past domestic violence and current tech abuse are ongoing and include anxiety, depression and PTSD.

These mental-health effects are remarkably similar to those found in cases of predator trolling on women like Badham and Dawson – who were ostensibly attacked online by strangers. While the precise scenarios are different, the parallels are crystal clear. This is technology used for the coercive control of women.

#

In 2017, Mitchell found Justine's profile on an online dating site. He created a demeaning meme from it, which he posted to Facebook along with her username. She then discovered her own Facebook friends were screenshotting her posts and giving them to Mitchell so he could keep tabs on her. 'I don't trust anybody because I've been hurt so badly by so many people who have betrayed me. When you're talking to people, you take them on face value and I can't do that anymore. It made me want to kill myself,' Justine says.

This isn't hyperbole. Eight years earlier Justine did try to commit suicide and cyberhate was a major factor in her downward spiral. 'My honesty, and my vibrancy and my passion for life were completely taken away … It absolutely destroyed me,' she says. 'It completely changed who I was.

'It never stops,' she continues. 'It never leaves me. I divorced him in 2008 and here I am in 2018 and I'm still frightened of him. I'm still suffering abuse from him. I'm still a victim of him and I don't know how to get away from that.'

In Karen Bentley's experience, this is exactly what tech abusers are shooting for. 'If you're living with your perpetrator you can see it [the abuse], but when it's happening online, that's when it starts to make you feel crazy because he can do it anonymously or he can get other people to do it for him,' she says. 'It's unknown, so your imagination can just go wild and that is the tactic ... to incite that fear and terror.'

Justine isn't the only one who has had trouble getting social media companies to assist her – and it raises an interesting question about whether, as a community, we're inadvertently outsourcing decisions about justice and law enforcement and hate speech into private hands. Should private companies – as opposed to policing and government agencies – have dominion over whether domestic violence perpetrated online 'violates their policies'?

The Northern Territory (NT) Police Force submitted evidence to the 2018 Australian Senate hearings into cyberbullying, which stated:

> There have been instances in the Northern Territory where offences ... have been broadcast from social media platforms.
>
> Requests to remove these posts from social media have been declined by Facebook on the grounds that Facebook did not believe the material published on the page breached community standards. No further recourse is available to have these decisions reconsidered.

The NT Police Force had to abandon certain investigations because social media companies either wouldn't give them the information in a timely manner or wouldn't provide information at all. 'This is an unsatisfactory outcome for the victim and fails to hold offenders to account for their actions,' the document reads.[10]

This isn't just an issue for NT police, it's an issue across the whole country. So even where there's a commitment to investigate cyber-hate – or other crimes, for that matter – police can find themselves at the mercy of overseas-based companies and their (sometimes erratic) enforcement of their policies.

As you might expect, the industry itself takes a different view. Speaking at the same Senate hearings, Nicole Buskiewicz, managing director of Digital Industry Group Inc. (DIGI) – whose members include Facebook, Google, YouTube, Instagram, Microsoft, Oath and

Twitter – stated social media companies were committed to working with police.

> Our industry will ... continue to disclose metadata to Australian law enforcement agencies, following legal process, to enable investigations to be made into crimes that involve any DIGI member service. Collectively, DIGI members received 3259 requests for metadata from Australian law enforcement agencies in the first six months of 2017.

She did not, however, say how many of those requests were met or in what time frame. Law enforcement, like social media, is struggling to keep pace with the ways in which the internet is used to inflict violence. Justine says, 'The cops don't care about cyberhate. They say, "Are you in immediate danger?" The technology has taken off and law enforcement isn't fucking catching up.'

The SmartSafe report suggests police may throw the onus back onto the victim. For example, instead of holding a perpetrator responsible, a police officer may instead suggest a cyberhate target 'should stop visiting Facebook or using devices'. Similar sentiments have been expressed in Australian Federal Parliament.[11] There are two glaring problems with this (and that's just for starters – we'll address more in the next chapter). First, being online isn't an optional extra. Even the United Nations has recognised internet access – and the preservation of it – as a human right that's crucial to free expression and the sharing of information.[12]

Second, brushing aside cyberhate associated with domestic violence belies the true risk associated with stalking. The SmartSafe report suggests that police may perceive the risk posed by cyberhate as lower than a physical threat, but warns, 'While non-physical abuse, such as technology-facilitated abuse and stalking, may be considered as less serious than other forms of abuse, stalking by an intimate partner has been linked to an increased risk of homicide.'[13]

Investigations by the New South Wales coroner show 43 per cent of domestic violence homicides committed in the state between 2010 and

2012 included stalking. The report points specifically to 'evidence of technology-facilitated stalking'.[14]

When I write to Justine a week after our interview to thank her for telling her story, she replies: 'I don't think my story is the worst. At least he hasn't killed me.'

'Justine,' I respond in despair, 'that's not a good measure of whether it's bad.'

10

Not much cop

J USTINE FOUND HERSELF alone when she needed to reach out for help. If only her case was an isolated incident. When I was first asked to write a book on cyberhate and trolling, my initial instinct was to say no. How could I justify keeping my family in this dark world any longer than we had to be? Then I re-read the emails in my inbox from predator-trolling victims. Although the stories were vastly different, some common threads ran through. Almost universally victims had one thing to say: *I couldn't – and can't – get help.*

On the surface, this seemed hard to understand. In the face of such extreme abuse, with such devastating consequences, why wouldn't police help? Plenty of answers crossed my mind. Perhaps they didn't know how, or lacked the technical training to find perpetrators. Perhaps police didn't understand the state and federal laws that applied. Perhaps the paucity of language around cyberhate was part of the problem. Perhaps, much like the way domestic violence was ignored thirty years ago, police thought it was a trivial domestic matter and that there were bigger fish to fry.

Once I dug in and started investigating, all of my suspicions turned out to be true. And, worse still, they were overlaid with complex societal prejudices. The only saving grace is that there are hopeful signs that things might be changing.

Nigel Phair, director of the Centre for Internet Safety at the University of Canberra and a former long-time member of the Australian Federal Police, variously describes Australia's current law enforcement response to cyberhate as 'pathetic', 'completely inadequate' and 'piecemeal'.[1] When it comes to police he suggests 'their days are full of policing terrestrial crimes' and frankly they are 'still trying to grapple with what cyberhate is ... let alone building the capacity and capability to investigate such matters'.

In her book *Hate Crimes in Cyberspace*, cyberhate expert and legal scholar Danielle Keats Citron notes few predator-trolling victims come forward because they are uncertain of whether it constitutes a crime and whether they will be taken seriously. She cites a study from the University of Bedfordshire, in the United Kingdom, that found more than '60 percent of survey participants reported receiving no help from police complaints'.[2]

In the United States, the problem is remarkably similar. Nearly half the population thinks law enforcement should play a major role in addressing online harassment and yet Pew Center research finds 'a sizable proportion of Americans (43 percent) say that law enforcement currently does not take online harassment incidents seriously enough'.[3]

In his powerful 2013 article 'The End of Kindness: weev and the Cult of the Angry Young Man', Greg Sandoval documents numerous cases of extreme predator trolling against victims such as US developer and blogger Kathy Sierra, US activist Holly Jacobs and UK-based journalist and activist Caroline Criado-Perez.

> When Jacobs went to the police, they found many reasons not to help her ... Police didn't arrest anyone six years ago when Sierra went to the police about the death threats she received. In Criado-Perez's case, the journalist received hundreds of threats, and UK police made a single arrest.

Sandoval goes on to reflect specifically on the situation in the United States, concluding, 'When it comes to combating internet harassment in general, the country still has a long way to go.'[4]

Game developer and cyberhate target Zoë Quinn also struggled with police responses to her plight. She questions whether targets should even bother going to the police. On the one hand, she says, 'If you don't, people will claim the abuse wasn't real because there's no police report about it.' Yet if victims do report, Quinn believes they must be prepared for a drawn-out legal process if the case goes to trial, and understand the current state of play, which offers 'little chance of seeing justice because legislation and law enforcement have not yet caught up with the pace of online crime'.[5]

Mark can shed a bit of light on law enforcement response: he has had contact with police services in Australia, the United States and the UK because of his trolling activities. He says that police in Australia and the United States 'largely don't care' and 'have better things to do than go after people saying mean words on the internet'. But, he says, it's a different story in the UK: 'It gets Orwellian.' After he abused a UK public figure online a couple of years ago, authorities there tried to take defamation action against him. 'In my eyes, and the eyes of a lot of people, the UK authorities have used their hate speech laws to clamp down on anyone expressing opinions online that the government disagrees with.'

As evidence of this he sends me a screenshot of a 2017 Facebook post from Cheshire Police, warning the public to think carefully about what they post on social media: 'Although you may believe your message is acceptable, other people may take offence, and you could face a large fine or up to two years in prison if your message is deemed to have broken the law.' The repeated warnings were prompted by a number of malicious social media messages investigated by the branch the previous year.[6] This proactive approach in deterring the public from attacking each other online – and reinforcing the community value of respect – is music to my ears.

What I've become used to – what I have firsthand experience of – is the opposite: cyberhate targets reporting that police blamed them for the online harassment they receive. When it comes to female victims, this plays right into the stereotype that we are hysterical or overreact to minor issues – like people being 'mean' online. Not only does this response fail to take into account the extreme, real-life impacts of predator trolling, but it's peak victim blaming. Just think back to Charlotte Dawson and how she was treated by the media after being trolled and attempting suicide. Within days of her acute mental health crisis she was cajoled onto television and then effectively victim-blamed for responding to her predator trolls.[7]

Dr Emma Jane documents the way cyberhate targets are victim-blamed in her work. One of her case studies is 42-year-old librarian and activist Kath Read, who tried to report her abuse – which was spilling into the offline world – to police. A 'male officer told her to, "Get offline and stop being so confident"'. Likewise, 43-year-old erotic filmmaker and university lecturer Anna Brownfield took threatening emails from an online stalker to police, and the response was, 'Well, in your industry what do you expect?'[8]

What's incredible to me is that cyberhate targets could go largely ignored in the face of such extreme impacts. Not only are the harms against them both mental and physical – they are economic too. And they are costing the whole country. That might seem like a big statement, but I have the data to prove it. You'll remember that when I asked the Australia Institute to do polling on my behalf, I asked them for more than just the incidence of cyberhate in Australia. I asked how much it costs.

This wasn't incidental. What I know from mapping out the stories of cyberhate targets as a group – rather than just individually – is that victims frequently endure the wholesale destruction of their lives. And money plays a large part. Not only do cyberhate targets report needing to take unpaid time off work, or even losing their job or multiple jobs, but they also shell out cash to pay for myriad other expenses, such as (but not restricted to) medical fees, legal fees, child care, moving house and interstate travel and accommodation to attend court.

Victims of predator trolling may also employ third parties to assist them in dealing with the cyberhate. Victims who have to be online as part of their work might employ someone to manage their social media accounts. Or, as radio host Mel Greig did, hire a security guard.

Other predator-trolling targets, like 47-year-old Carmen, who has been a target of ongoing cyberhate since 2011, employ a private investigator or IT expert to try to confirm the perpetrator's identity and gather evidence. If she adds up lost income, legal and medical fees, Carmen tells me, plus travel to attend court hearings over the last seven years, the costs would be in excess of $200,000. Carmen had been a successful freelancer but her reputation, she says, has been ruined online. 'The last two years have been progressively worse in terms of not working and last year I only worked about three weeks in the entire year.'

Van Badham probably says it best: 'Trolling becomes your own personal economic liability, and it becomes a liability to your job opportunities and your work performance.'

Taking into account two types of expenses – medical costs and lost income – TAI's most conservative estimate is that Australians who are at the receiving end of cyberhate and online harassment have borne an aggregate cost of $330 million. The high estimate – again, based solely on medical costs and lost income – is that, to date, cyberhate and online harassment has cost adult Australians $3.7 billion. Read that again. THREE-POINT-SEVEN BILLION. Yes, it's a pretty penny.

Keep in mind our nationwide polling did *not* cover the legal and logistical expenses that individuals may incur. Nor did it consider costs to the community, such as the way cyberhate cases are increasingly tying up law enforcement personnel and, more broadly, the justice system. Data obtained from the New South Wales Bureau of Crime Statistics and Research shows that in 2017, 1635 charges were finalised in that state under section 474.17 of the *Federal Criminal Code Act*. (This is the part of the law that makes it illegal for individuals to use 'a carriage service to menace, harass or cause offence' to another person.) If we look back to 2013, there were just 1171 finalised charges – which represents a 40 per cent increase over the five years to 2017. In fact, the number of cyberhate cases being brought before the courts has been steadily rising each year, with the majority of defendants being found guilty. More severe penalties – such as fines and jail terms – are also slowly increasing. Interestingly, the New South Wales government has announced it will toughen laws to protect people from cyberhate and increase the maximum jail time to five years.[9]

While this announcement and these statistics are certainly a positive in terms of deterrence and holding perpetrators to account, they must be kept in perspective. A *Sydney Morning Herald* article from 2016 reported the most common punishment under this legislation was a $700 fine and this was 'far from the maximum prison term of three years'.[10]

TAI figures show the financial cost of cyberhate to the community is profound – and it's cash better spent elsewhere. These significant dollar figures effectively serve to throw a hot and bright spotlight on our societal attitudes to predator trolling. If it's costing us so much – socially and financially – why don't we demand better responses from police?

Through representing cyberhate targets (and becoming one himself), lawyer Josh Bornstein came to the realisation that police don't have the resources to deal with the scale of the problem. 'From my experience, there's a lack of skills. They're struggling with how to pursue perpetrators and they're not being sent a clear message … from legislators and the community that this has to be a priority. And that will mean properly resourcing them and properly training them, so I don't blame the police,' Bornstein says. 'This is part of a broader malaise.'

The Law Council supports this theory, submitting evidence to the Senate hearings into cyberbullying that 'research shows that police often refuse to lodge complaints from disgruntled victims of cyberbullying because of their lack of knowledge of the various laws applicable to incidents of cyberbullying'.[11]

And yet, there may be a glimmer of hope. Some stories are emerging of more appropriate, and effective, responses to cyberbullying complaints. Take comedian and writer Catherine Deveny. After making controversial comments on Twitter and Facebook about Anzac Day in 2018 – describing it as 'Bogan Halloween' and a 'fetishisation of war and violence' – she was doxed multiple times. Her home address was posted all over the internet and she received an avalanche of credible rape and death threats. She was the focus of several Facebook hate groups. One night, five men in a ute turned up to her house. One of them knocked on her door and videoed himself doing it.

Within forty-eight hours of Deveny's original comments being posted – and the resultant blow-up of public vitriol – Victorian counter-terrorism police reached out to her. They got her statement and started investigating. Police patrolled outside her house and work events.

An investigator from the Office of the Federal eSafety Commissioner also got in touch.[12] In contrast to many who'd gone before her, Deveny received significant and appropriate support. After hearing so many dire stories, it's great to hear one like this. Wouldn't it be amazing if all predator-trolling victims could rely on getting this kind of assistance?

In fairness, there are also some positive signs from other countries: the London Metropolitan Police has created a specialist five-person cyberhate team, and Colombian police formed 'C4' – the Command and Control Center for Cybersecurity (this body is a kind of one-stop shop, where all agencies dealing with online crime, including cyberhate, are under the same roof).

Australia is taking note. Enter Detective Chief Inspector Carlene Mahoney, who works for New South Wales Police. She's also the holder of a PhD that examines the threats social media poses to law enforcement. That's right – police can be on the receiving end of cyberhate, too. Mahoney says, 'We received information that bikie members from a well-known bikie gang ... were taking photos of all our [police academy] students as they were walking off the parade ground and taking that back and running those images through facial recognition. And what they do is start to create a profile and then sell that information off to organised crime. So, basically [it's] affecting our covert [policing] capability.'

All in all, Mahoney has spent plenty of time thinking about social media and how it affects police and policing. She's thought about the dangers to police officers of being on social media themselves and using social media as investigative tools, and has trained police to help members of the public who are cyberhate victims. She says things are rapidly changing on the policing frontline.

NSW Police has tried to ensure its officers don't need special technical skills to take down the complaint when a target comes in to report cyberhate. According to Mahoney, every police officer 'has access to a cybercrime toolkit', which is an internal document that guides them through a step-by-step process so they can investigate online offences. The toolkit makes it clear when to escalate a case. Serious threats are triaged to a specialised policing unit – the NSW State Crime Command's

Cyber Crime Squad. Mahoney explains this squad has 'basically doubled' to about fifty detectives in the last twelve months and is responsible for investigating offences committed on the internet and via social media. Intelligence officers and detectives are given intense training for social media investigation. This is welcome news, yet during my own research for one of the case studies in this book, my questions about how NSW Police investigates cyberhate cases went unanswered despite repeated requests.[13]

Mahoney says NSW Police are leading Australian efforts to improve capacity when it comes to cyberhate and, to this end, have been looking at overseas initiatives like those in Colombia and the UK. There's a contradiction here, though, because although she says police are 'building capability' when it comes to cyberhate, Mahoney notes 'we don't get a lot of reports on cyberbullying … it's not our biggest cybercrime'. Crimes like online identity theft, financial crimes and data breaches are reported to police far more frequently than online harassment.

Reflecting on the 1.3 million Australians who have been cyberhate victims, I have to conclude this lack of reporting isn't to do with whether people are receiving extreme online abuse. They clearly are. What they aren't, generally, is willing to go to the police.

Danielle Keats Citron writes:

Victims often do not report online abuse because they assume law enforcement will not do anything to stop it. Their intuition is regrettably accurate. Law enforcement agencies often fail to follow up on victims' complaints because they are not trained to see online harassment as a problem and feel uncomfortable getting involved, even when the law suggests they should.

In Citron's mind, community attitudes – in which victims are blamed for their predicaments or seen as hysterical and oversensitive – are directly responsible for this 'lacklustre law enforcement response'.[14]

'We are now looking at how to train our police officers to be more victim-focused,' Mahoney tells me, and this includes being aware of whether cybercrime targets need 'a mental health team to come and make an assessment'.

From this vantage point, it seems like a slow start. However it's certainly positive to see a growing awareness among police that predator trolling can have real-world, enduring effects on the mental health of victims.

The SmartSafe report suggests police responses across the country are patchy. However, the document also points out that when police do 'thoroughly examine evidence of technology-facilitated abuse, it can make a significant difference on the outcome for the victim'.[15]

Aside from reporting hateful content to social media companies and local police, one of the other things cyberhate targets are often instructed to do is report to ACORN – the Australian Cybercrime Online Reporting Network. According to its website, ACORN is 'a national policing initiative of the Commonwealth, State and Territory governments … that allows the public to securely report instances of cybercrime'.

In reality, though, it's a red herring. Time and time again, victims like Carmen tell me they haven't found success with this reporting mechanism. Even those in government will tell you – quietly, behind closed doors – that they know how hopeless the service is. Not only does Nigel Phair criticise law enforcement, but he's equally scathing about ACORN, describing it as 'a disappointment at every level'. 'For the few consumers who do know about it, it provides no comfort to them that anyone actually cares about their issues, let alone is doing anything about it,' Phair says. 'For police it doesn't provide significant triaged advice to determine whether an investigation should take place.'

Phair calls for ACORN to release 'granular statistics … particularly with respect to [the] number of investigations undertaken and the results of those investigations'. As he suggests, the rate of prosecutions and convictions from ACORN seems the simplest way to gauge its effectiveness. I'm curious to know what statistics the organisation has on this, but on enquiry I'm told that the Australian Criminal Intelligence Commission 'is not placed to comment on the effectiveness of police agencies [or] data on prosecutions undertaken by police agencies'. Rather than going to each state police force, it seemed logical to contact the minister responsible for ACORN, Angus Taylor. Despite assurances from one of his staff that she would be 'happy to help' and provide me with some information, the eight questions I sent through went unanswered. This ambiguous messaging, plus various other murmurs from my contacts, leads me to believe changes may be afoot with ACORN. However, at the time of printing, no on-the-record information was offered.

Another place Australians can go for help is the Office of the eSafety Commissioner, which was formed by an act of Parliament in 2015. Australia is the 'only country in the world to establish a government agency dedicated to protecting its citizens online'.[16] The eSafety Commissioner, Julie Inman Grant, is an American native who has spent more than two decades working in policy and safety roles inside tech industry giants like Microsoft, Twitter and Adobe. As the legislation currently stands, the Commissioner has take-down powers for children. This means her office has the legal power to help get cyberhate against Australian kids removed from the internet.

Before you get too excited, though, this same power doesn't extend to cyberhate against adults; the legislation wasn't drafted to cover them. Considering the office has seen a 95 percent month on month increase in complaints since October 2017, maybe it *should* apply to everyone.

In fact, the Senate's Legal and Constitutional Affairs References Committee recently recommended the Australian government consider 'expanding the cyberbullying complaints scheme to include complaints by adults'. Given the scale of cyberhate in Australia, and its associated financial and personal impacts, this seems urgent.

The same report notes there is a patchwork of state and territory offences that may apply to cyberbullying, such as stalking, harassment, assault, threats and defamation. The document – which resulted from wideranging hearings into cyberbullying and the adequacy of current Australian laws – calls for consistent laws across the country. The report's authors further propose 'increasing the maximum penalty for using a carriage service to menace, harass, or cause offence under section 474.17 of the [Federal] *Criminal Code Act 1995* from three years' imprisonment to five years' imprisonment'.

Here we need to note that section 474.17 has been around for more than ten years. So 'its effectiveness as a deterrent is obviously questionable'.[17] If this is the case, Josh Bornstein believes we need to consider further legal remedies. He's deeply concerned about the damage being inflicted on victims.

'The existing laws need to be tailored specifically to cyberhate and rather than having a general law … be sufficiently broad to cover the gamut of trolling,' he says. This would send 'a strong message to the police and to the prosecuting authorities and also to the public'.

Inman Grant is hesitant to suggest further legislation to deal with cyberhate and is concerned by the idea that 'we're going to arrest our way out of this problem or that laws are the panacea'. 'By their very nature, criminal laws are applied after the damage has been done, which is why prevention and early intervention through various support services, in the first instance, are so important,' she says. She describes law enforcement responses to online harassment as 'very patchy' and says it depends on who you get at the constable's office. 'They're not resourced to deal with this kind of stuff,' she says. 'I worry if there's more legislation to criminalise and people start going to the police, they're just going to be disappointed.'

I'm inclined to agree with her. It makes me think that perhaps the problem isn't the legislation itself. It's the way the current laws are – or in many cases aren't – being used to their full potential by police and by the judiciary.

But Bornstein believes social media companies should be liable for cyberhate and if they were, we'd see a radical change in their behaviour. 'If Facebook and Twitter and any other social media platform faced the prospect of multiple lawsuits for facilitating these trolls … these companies would have to devote enormous resources to preventing these problems, and that would change the game. If they had a duty of care, then I think their corporate behaviour would be very different.' Similar calls for a legislated duty of care are coming from Europe. Quite simply, this legislation would put the onus on tech companies 'to prevent reasonably foreseeable harms'.[18] And if they didn't, they would be liable.

As a workplace relations lawyer, Bornstein relates it back to 'what happened when companies could just get rid of workers who got injured in the workplace and who faced no liability for workplace injury'.

'When laws were introduced to provide for workers' compensation and provided the right for employees to sue those companies for the damage, that had a huge effect.

'It will be the same with social media companies. If they are made liable for the damage that cyberhate and trolling causes, that will have a massive effect on their business model … and they will try and minimise their [compensation] payouts,' he says.

The flipside of this, of course, is that we'd potentially be granting – or even forcing – social media companies to play an even greater role when it comes to surveillance, censorship and policing the behaviour of their users (trolls included). This is a point made repeatedly by trolls themselves – like Meepsheep, for example – and by numerous experts in the Pew Center report into trolling, fake news and free speech.[19] The question is, do we want that?

In addition to a legislated duty of care, Bornstein believes individuals must have a clear pathway to sue. At the moment, he says, people are racking up huge legal bills because this is missing. 'My view is if you had civil laws, which allowed you to sue the perpetrator … then that would be a gamechanger.'

It strikes me that perhaps we need all these things. Alongside legislation – which serves to send a message about what the community will and won't tolerate – we do need public education. Cyberhate is serious and doesn't stay online. The harms are real and they affect everyone. Not to mention costing billions of dollars. This is not just women being hysterical. We urgently need a broader, ongoing conversation about how misogyny feeds into gendered violence, online and offline. Inman Grant suggests prevention is better than picking up the pieces afterwards – and she's right.

There's no question that community attitudes play into policing attitudes. So police also need education about the personal impacts, community costs and legal frameworks that apply to predator trolling – as well as the technical skills and resources to investigate it.

11

Champions of free speech controlling the message

O N 9 FEBRUARY 2018 I gave evidence to the Australian Senate committee hearing into the adequacy of existing cyberbullying laws. At the time it was a big deal. I, along with the two other women speaking alongside me, came with my statements carefully thought out and written down.

I've often found in life that so many of the most crucial and revealing moments occur not as part of the big ceremony or scheduled proceedings. Rather, they happen in the spaces in between. In the cracks. This day was no different.

The hearings were held deep in the bowels of Parliament House in Canberra. Through security doors, across noisy wooden floors and past formal paintings of previous prime ministers. Up flights of stairs. Alongside journalist and academic Jenna Price and reputation manager and CEO Liza-Jayne Loch, I sat at a table facing the senators. The three of us were representing the non-profit volunteer organisation Women in Media. The microphones hung from the ceiling, recording us; our feet were on the soft carpet. The glasses of chilled water. We read from our prepared statements. We answered questions.

Directly after our evidence, representatives from Facebook and non-profit Digital Industry Group Inc. (DIGI) were due to have their say. Noticing Mia Garlick, Facebook's Director of Policy for Australia and

New Zealand, I walked up to introduce myself. She was surrounded by a wall of mostly female staff.

'I just gave evidence,' I said, smiling.

'I heard your evidence,' she said, staring straight at me. She was not smiling.

I'm writing a book about cyberhate, I said, and would like to interview her. Could I have her business card? She said she didn't have one on her.

'What's the best way to get in touch, then?' I asked. 'Can I get your email address?'

My paper and pen were poised. But she didn't start spelling out her email address. She paused and mumbled something about how I could get it from Jenna Price. 'She's got it,' Garlick snapped and it was clear our conversation was over.

This brief interaction turned out to be a marker of what was to come. Beyond public relations spin, it's hard to get any real, in-depth and on-the-record answers from the social media companies about how they are tackling cyberhate. Despite their insistence on being platforms for and champions of free speech – 'Twitter stands for freedom of expression for everyone!'[1] – they are hell-bent on controlling the message. The companies remain largely unwilling to be held to account. This doesn't mean I don't try to get answers. I do. In the months of gathering information in order to understand how the platforms are dealing with predator trolling, I'm reminded of when my sister used to make mosaics from shards of coloured, smashed ceramics. She'd collect the strangely shaped pieces and move them around until the pieces fitted together to form a picture.

Predictably, social media companies aren't crazy about Josh Bornstein's notion of further liability. Facebook's submission to the Australian Senate hearings states: 'Given the strong commitment of industry to promote the safety of people when they use our services, we believe that no changes to existing criminal law are required. If anything, we would encourage the Committee to consider carve outs from liability for responsible intermediaries.'

In plain English, Facebook isn't just seeking the status quo – it's suggesting exemptions from prosecution. Also notable in this statement is the use of the word 'intermediaries' to refer to themselves (as opposed to simply accepting their role as a publisher). Interestingly, Amnesty International also rallies against the imposition by states of legal liability 'for companies who fail to remove abusive content' and says it 'sets a dangerous precedent and risks causing more harm instead of addressing the core of the issue'.[2]

Under the current system in Australia, social media companies are viewed as the eSafety Office's 'partners' but when it comes to cyberbullying they can be given legally binding notices or fines if they don't comply with requests from the Commissioner.[3] 'We haven't had to use our formal powers once,' Julie Inman Grant says, adding that the system of treating social media companies as partners and giving them 'the benefit of the doubt' is working. 'They don't want bullying. They don't want that happening on their platforms.'

Encouragingly, the eSafety Office claims it has a 100 per cent compliance rate when it comes to getting cyberhate taken down.[4] Yet I've seen that for individuals like Justine, who try to attempt this without a government body behind them, the outcomes are not so flash.

This isn't to say that Inman Grant thinks the social media companies are at the top of their game when it comes to addressing online harassment. 'They've made some incremental changes … but they haven't been monumental changes,' she says. Grant sees the current historical moment as a 'tipping point' of public anger, and is adamant: 'Our expectations are for our technology leaders to do better. We need to see full-scale change. We need to see meaningful transparency or radical transparency, if you want to call it that. Online safety is not a destination, it's a constant journey.'

One of the things the eSafety Commissioner talks passionately about – and I come to agree with – is a concept she calls 'safety by design'. Her idea is that instead of being retrofitted after the damage is done, tech platforms must be engineered to protect us from the get-go. This strikes me as just like cars fitted with mandatory seat belts and airbags in case we crash while driving them. Late at night when I'm writing and peeling back all the painful consequences of predator trolling, I can't help wondering how different things might have been. How many lives might have been saved if social media companies had, right from the start, internalised the Latin phrase all medical students are taught, *primum non nocere?* First, do no harm.

To explain what happens in the absence of safety by design, the eSafety Commissioner takes the examples of live video streaming platforms Periscope and Meerkat, and contrasts them with the rival product Facebook Live. Facebook Live is, for her, a 'perfect example' of the failure to implement safety by design.

When Facebook Live came onto the market, Periscope and Meerkat were already in operation and therefore, she says, it should have been clear that user safety would be a major issue. 'Why did it take almost a dozen live-streamed rapes, murders and suicides for them [Facebook] to say, "Okay, well, we're going to hire 3000 moderators"? They were so focused on getting out to market and gaining market share that they didn't do the proper risk mitigation and risk management and try and build those in.'

Facebook responded to this criticism via email, stating: 'All new features – including Facebook Live – go through rigorous internal review involving specialist privacy, safety and security teams.'

Neither Facebook nor Twitter agree to nominate a representative for me to interview on the record. To give Facebook its due, the staff do attempt to answer my direct questions and have ongoing correspondence and phone calls with me over many weeks. However, both platforms are guilty of providing long, prepared written statements which often smack of public relations spin. Twitter directly addresses only two issues I raise with them – the first is regarding the purchase of advertisements to perpetrate cyberhate, and the second is related to outsourcing moderation overseas. My other thirteen questions, based on the comments and experiences from case studies and experts in this book, are not directly answered by the platform. Given these deficits, only limited portions of these statements can be included in these pages.

In case you're wondering why these two platforms are singled out, the majority of cyberhate targets I've spoken with have been predator trolled on either Twitter or Facebook (or both). This may be due in part to the scale and saturation of those platforms – Facebook in particular, with its 2.2 billion global users. (Twitter has approximately 336 million active users.)[5] It may also be due to their intrinsic characteristics. Unlike other, more visual, social media platforms, Twitter and Facebook are word-heavy. This isn't to say trolling doesn't occur on other platforms like YouTube and Instagram – it does.

At various times I write to both Twitter and Facebook, expressing my frustration at their insistence on tightly managing the message. In an email to a Twitter spokeswoman based in Singapore – who won't be named and did not directly answer my specific questions – I write:

> The book makes very serious claims – investigated and backed up with evidence – about the real-life impacts of this kind of speech on social media platforms.
>
> The bottom line is that Twitter hasn't provided someone for me to interview. So I can't put all the numerous concerns raised by my interviewees directly to anyone … it's your own call as to how this will reflect on the public's perception of how seriously Twitter takes predator trolling and cyberhate.

Needless to say, she does not reply. After months of highly controlled communication with me, a Facebook staff member – who also insists on not being named – asks me why the media doesn't accurately report on what Facebook is doing in regard to user safety; I nearly laugh.

In part my response reads: 'This is all about how much trust is in the bank – which is low at the moment due to issues you are already aware of.' (We had discussed Facebook's data breaches – and how dimly the public viewed them.) Getting accurate coverage, I explain, is more likely 'if you have those human relationships with journalists' and allow leadership to be interviewed because 'this gives the appearance of being in open and honest communication with the public'.

After three months of corresponding with Facebook, the company offers me a meeting with Mia Garlick. This is not the interview I've requested but it's better than nothing. Perhaps Garlick won't remember our last encounter, but on the day I'm nervous. I put on more makeup than usual – my sister fondly calls this my war paint – shapewear and a floral shirt.

The building's companies are listed in the foyer of this nondescript high-rise in Sydney's CBD. Facebook is not listed. As the troll hunter pointed out to me, unless you know the address, it's not easy to find. Beyond the big wooden-framed doors on the eighteenth floor, it's like a separate universe. Deliberate funkiness. There's a big wooden 'f' on the wall, in Facebook's signature font, surrounded by fake grass. A vase of orange orchids stands in a clear glass vase on the beach-coloured reception desk. Behind the desk is a high wall covered in a huge, modern mural suggesting flowers and vegetation. The phone doesn't stop ringing.

The receptionist asks me to electronically sign a five-screen-long non-disclosure agreement. This form effectively stops me sharing 'confidential information' gleaned in the upcoming meeting.

She gives me a green bottle of sparkling water and directs me to a blue-and-grey couch with colour-coordinated throw pillows of different sizes. I find myself peering into a giant bowl of lollies – Fantales and Minties – on the coffee table. There's something about these sweets, staring back at me like dozens of faces, that makes me hyperfocused on why I'm here. The predator-trolling targets. Their names march on and on, like a parade. Charlotte Dawson, Van Badham, Josh Bornstein, Sherele Moody, Mel Greig, Carmen, Eva, Justine. Others I've only read about: Anita Sarkeesian, Zoë Quinn, Jessica Valenti, Lindy West.

Finally, I'm collected from reception by a public relations representative and shown to a boardroom behind glass doors. Floor-to-ceiling windows look over the city. Garlick greets me. She's wearing a black cardigan with a white top underneath, and a chunky blue ring on her right hand with a wide resin bracelet to match. Her hair slightly slicked back. Those same startling blue eyes.

There's a note of tension in the room and I crack a bad joke about having slept badly because of drunk kids in the city. Both Garlick and the PR person laugh politely and visibly relax. The pair of them reiterate the message they've given me via email: *Nothing is quotable.*

And that's a crying shame because, one by one, Garlick graciously answers every single question that I have. In detail. Unlike the prepared statements Facebook sends me both before and after this meeting, this face-to-face conversation shows Garlick to be authentic. She's passionate about her work and believes in it. She's thoughtful and well informed. Her answers – which I'm, of course, unable to share – go a long way to making Facebook's case in relation to what the company *is actually doing* about cyberhate.

Once a journalist, always a journalist – even in a situation where you can't quote. During the meeting I take down more than a thousand words of notes. Towards the end of our allocated time, I'm told that if I wish to have these exact same questions answered officially, I need to send them again via email (for the third time).

Facebook brands itself as a place 'where people from all over the world can share and connect'. Clearly, journalists are not the people they have in mind. On the contrary, this rigmarole leaves me with a distinct and unprovable hunch: this unwise attempt at containing the media – and, by proxy, the public – must be deliberate. Is it a directive from the California head office? What other sensible reason could there be for this behaviour?

Social media is the missing piece in the discussion about predator trolling. As a community, we seem to be quite content to blame victims. To blame pale police responses. Occasionally the perpetrators too. Yet we are unwilling to analyse the role of these private companies in providing a platform for the perpetration of cyberhate.

As I'm starting to understand, they don't make this task easy. After witnessing the company's responses at the Senate hearings and then communicating with them at length myself, it's hard not to conclude that this obstruction is by design: *There's nothing to see here. Move along.*

Facebook, for example, has consistently denied being a publisher, instead claiming 'we are in the business of connecting people and ideas'.

'On Facebook,' the company submitted to the Senate, 'people choose who to be friend [sic] with, and which Pages or Groups to follow. Consequently, people make a decision about the types of content that they can see in their News Feed … We do not write the posts that people read on our services.'[6]

The issue of whether social media companies are or aren't publishers is a thorny one – and it's being debated around the world.[7] The reason for this is that traditional publishers – like newspapers and TV stations – can be held responsible for false, misleading or malicious content shared on their platforms.

Writing in *The Guardian,* Emily Bell, director of the Tow Center for Digital Journalism at Columbia University, articulated what many people already believe. Social media companies *are* publishers because they 'monetise, host, distribute, produce and even in some cases commission material'. Teasing out why this is a particular problem when it comes to news and information, she continues, 'By acting like technology companies, while in fact taking on the role of publishers, Google, Facebook and others, have accidentally designed a system that elevates the cheapest and "most engaging" content at the expense of more expensive but less "spreadable" material.'[8]

In short, this prioritises shoddy content while suffocating quality journalism. To unpick what this means, we must acknowledge something else: huge swathes of people around the globe use social media as their primary news source. For example, 41 per cent of people in the UK, 46 per cent in Australia, 51 per cent in the United States, and 66 per cent in Brazil.[9] If, as Bell suggests is the consequence, we're no longer getting quality information, our ability to move through the world as informed citizens, able to make democratic choices, is severely limited.

This prompts another question: Should website operators be accountable for what's on their sites? Of course, the answer is its own can of worms. Under Section 230 of the US *Communications Decency Act of 1996*, social media companies are not responsible for anything third parties or users publish on their platforms.[10] (Because the internet was created and regulated in the United States, this legislation effectively impacts anyone anywhere in the world who uses the internet.) Section 230 has recently been amended, but only as it applies to sex trafficking. However, there's widespread disagreement among experts as to how the changes will play out and whether free speech on the internet will be affected more broadly.[11]

Although some like to claim 'Section 230 ... is responsible for creating the modern internet that we know and love', it's still baffling as to why social media companies are able to shirk responsibility for the extreme harm perpetrated via their sites.[12] Imagine if such harms were routinely inflicted on members of the public visiting other types of privately owned spaces – like shopping malls or amusement parks.

To be fair, Section 230 was never created to protect tech companies from policing their platforms – just the opposite, in fact. Back in the 1990s, when Section 230 was drafted and made into law, US legislators believed the then fledgling internet must be allowed to flourish without censorship. One of these lawmakers was Senator Ron Wyden, who co-authored the legislation. In a fascinating interview with The Verge, he explained that the intent was to provide both 'a sword' and 'a shield'. The shield was designed to allow tech companies to secure vital capital, he says, while the sword protected them from liability from content posted by users. It gave them the freedom to moderate. But, in exchange, tech companies had to police their platforms.

'[W]hat was clear during the 2016 election and the succeeding events surrounding Facebook, is that technology companies used one part of what we envisioned, the shield, but really sat on their hands with respect to the sword, and wouldn't police their platforms,' Senator Wyden says.[13]

Here, Wyden is referring to Facebook's massive data breach – revealed by a Cambridge Analytica whistleblower – which many experts have suggested influenced the outcome of the US presidential election.[14]

Speaking to the US Senate in March 2018 about Section 230, Wyden disputed the oft-made claim by tech companies that the volume of content on their platforms was too great to monitor. (More than 4.75 billion pieces of content are posted on Facebook each day and users send more than 500 million tweets in the same time period.[15]) He retorted that the spread of hateful content had become 'a direct function of their business models'. 'The companies have become bloated, uninterested in the larger good, and feckless … There have been far too many alarming examples of algorithms driving vile, hateful, or conspiratorial content to the top of the sites millions of people click onto every day.'[16]

Accordingly, Senator Wyden supported the recent changes to Section 230 and warned: 'The industry better start using the sword part of the two-part package, or else it isn't going to be in their hands.'[17]

As yet, the tech companies have failed to quell increasing criticism of their practices. Far from it. The standard tepid rejoinder seems to be:

'We messed up, but we're trying to improve.'[18] In an interview that also took place in March 2018, Facebook CEO Mark Zuckerberg seemed either unbelievably naive or disingenuous in light of the persistent international malfeasance on his platform. He told the technology news website Recode he was 'fundamentally uncomfortable sitting here in California in an office making content policy decisions for people around the world'.[19] Let's remember that this platform is one Zuckerberg co-created.[20]

For me, his naivety and/or disingenuousness was perfectly captured in a satirical tweet sent by a woman using the Twitter name 'Skelly Belle'. Zuckerberg was testifying to the US Congress in the wake of the massive Facebook data breach. During his testimony she posted a photo of him looking decidedly uncomfortable, with the caption: 'When you just wanted to create a website that rates women as hot or not and degrades people on your college campus but you end up being grilled by the Government years later about contributing to a worsening genocide in a foreign country and you can't handle it.'[21] The genocide reference is to the mass murders and gang rapes of the Rohingya Muslims in Myanmar, in which the United Nations implicated Facebook.[22]

It appears Facebook leadership is far out of its depth when it comes to everything from spreading fake news on its platform to interference in democratic processes, massive data breaches and the spread of hatred leading to mass murder. 'Things like, "Where's the line on hate speech?" I mean, who chose me to be the person that did that?' Zuckerberg told the website Recode. 'I guess I have to, because we're here now, but I'd rather not.'[23]

Yet despite claiming to not know where the boundary is when it comes to hate speech, Zuckerberg has repeatedly claimed it 'has no place on Facebook'.[24] Outlining his vision for the company over the next decade in a Facebook post, he appeared to expand on this platitude, stating: 'Keeping the global community safe is an important part of our mission – and an important part of how we'll measure our progress going forward.'[25]

What are we to make of these sentiments, side by side? My take is that Zuckerberg is saying what he thinks people want to hear, but his heart isn't in it. He's created a global monster but is not fond of taming it – and he doesn't want anyone else to do it either.

Julie Inman Grant was once a Silicon Valley insider, and in October 2013 she told the National Press Club in Canberra:

> [T]he default position of the tech industry is that it wants to be left alone by government. There continues to be a fervent belief by industry that a completely unregulated environment is the best way to innovate and drive profits, as well as create jobs and maintain the sanctity of the First Amendment.[26]

Of course, profit is a major factor in tech companies – and likely a substantial reason Zuckerberg would perhaps 'rather not' adequately police his platform. Frank Pasquale, Professor of Law at the University of Maryland and author of *The Black Box Society* explains: 'Very often, hate, anxiety and anger drive participation with the platform. Whatever behaviour increases ad revenue will not only be permitted, but encouraged, excepting of course some egregious cases.'[27]

Sometimes, when I'm watching the daily dog-piling of someone like journalist Sherele Moody, it's hard not to wonder whether Pasquale has a point. If predator trolling and the incitement of discord by third parties weren't serving the platforms in some way, wouldn't these behemoths have found a way to stop it by now?

Of course, when I repeatedly put this to Facebook, staff there furiously deny it. One spokeswoman says to me: 'Those comments are insulting to the thousands of people who've come to work every day [at Facebook] for the last fourteen years – policy people, leadership, safety experts, engineers – to make the platform safer. It's bad long-term business if people have had a bad experience on our service. If people don't find Facebook useful, they are not going to use it. Our long-term future is to continue delivering a service that people enjoy and feel safe using.'

Still. Even Twitter's current CEO, Jack Dorsey, understands his platform has been failing to keep people safe. In a series of tweets from 2017, he said:

We see voices being silenced on Twitter every day. We've been working to counteract this for the past 2 years ... We prioritized this in 2016. We updated our policies and increased the size of our teams. It wasn't enough.[28]

#

Let's go back to the Australian Senate hearings into the adequacy of existing cyberbullying laws, held in February 2018. Officially these hearings were held by the Legal and Constitutional Affairs References Committee. Before you decide the name of this committee is so long and boring that you'll skip ahead: STOP. This is about what we don't know. What the social media companies don't tell us and, standing in that void, the questions we're left with. Questions about why social media companies say we're safe on their platforms, but we aren't. Why they continually say they are fixing cyberhate, yet nothing seems to change.

Alongside Jenna Price and Liza-Jayne Loch, I speak to the Legal and Constitutional Affairs References Committee about how often female journalists are attacked online, how hard it is to get the cyberhate taken down in a timely fashion and how extreme the impacts can be on individuals.

We call for legal change and transparency from social media companies, especially in regard to their complaints handling. How many complaints do social media companies get? How many are upheld? Release all the data, we say. We tell stories of how hard it is to get cyberhate taken down – and how slow the process is.

'[S]peed of response is key, and taking down the images and the attacks is key, but it takes a long time. And ... if they don't agree with you then you have to appeal, and that takes more time, and in the meantime your image, in whatever version it is, has been plastered all around the internet,' Price tells the hearing.

For my part, I outline the real-life harm done to the victims of predator trolling, including causing people to harm themselves or to lose their jobs, and as a contributing factor to suicide.

As if we come from different planets, our testimonies are often dia-metrically opposed to those given by the social media leaders who follow us. Mia Garlick gives her evidence alongside Julie de Bailliencourt, head of Global Safety Outreach for Facebook, and Nicole Buskiewicz, managing director of DIGI. Buskiewicz opens her discussion by tell-ing the committee that the safety of users is 'the industry's top priority' and 'all DIGI members have specific policies that prohibit the use of their platforms and services for any kind of harassment or menacing behaviour like cyberbullying. The vast majority of reports are reviewed within the time frame of twenty-four hours. Some may go to forty-eight hours. We try to go even faster on very sensitive reports, such as bullying. Suicide prevention is the one we try to get to in minutes,' she says.

Facebook's de Bailliencourt concurs – she says the company's policies are 'strong' and 'we enforce these aggressively'.

Not only are these claims in direct contrast to the evidence given by Women in Media, but they also negate what the trolls tell me. Although Meepsheep has been permanently banned from Twitter, he still believes, 'Social media companies don't take down fake accounts fast or deal with cyberhate well. Trust me from being on the other side. And the measures they do implement don't work.'

This means the tardiness of social media companies in dealing with online harassment becomes part of the trolls' arsenal. Inman Grant is unequivocal on this point: 'They're [predator trolls] totally gaming the system and they're finding out the vulnerabilities. And, full stop, these companies can do more. What it comes down to is the will of the leadership [of tech companies] to make online safety a priority.'

To date, predator troll Mark has had more than 260 Facebook accounts suspended and has also been kicked off Twitter at least fifty times. He says social media companies 'went from doing nothing to being overbearing and authoritarian and banning anything that went outside of what they deemed to be appropriate, largely due to an over-reliance on computers handling reports. The response time varies greatly from case to case,' he says, 'and I'm sure that is due to their moderation algorithms that they will never be open about.'

At the hearings, the social media representatives reiterate the view that the current laws are adequate. They claim to cooperate with authorities and work with users to keep people safe. Data points help them identify fake accounts.

Garlick tells the senators that Facebook prohibits credible threats and hate speech and takes that content down. She says the platform is working to apply its policies consistently and is 'developing new tools to assist people who are experiencing harassment on the platform'. Facebook does have detailed policies explaining what type of material it allows, with provisions covering direct threats, self-harm, bullying and harassment, and fake accounts. The social media company acknowledges '"inauthentic" accounts are typically created to harass, bully or for other harmful purposes'. It also offers tools to help individuals 'manage their experience on Facebook', including privacy controls and blocking and reporting mechanisms.[29]

You've heard arguments from lawyer Josh Bornstein that we need more regulation. And counterarguments from the eSafety Commissioner that we don't – it won't help and there are other, more effective ways to solve the problem. The conversation at the hearings moves on to this same conundrum.

'From our perspective,' Garlick says, 'regulation doesn't drive updates or improvements in terms of our policies or our tools. For us it's about people having a positive experience on our services, so we listen to feedback from the community.'

The committee's chair, Senator Louise Pratt, remarks that pressure from the European Union has seen social media companies responding to cyberhate far more quickly in those nations than they previously had. Data released by the EU at the start of 2018 shows that in response to the Code of Conduct on countering illegal online hate speech, tech companies including Facebook, Twitter and YouTube 'removed on average 70 percent of illegal hate speech notified to them' within twenty-four hours. This was up from 28 per cent two years earlier.[30]

Separate to this, Germany has taken an even stricter approach, passing a law that requires social media companies to take down hate speech within twenty-four hours or face the possibility of a 50-million-euro fine.

Critics are claiming it violates free speech and privatises enforcement of the law.[31]

Drawing on the EU figures, Senator Pratt asks the social media representatives, 'How do those figures compare to the amount of content that's taken down in Australia?'

'Wow! This is a good question,' de Bailliencourt replies. 'I don't know the figures offhand.' She says she will take the question on notice.

De Bailliencourt and Garlick both also tell Senator Rex Patrick they do not have a record of the number of complaints and take-down requests for Australia. Instead of providing numbers, de Bailliencourt says Facebook's 'measure of our success' is 'how quickly we're able to provide support to people'.

To me, listening in the audience, her response is anxious, repetitive and babbling: 'The numbers in themselves are quite meaningless; for us the focus is on the strength of our team and coming back to the people who need our support.'

This is also frustrating because although social media platforms rely on the public for their existence – to make money – we're unable to get adequate information with which to judge whether we're safe in their care. And if we're not safe, are things at least improving?

In a remarkably similar refrain, Twitter responds to Amnesty International's requests for 'the absolute numbers of reports and the proportion of accounts that are actioned' by stating that 'this type of information can be both uninformative and potentially misleading'.[32]

Amnesty therefore concludes, 'Twitter does not publicly share any specific data on how it responds to reports of abuse or how it enforces its own policies.'[33]

Julie Inman Grant's view is more nuanced. 'I do know from working inside Twitter that those numbers are jealously guarded because there is a huge risk to these companies,' she says, sensibly pointing out that when a social media company has a large user base, the numbers of complaints will also be large. 'And big numbers put out there without context can be incredibly damaging. There needs to be a lot of context and detail.'

In her mind, it's not just about how much abuse was reported and how much was then taken down. Instead we need to know how complaints are triaged. Are the most urgent ones dealt with first? And what about the less urgent ones? Inman Grant also wants to ensure the burden of dealing with complaints sits with tech companies, and isn't just dumped onto users.

Meanwhile neither Senator Jordon Steele-John nor Senator Patrick buy into the notion that social media companies don't retain and analyse data relating to cyberhate. Patrick says to the social media representatives: 'Respectfully, if you say that you're customer-driven but you're not collecting data about the volumes of customers that are being affected by this, there is a disconnect there.' Moments later he adds, 'I still have difficulty understanding why you wouldn't collect data on the number of complaints … because you can't possibly know where to direct resources.'

Garlick repeats her earlier refrain: they'll respond later. Despite starting the afternoon pleased that I can have a say in this official process, I'm discouraged to hear these women repeatedly failing to answer direct questions.

Facebook and Instagram do later provide a written response to the questions taken on notice at the hearings. The document contains none of the additional complaints data requested by the senators: 'We understand the rationale behind your requests for us to provide more details around data showing reporting trends, however unfortunately at this stage we are not able to do so.'[34]

Perhaps in response to public pressure after the Cambridge Analytica scandal, Facebook released its first *Community Standards Enforcement Report* in May 2018. Among other things, the report reveals the company had 'disabled about 583 million fake accounts' and removed '837 million pieces of spam … nearly 100 percent of which we found and flagged before anyone reported it'.[35] At around the same time, Twitter announced it was suspending 70 million suspicious accounts (although academics have shown this did little to solve the problem).[36] Facebook has also announced the company is altering its appeals process.[37]

While these actions seem to be steps in the right direction – and better than nothing – there are still reams of key questions left unanswered. We don't have a clear understanding about how moderation decisions are made on social media. Are there clear and timely avenues for appeal? For its part, Facebook has tried to be more transparent about enforcement of its policies, but ambiguity remains.[38] Why does a photo of a breastfeeding mother get removed from Facebook when tech abuse against domestic violence victims remains?

A new German documentary titled *The Cleaners*, directed by Moritz Riesewieck and Hans Block, suggests social media moderation is heavily outsourced to the Philippines – to the tune of 100,000 workers. Hordes of young and poorly trained staff make split-second decisions, often in difficult working conditions, about whether content violates a platform's policy.

The platforms tell us most flagged content is reviewed quickly – within twenty-four hours. Complaints may be dealt with rapidly, but are they getting it right?

According to the film's directors, some of the workers have strong biases, with one extremely religious moderator openly admitting to seeing herself as a 'sin preventer' and another favouring the 'violent anti-crime and drugs stance' of Filipino president Rodrigo Duterte.[39] Is an eighteen-year-old who has strong cultural and social prejudices, coupled with little life experience or training, really best placed to make decisions about speech and the harm it may or may not cause in other countries?

Domestic violence survivor Justine, who remains in danger from her ex-partner, told me that nothing she reported to Facebook had ever been taken down.

In February 2018 I wrote an in-depth article about a woman called Christi. She was born with a complex birth defect called imperforate anus, which affects the bowel (among other parts of the body). In the story, Christi explained how her whole life had been marred by this disability and she was fighting for things to be better for children who are born with the condition today.[40] The article was posted to the news outlet's Facebook page and streams of vile and demeaning predator trolling ensued against Christi. When I reported this as hate speech against a woman with a disability – which is clearly against Facebook's policies – I got the same response as Justine. Facebook's moderators told me that of the seventeen comments I reported, none of the abuse violated their rules. This leads me to wonder: for the sake of speed (and possibly from lack of context), are the majority of social media complainants simply being told their issue doesn't violate company policies so moderators can move on to the next complaint?

This issue, largely unaddressed in most public discussions about social media, is bothering me so much I email lawyer Roger Blow, a commercial litigator with specific expertise in online liability. In an email, he concurs: 'All too often they seem to spit back a simplistic rejection of the complaint, sometimes in circumstances where the complaint is clearly very necessary.

'I have long feared that there is a degree of "reject the first complaint and see if that resolves the situation" – as looking into each complaint properly of course takes some time and requires teams of employees to do it (properly), which eats into profits.'

Meanwhile Facebook has announced that it's doubling its 'safety, security and review teams to 20,000 [people] as part of a larger company investment in this space'. This will include 'an expansion of our engineering, product and program management and policy teams'. The platform's vice president of operations, Ellen Silver, claims those who review 'objectionable content' are a 'mix of full-time employees, contractors and companies we partner with'. She says these people speak fifty languages, cover every time zone and are well supported and trained.[41]

Twitter acknowledges it has moderation staff in the Philippines but, like Facebook, is adamant it is sufficiently supporting employees by providing 'regular on-site counselling, training, and person-to-person support, particularly for those whose work may involve reviewing sensitive content'.

As for us, the public, we still don't know how many cyberhate reports the platforms get, the precise nature of those reports, how they are triaged or how the problem is resourced in comparison to the scale of the issue. Numbers like '20,000 safety staff' don't mean anything without a sense of the nature and number of cyberhate reports those staff are dealing with.

In its final recommendations to the Australian government, the Senate committee proposed 'requiring social media platforms to publish relevant data, including data on user complaints and the platforms' responses, as specified by the eSafety Commissioner'.[42] The committee also recommended maintaining 'regulatory pressure on social media platforms to both prevent and quickly respond to' cyberhate, and legislating a duty of care, as Josh Bornstein proposed.

#

After the hearings, I text Bornstein in disbelief at the seemingly endless capacity of Facebook and DIGI to obfuscate in the face of clear questions from the senators. He responds with only three words: 'Standard monopoly behaviour.'

Alongside a growing chorus of others – including the US president – Bornstein believes social media companies have too much power.[43] 'Over and above cyberhate, the Facebooks, Twitters, Amazons of this world, they are incredibly powerful and, I would argue, too powerful. They're monopolies in their fields. They swallow up any competition or crush it. They have enormous political sway and they don't pay proper tax,' he says.

'This era is very much reminiscent of the era in political history in the US during the Gilded Age, when Theodore Roosevelt, in the early 1900s, was dealing with monopoly oil companies and train companies, energy companies, who mistreated their workers, crushed any competition, bribed politicians and were thumbing their nose at proper standards of corporate behaviour.

'Roosevelt, who's a political hero of mine, took them on and started to legislate them to regulate them and break them up. And so, there's a strong argument that these companies should be broken up. They are simply too immense and too powerful.'

Along with the other social media companies, the committee invited Twitter to give evidence at the Senate hearings. In one respect, this is an acknowledgement of the platform's unique place as a conduit for public discourse. On a darker note, it points to the company's unenviable role as 'a platform where violence and abuse against [women] flourishes, often with little accountability'.[44] Perhaps the Australian senators were also conscious of Twitter's potential to damage democratic processes. Just like Facebook, Twitter played an unhealthy part in spreading fake news before and after the 2016 US presidential election.[45]

Despite these compelling factors, the company declined to appear at the Australian Senate hearings into cyberbullying. A representative wrote to the senators, stating that Twitter would 'let our contribution through DIGI's [Digital Industry Group Inc's] submission and testimony stand'.

A nameless Twitter spokesperson writes to me that since January 2017 the company has instituted 'around 100 experiments and product changes, dozens of new policy changes, expanded our enforcement and operations, and strengthened our team structure to build a safer Twitter. We've made good progress but we know there's still a lot of work to be done'. The email goes on to claim Twitter is committed to striking 'the right balance of protecting freedom of expression and keeping our users safe'.

Somehow, the company's continual unwillingness to answer questions – from journalists and senators – makes these claims harder to believe. According to Amnesty's *Toxic Twitter* report, Twitter has made 'several positive changes to their policies and practices in response to violence and abuse on the platform over the past 16 months' and despite this, 'the steps it has taken are not sufficient to tackle the scale and nature of the problem'.[46]

'Twitter's inconsistency and inaction on its own rules not only creates a level of mistrust and lack of confidence in the company's reporting process, it also sends the message that Twitter does not take violence and abuse against women seriously.'[47] (Although Amnesty's report is ostensibly about women, my research indicates these sentiments likely apply to predator-trolling victims of both genders.) Later in the same report, Amnesty calls for transparency, declaring that social media companies can't just *say* they are protecting human rights – they must show us how their reporting and appeal mechanisms work.[48]

After months of trying to get answers, the hill seems steeper than ever. When it comes to accountability, only the eSafety Office seems to offer any hope. (So much so that there are calls for similar statutory agencies to be set up in the United States, Canada, Korea, the UK and Ireland.[49]) What we don't know – and what I can't report – seems far greater in quantity and weight than what these purported champions of free speech will actually reveal.

Notes in the margins
White women are cancer

THE XANAX TROLL – XT – and me: against all odds, we get on like a house on fire. Despite all the things we don't agree on. Which, let's face it, is most things.

For a while, I try to resist falling into a kind of friendship with him. I stay offline for days at a time, fiercely sinking my teeth into the offline world. Going for runs through the bush, under the grove of eucalyptus trees. Thankful for the shade on these searing mornings, the crimson parrots rising out of the grass and the kangaroos grazing on a clear morning.

Inevitably, I get stuck with something in my writing. Some things are so hard to determine from the outside. As I work, question after question arises: *Where does a particular person fit in the hierarchy? Is this a troll who is respected? Or cast out? What does it mean when he uses language like this?*

XT will always help. We end up talking online, sometimes for hours. And not just about trolling. About music (he loves the Grateful Dead and country singer David Allan Coe). And strange mothers. Sorority girls. Anger and despair. Mental illness. Books. Arthouse movies.

Then we have a fight. A big one.

It starts with a tactical error on my part. I've been reading piles of 4chan and IRC chatlogs. The relentlessly violent dialogue – largely directed at women – imbues me with a sense of hopelessness. A kind of slow, rising panic. There's one particular sentence, written by an anonymous poster: *White women are cancer.* He goes on to say white women are 'ruining the west' because they 'pretend to be a separate victim group from white men' and 'don't take care of their body, sleep around, outsource their kids to day care and completely lack any basic women skills'. (An aside: who knows what 'basic women skills' actually are?)

Overall, other posters in the group seem to agree, adding in their own supporting 'arguments':

> *Women have no sense of loyalty.*
> *White traitors will be the ones to destroy us.*
> *Every woman no matter the color is a disgusting slut.*

Over a couple of days, the thread gnaws at me. I find myself thinking about it in the shower and while making Vegemite sandwiches for my kids. *White women are cancer. White women are cancer.*

The logical person to discuss this with is XT. He's familiar with this kind of anti-women discourse – a few years back, he toyed with joining ranks with the 'incels', or 'involuntary celibates', as they're known. These men gather in online forums to share their hatred for women; they believe women owe them sex and endlessly discuss how to get laid, often suggesting force as the means to this end. But XT isn't online when I want to chat – it's probably the middle of the night there. I write anyway, the words spewing out almost by themselves.

'It's so fucking misogynistic,' I write, 'I can barely read it.' I link to the 4chan chatlogs, as well as to Michael Edison Hayden's article about endemic misogyny within the alt-right. Then I continue the stream of consciousness: 'And so, I don't understand this. Why do they hate women so much? And yet they seem to still want women – even if it's just for sex.'

In this rambling monologue I ask whether this is to do with incels' lack of social skills or whether, somehow, women make these young white men feel marginalised and inadequate.

My problem is a wilful blindness to my own state of mind. After hard months of writing, my mental health is fragile. These questions are too raw to ask right now. Or, more accurately, they are easy to ask. What's missing is the ability to consider how I'll manage the answer.

The next day, XT writes back. 'Women are inaccessible to them and women can actually be pretty cruel to men like that IRL. It's a cycle,' he says. The perceived behaviour of women makes incels hate them more.

XT has manners. Maybe he knows this conversation could be volatile and wants to move on to something else. He politely asks me how I am – and I'm great because I'm drinking wine with my best friend in Melbourne. He wants to know what the city is like.

'I'll take pics of the city tomorrow for you, if you like,' I reply. 'It really has a soul.' Then, because I can't fathom that he might sympathise with the bile in these chatlogs, I go back and prod the bear. 'Women are not the enemy,' I say. 'There are assholes of both genders.'

Although he acknowledges this, he says, 'I don't think the guys you are talking about really recognize that though.' He expresses a desire 'to represent ... the legitimate grievances of dudes like that'. 'They just weren't taught how to express [them] in a healthy way,' he says, before adding, 'Women make them feel powerless.'

This answer splits me straight down the middle. It offers what I value most – honesty. It also makes me the enemy.

'It's hard to feel like they hate all women,' I write. '*White women are cancer.* And they're talking about raping and punching women. And that all women deserve to be punched if they don't obey. And if you are a woman, you're always so afraid of coming to harm. Most of us have been sexually assaulted, or come close to it. So this kind of dialogue is frightening in a visceral way that's hard to describe. Also, I just think that women ARE accessible to them.'

We're carefully using the word 'they', to set him aside. Until this moment, I've understood XT is associated with the angry young men writing these comments. But he's not quite one of them. He stands a little apart.

But then he shatters the illusion: 'To be fair white women kinda are cancer on society.' After a moment he continues. 'White women do not stand out as being particularly intelligent. White women are generally the most childish and annoying people on the planet. So in the world of trolling for example, there's never been a white chick who could troll or hack.'

Reeling, I say, 'You know, you are ALWAYS telling me that each person is different and their motivations are different. SO you can't tar everyone with the same brush. I could have treated you like you were just the same as all the other trolls. But I didn't. Because you aren't.'

One of the distinctions XT has always made to me is that he isn't a predator troll. He never set out to harm individuals. When he told me this, it seemed to matter. Now I wonder: *Is this an arbitrary distinction I'm holding on to for my own convenience?*

XT ignores my point about individuality and keeps going with his train of thought. 'There's Asian chicks and other brown girls who can hack,' he tells me. 'But not white chicks. Any white women online generally just want attention ... It seems most white women are painfully immature.'

After the Xanax episode, our relationship developed a gentleness. The combativeness dissolved. We left room in it for each other's differences. Walked around them. Sometimes he'd tell me personal things. Like how, as a kid, his mother was violent and drunk. How much he loved his former girlfriend, and she cheated on him right after they met.

This current conversation feels vicious, though. Attacking. Maybe I've let myself be lulled into a false sense of security. Dumbfounded, I simply say, 'Wow.' And then, with a kind of sadness creeping into my throat, 'I thought you were more open-minded than that.'

Then it sinks in.

'That's just patently bullshit,' I say. 'You're a really smart guy. Why are you getting sucked into crap like that? Just because male–female relations are hard doesn't mean all women are bitches. And what you are talking about relating to women and tech is a TOTALLY different thing. Women are discouraged from science and tech from a very young age. It's not that they CAN'T. It's that society doesn't say it's okay. You can't say that because there aren't many white female hackers, women are stupid. That's not causal. IQ isn't to do with gender or skin colour.'

He replies, 'I'm not saying women are stupid. I do think that western culture is unfair to young women but now instead of telling them that they can't do anything, they're being indoctrinated with this idea that they can do ANYTHING but aren't taught how to actually teach themselves.'

'I can't believe I'm even having this conversation.'

'I think you're interpreting me as being a little more angry or something than I am,' XT writes. He might be right: this is a problem with online conversations that, for me, never goes away. I can't see his face or hear his voice; the body cues aren't there, so I'm guessing. He tells me about the young white women – under the age of thirty – he knows and how shallow they are. How they only care about their appearance. How they only talk about hating their fathers and their ex-boyfriends. How he can't find their souls or anything to talk to them about.

I tell him to have some brains and 'zoom out'. 'That's just your college. In your town. In one city. In the world. And the women you're talking about. They are young and scared and think their value is about how they look. They've been taught to minimise their brains,' I say.

He doesn't seem to be paying attention. 'It's not just young white women, either. White bitches in their 40s almost always talk with fake voices. It's possibly the most annoying thing.'

'If you knew the women I know,' I reply, 'you wouldn't say this stuff.'

The tears are close. This always happens with him: he brings me face-to-face with myself. And in this instance, the closeness is jarring. I hear it in my head: *white women are cancer.* The word cancer is a trigger for me. The doom of 2007 comes back in waves of colour. After the operation, a bad mistake made by one of the nurses. Nearly dying in my hospital bed because of it. My dear friend Poppy flying back from England just to be there, to hold my hand. Poppy driving me around the car park in my hospital gown just so I could leave the ward. The wide, clear tape across the width of my throat holding the skin together at the purple incision.

Does he realise I'm upset now, through these screens? The messages instant across swathes of ocean. His tone seems to soften. 'Probably not,' he says. 'I've just seen a lot of a specific and depressing world here. Kids destroying themselves without guidance.'

Changing tack, I say, 'It's always so hard for me to understand why, when a person feels marginalised, they then go ahead and marginalise other people.'

'When you're a socially ostracized white male you're not really recognised as marginalized,' he replies. 'It's easy to lash out at people who get all the glory and hype for being marginalized.'

While I take this point – and tell him so – this doesn't put the issue to bed for me. Far from it. 'I still just feel depressed that you actually think white women are cancer,' I say.

'I don't completely think that either. I think I'm just trying to paint a picture for you of the things young men see and how that might lead some of them to have beliefs like that,' he says.

'I guess I'm grateful for that even though it's pretty uncomfortable.'

He says, 'I didn't mean to make it uncomfortable. Lol.'

'This trolling book turned out so hard. And so confronting.'

'Sorry to ruin your morning. If I did :['

I close my eyes for a second and force myself to stop typing.

'Hey. It's okay.'

But it's not okay. I can't stop the tears.

I wake up in my hotel room the next morning. Crying again. Stupidly, I re-read the *White women are cancer* conversation from start to finish, and really wish I hadn't.

I'm at the point where the rubber band is just stretched too far.

Over and over I say to myself, *I'm done. I'm so done here.*

'I think I'm out for a bit, OK?' I write to him. Then, without giving him a chance to respond, I delete the apps on my desktop and phone.

#

Back at home, forty-eight hours later, I'm telling another friend of mine. A writer. A white feminist, like me.

'Fuck off, troll,' she says, furious.

My husband's response is different. Drinking wine with me, he listens as I pour out this story without taking a breath. My rage. My hurt.

'I'm out,' I say defiantly, and out loud this time.

Quietly, Donnie thinks about XT – what I've told him now and a few previous snippets. 'Didn't XT just break up with his girlfriend?' he asks. 'Was she white? Maybe he's just feeling misogynist because of that. Go back online and talk to him.'

Awash in angst, I can nevertheless see this seems calm and reasonable.

Gingerly, I go back to my desk very early the next morning. I reinstall the messenger app and send XT what, once upon a time, would have been a letter handwritten in cursive on stiff, crinkly paper and sent by post with a franked stamp. (Too bad we gave all that up for the likes of 4chan, Tumblr and Facebook.)

It says:

I don't even want you to be sorry. That's not the thing. The thing is that you actually think that most white women are bitches or cancer.

Firstly, I've had cancer, as you know. The doctor slit my throat to take it out. So that's awesome, relating the whole thing back to that #notatall

Second, when you were withdrawing from Xanax I stayed with you online.

Just imagine you're me for a second. I work 60–70 hours a week doing journalism and then my domestic load is about 25 hours (about). So it's a lot. I'm stressed and busy, just like you. When that happened, I was cooking my family dinner and playing with the kids. But I stayed with you online. Because I cared that you were safe. I don't want ANY thanks or congratulations for that. I wanted to. I chose to. The point is ... you're not seeing what's right in front of you.

You're ignoring the kindness and cherry-picking the evidence to suit your pre-decided stigma about white women. It's confirmation bias. (I don't know why you're doing that. If it's because of your ex-girlfriend or the kind of stuff people say in IRC – the culture around trolling and the alt-right.)

And you kept going on and on about how white women can't be hackers.

I mention one of his dear friends. She's white, an expert hacker and a troll. Then continue:

Not to mention that the first ever computer programmer, Ada Lovelace, was a woman. I can't believe I'm even defending this stuff? It's so crazy.

And I don't want to be grateful because I'm in the small percentage of white women that aren't bitches in your mind.

Compassion is a two-way street. And if you think white men are marginalised and need compassion, then give as good as you get. Give the compassion back. (And don't make sweeping generalisations based on a few shallow cows that you met at college who hate their fathers and their exes.)

If you (white men/the alt-right) want women to love and admire and have friendships with you, give it right back.

I'm happy to be your friend. You're fun and interesting and you can make me think about things in new ways. And I love that. But I don't want to be judged for WHAT I am (not who I am). I've never done that to you and I don't want you to do that to me either.

He writes back almost straight away.

Alright I understand what you're saying. Not to just apologize again, but I think that when you spend so much time online in these communities it's easy to be conditioned to the idea that most people are going to take whatever you say very lightly and to some degree it's easy to use outlandish statements in an inappropriate context. Which is also why it's easy to spew opinions without thinking about the personal impact they might have.

Obviously not all white women are dumb and/or bitches. I can see why that generalization would bother you. And statistically that's also impossible. At the same time, what I was getting at – which I've said probably 9000 times now – is that regardless of whatever objective truth there is, in my daily life (and I believe in those of most of these young men you're researching) white women are not particularly kind people.

That's just what seems to be the cold truth based on most of my experience. It's not 100% applicable across the board obviously, but white women can still be extremely cruel to young men. I've seen that in all sorts of places ... schools, workplaces, homes.

I know I keep apologizing but I am actually sorry about how I approached that. I think there are a lot of other ways I could have conveyed the point I wanted.

The first time I read his response, it's hard to absorb. Like blind-spot vision, there's only one word that comes into focus. *Sorry*, he says. Not once, but numerous times. A litany.

It brings me back. Makes me chew my thumbnail and stare at the rest of the text, willing myself to comprehend. Quite apart from his anger, XT is trying to articulate something about his world. Something *I asked about.*

Finally, I write, 'I'm pretty tough but I have a limit.'

'Looks like I found that,' he replies, 'lol.'

Not ready to lol yet, I keep going. 'And also, I'm deliberately open-hearted. That's a choice about who I want to be. But yesterday I was so fucking angry with myself. I was wondering ... Why did I even let this happen?'

'Let what happen?' he asks.

'Another journalist who writes about hackers told me ... *Don't trust trolls and you won't get burned.* I felt like I walked into the snake pit and was then amazed that I got bitten. It made me question myself: *Why am I friends, supposedly, with this person who thinks white women are cancer? What am I actually doing here?*'

'Well I don't actually think all white women are cancer,' he says, 'Also there's a really specific way the word "cancer" is used in this circle. And I think there were some translation issues with that.'

'Nope, there weren't,' I say. 'I understand because I've read so many chatlogs.'

XT says he won't press the issue, but he just wants me to consider one more thing: 'how much the media can vilify men'. 'This whole concept of "mansplaining",' he writes, 'which I'm not saying isn't a phenomenon. But white women do the same thing just as much and nobody is interested in that: "Whitewomansplaining".'

(Later on, my Asian husband belly-laughs when I recount this interaction. When he recovers, he says: 'I get whitewomansplained to all the time!' At the time, I don't laugh; I'm too affronted. But after a few days of rumination, I am willing to concede to both Don and XT that, yes, as a result of feeling powerless and disenfranchised, I have been guilty of this behaviour.)

'All of that makes me just want to crawl into a ball and go to sleep. Because it gets too bitter,' I write.

'Does it? I'm not trying to sound bitter,' XT replies.

'Everyone is just shouting and no one is listening,' I say. 'If people would just ask a few more questions and listen to the answers, the world would be very different.'

'That's pretty true. Yeah, I agree with that a lot,' he says.

And just like that, we're back to the strange place we always get to. Agreeing.

After pausing for a second, I ask something that would be crushingly forward, face to face, but seems to be okay online: 'Why do you want to be friends with me? I mean, in your head, what is the point of that?'

If this question alarms him, he doesn't show it. 'You're smart, interesting, and I think have a pretty good sense of humor, most of the time.'

I write, 'I was scared maybe I misjudged you. It's hard to understand why or how I've become friends with you, in a way. But I think that's okay. It was so far from what I was expecting. But I'm still grateful.'

'Me too,' XT says.

The morning is getting late now and the school run is looming. I have to go (in troll speak: 'G2G').

He says, 'See ya. And thanks again.'

'For what?' I ask, puzzled.

'IDK [I don't know]. For being so nice.'

Embarrassed, I brush this off. 'I'm complicated. Like most people.'

In this moment, and in many more to come, there's an almost imperceptible change in his language. He's softer. He says 'thank you' more often. He says 'good night'. He starts asking how I am – before I ask him.

He changes me too. It's harder and harder to remember he's a troll, and easier to think about sharing some thread of humanity.

Over many weeks we loop back to this topic of white women, again and again – often unexpectedly and sandwiched between other online chatter. Each time, the tension eases a tiny bit. Stitches in fabric that loosen with wear. Eventually, like so much online drama, we give this tense interplay its own hashtag, #whitewomencancergate or just #WWCG.

It removes the sting. And opens the door.

#

'Do I need to stage an intervention?' asks my dear friend and business partner, Sue.

We're in the studio, recording the last part of the online course we've been working on for months. By now, she's used to me babbling endlessly about trolls every time we take a recording break – the strange and disturbing things they do and say.

Sue is a journalist too and often has editorial insights for me. Today, though, she's worried that some of my quasi friendships with trolls – like the one with XT – step over the line. She questions whether, sometimes, I can be too open-minded, and jokingly suggests that maybe I've got Stockholm syndrome. Although she laughs, I can tell from the tightness in the corners of her mouth that she's serious.

'You are so engrossed in the work and the story that you forget these people are not safe, and that they ruin lives. That they're not normal people to be friends with,' she says. 'My assumption is that they are probably psychopaths of some sort. So not your ideal friends.'

She looks me in the eye. 'I think your desire to understand them drives your behaviour but then once you're in, you are drawn to something else too. Perhaps this is because you find multi-layered people interesting and aren't threatened by complex personalities as a rule.'

I'm not sure how to respond, so just keep listening.

'It could be the same appreciation of "grey" and "fuzzy" that probably makes you a good investigative journalist,' she muses. 'It's interesting to me as you wouldn't be so benevolent to, say, one of those mansplaining academics who always write to you.'

Sometimes the people who love you know you better than you know yourself.

#

There's something in cybersecurity journalist Lorraine Murphy's writing that stays with me. Sentences float back days after reading her written profile of TriCk – otherwise known as Junaid Hussain, the British Pakistani hacker and troll who joined ISIS and was killed in a drone strike in 2015. *'And he was my friend. We met on Twitter.'*[1]

I direct-message her on Twitter. Graciously, she responds. In the first instance, I'm just trying to clear up my own confusion about something one of the trolls has told me: Was TriCk a member of Rustle League?

'No,' she says, 'he wasn't in Rustle League. He was in Team Poison, and they sometimes worked together on pranks and things. He definitely did some trolling, but it wasn't where his heart lay. He was all about hacktivism.'

Then, because she seems so open, I spit out the thing that's really bothering me. 'Well, one thing that I think is weird – and I liked about your article – is that these people (hackers, trolls) often aren't who you expect.'

Instantly, Murphy agrees: 'Indeed, the internet teaches lots of lessons about jumping to conclusions.'

'I mean, it SURPRISES me that I like some of them so much,' I say. 'And I've become friends with some of them. So how do you understand that yourself, from your own experiences?'

'I understand charm to be a completely independent characteristic from goodness,' Murphy replies. 'I literally reported to [hacker] Adrian Lamo, worked for him as a volunteer for years, while also being one of the key people on the "Free Chelsea" Twitter movement.'

Adrian Lamo was the person who reported US soldier Chelsea Manning to criminal investigators after she passed confidential military information on to WikiLeaks. Among multiple charges, Manning was convicted of 'aiding the enemy' and imprisoned from 2010 to 2017.[2]

She continues, 'Every person is trustworthy about some things, but not others. It's part of adulting to figure out where their limits are. Like, weev was extremely kind to [Anonymous hacker] Kahuna in prison. Shared his food, introduced him to people, gave him very important advice. But he's still weev, and was a Nazi even then.'

My uneasy and occasional sympathy for some of the trolls, coupled with my dismay at the harm they inflict on individuals, is partially captured by attorney and academic Dr Seth Abramson in his 2017 Medium article about 4chan trolls:

> If you sense here some empathy for these jerks, this is why: they're fundamentally unhappy young people whose subtle indoctrination into a cult is explainable by virtue of their juvenile anxiety, confusion, and pathological inability to assimilate into normative human culture. And those very human frailties will nevertheless end up destroying their lives in the long run.[3]

Just a few days after I start talking with Murphy on Twitter she sends me a link to a post she's written on her blog, The Cryptosphere. Adrian Lamo is dead. Underneath a screenshot of a Facebook post written by Lamo's father – 'he was my beloved son' – the first part of her post reads:

> Could be his hard living lifestyle just caught up with him, could be an accidental overdose. If it were deliberate, I'm sure Adrian of all people would have left a note.
>
> People would be shocked to learn just how normcore his final year was. Holding down a steady job (that he enjoyed and was a natural for). Seeing friends IRL. Going to Little League to watch a pal coach his team. Attending church and getting baptised. Having family dinners together on Thanksgiving and Christmas with his local informally adopted family, who had helped him get established, get his own place, and live something approaching an ordinary life.[4]

After checking she's okay – just like TriCk, Adrian was her friend – my next question is: 'Why do so many of these guys end up dead?'

She says, '[The] lifestyle is hard on the system. And [the opioid drug] fentanyl can surprise any drug user.'

When Murphy says this, my mind reflexively snaps to XT. His withdrawals from Xanax. I know he's been taking other, softer drugs recently. I write to him on one of the apps we're using: 'I feel like your mother saying this but just don't die, okay?'

He says, 'Yeah I'm not going to, lol. After the Xanax episode I don't want to touch any hard drugs again.'

Once I say goodbye, I have a terrible feeling. A stomach knot, like leaving someone you care about at the train station or airport. Despite my extreme discomfort and unwillingness, something has unhardened within me and is making some space for him. Perhaps even more disconcerting is that this is reciprocated. There are flashes of humanity in some of the trolls' behaviour, reaching out to me like hands across the cold water. They help me. They help each other. They even help strangers.

Part 3

TROLL HUNTING

12

Hunting a terrorist troll

WHEN PROMINENT AUSTRALIAN employment lawyer Josh Bornstein woke up on Friday, 10 April 2015, the first thing he saw was 'my Twitter feed going feral with death threats and emails from all over the world, threatening me, and attacking me, and criticising me'. To his horror, some of these critics were well-known people like US feminist and author Naomi Wolf. While Bornstein slept, Wolf – who has since apologised – labelled Josh 'deranged', 'genocidal' and 'psychotic' in a Facebook post.[1]

Bornstein was about to discover firsthand just how hard it can be to get the help you need from law enforcement. How easy it is to have your reputation smeared online and how tough it is to hold up in the face of predator trolling. He was about to get a close look at one of the young, angry and marginalised white men who turn to attacking strangers in their despair. And how those young men can fall through the cracks.

Like anyone waking up to piles of online slurs, Bornstein says he felt disoriented and shocked. Fairly quickly, though, he managed to regain his composure enough to start putting the pieces together. 'In my day job, most people who come to see me are derailing at work or have suffered sexual harassment, or bullying or being sacked. They are the subject of disciplinary proceedings and are traumatised or worse. So I'm used to seeing people who are very agitated, upset, in crisis,' Bornstein explains. 'I often go into a crisis-management mode for my clients.'

In this instance, however, he was forced to switch into crisis-management mode for himself. He quickly discovered someone posing as him had posted a racist opinion article on the website of the Jerusalem-based newspaper *The Times of Israel.*

'I detest racism. I've fought it all my life,' Bornstein says, shaking his head. Although it's now three years after the article was published, his incredulity is still palpable. As he wrote in *The Guardian* a month after the attack, the original opinion piece contained 'a graphically violent and racist diatribe against the Palestinian people ... calling for their "extermination"'. 'The despicable article was attributed to me and was accompanied by my photograph. It was quickly disseminated in the hothouse that is Middle East politics and spread throughout the globe,' he wrote.[2]

I am a secular atheist FFS [for fuck's sake], Bornstein tweeted in an urgent, pressured response to the hate and anger filling his feed that April, I didn't write that shit.

Another read: I have not written anything for The Times of Israel. Ever. WTF???

This latter point would have been news to the newspaper's staff and readers. As with numerous other online news outlets, people can apply to become *Times of Israel* bloggers. The person claiming to be him had done just this. In order to appear credible, the impersonator had previously reposted a number of articles the real Bornstein had written for *The Guardian.* The hoaxer did this to lay the groundwork before posting the racist rant about Palestinians. 'It was a very calculated, careful, well-planned attack,' Bornstein says.

After realising something had gone badly wrong, the *Times of Israel* contacted Bornstein and apologetically tore the hoax article down. One of the people spreading the phoney article on social media had a Twitter account with the handle MoonMetropolis.[3] Remember that name.

#

Nearly 900 kilometres away, an SBS journalist named Elise Potaka was hard at work researching and reporting on Australian jihadists. Early in 2015 – around the same time as the attacks on Bornstein – Potaka noticed a Twitter user with the online alias Australi Witness, who was attracting attention from journalists and terrorism experts.[4] Some of the media seemed to be quoting Australi Witness as if he were a genuine jihadi.[5]

As someone who'd been following and talking to jihadis for some time, Potaka had a sense of the ideology. To her, there was something odd about the way Australi Witness presented: 'I'd followed a lot of them on Twitter and … understood the language they would normally use.'

The now-suspended Twitter profile of Australi Witness claimed he used to work for Amnesty International. He also seemed to claim lawyer and anti-Islamophobia campaigner Mariam Veiszadeh was a friend. (This turned out to be untrue.)

To Potaka, this made no sense. Islamic State supporters hate Shias, and Veiszadeh is Shia Muslim, and 'all of the ISIS guys are Sunni Muslim. So why would this Australi Witness, by all accounts an ISIS-supporting Australian, like Mariam?'

Potaka and I are sitting on a Sydney balcony on a strangely cold January day in 2018 drinking cups of tea that quickly lose their heat. She's wearing a mustard-coloured cardigan wrapped tightly around her. Occasionally, mid conversation, she will gather up her thick black hair into a bunch and let it go.

One of the people Potaka had interviewed for a documentary in 2014 was the young Perth-born Islamic preacher Junaid Thorne. In April 2015, around the time of the *Times of Israel* hoax, Thorne let Potaka know via Facebook Messenger that someone had set up a fake Twitter account in his name. He warned her not to follow it.

'This is where the story kind of gets a bit convoluted,' Potaka says with a slight smile. She's not wrong. I've already said to her at least half a dozen times: *This story is confusing.* It requires concentration to keep the strands straight.

With the instincts of a journalist, Potaka couldn't help herself; she wanted to track down Thorne's doppelgänger. She thought: 'I'll just have a little bit of fun, just to see if I can suss out what this weird impersonator is doing with this fake Junaid Thorne account. So,' Potaka tells me, 'I sent a message [to the fake account] saying, "Do you remember what I said to you last time we met?" and I didn't hear anything back.'

Over a few days, Thorne and Potaka kept chatting on Facebook Messenger about the oddness of Thorne finding himself with an impersonator. 'And then suddenly ... Junaid sends me a message mid chat. He says, "Why are *you* chatting to me from two Facebook accounts?"'

As if things couldn't get any stranger, Thorne sent Potaka a screenshot of a fake Facebook account in her name.

When Potaka took a look at her own fake account, it was nothing but a shell containing her stolen profile photo. The account had no friends. It linked back to a single Facebook account, under the name of MoonMetropolis.

Bizarrely, the fake Elise Potaka Facebook account had sent the real Junaid Thorne Facebook account a message asking, 'Do you remember what I said to you the last time we met?'

'This is how I linked the fake Junaid Thorne Twitter account to this person who was then impersonating me on Facebook,' Potaka explains.

#

For Bornstein, the waves of trolling continued. His impersonator went on to set up a fake Josh Bornstein Twitter account and attempted to set up a fake Facebook account. 'I was getting death threats inspired by someone who clearly wanted to hurt me, and at one point another Twitter user, with the handle Australi Witness, incited ISIS followers to attack me. Australi Witness then participated in an online Twitter exchange trying to establish where I lived.'

When a sponsored tweet calling for the death of all Muslims was posted under a fake account set up in his name, Bornstein assumed the police would jump on it because now there would be a paper trail. Someone had paid Twitter for it. He waited forty-eight hours but didn't hear a peep from the police.

Finally, he contacted them to ask if they'd obtained the payment record. They said they hadn't and he never got a straight answer why not. Far from allaying his concerns, Bornstein says, the police involvement simply made him more alarmed: 'They were so clearly out of their depths.'

As he discusses how law enforcement dealt with the issues he faced, Bornstein's measured voice wavers and cracks. He talks almost imperceptibly faster. The Australian Federal Police instructed him to go to the local police, which he did. All contact was by phone and email. Victorian police told him there was 'a dedicated joint federal police and state police taskforce looking at this issue and investigating, and they were very concerned about the identity of this person, Australi Witness, on Twitter, who was inciting attacks by ISIS'. Bornstein says he was told the impersonator had been located in Perth, then Melbourne, 'and that they were closing in and were going to make an arrest'.

'I worked out, after a time, they didn't know what they were doing. He was outsmarting them. They were being completely outmanoeuvred.'

As far as possible, Bornstein tried to protect his wife and children from how extreme the cyberhate had become, but the onslaught took a massive personal toll. 'I was terrified, of course.' He found himself behaving like the clients he'd worked with who'd had their lives destroyed by workplace bullying. 'I became hyper vigilant, so that when you walk out into the street you wonder, are you being watched? When you put out the rubbish, you wonder, is it safe to do so?'

Bornstein tells me that after a few months, his health started to deteriorate: 'Every time I looked at my phone I'd get anxious and I lost weight, I wasn't sleeping.'

The lawyer followed the same advice he regularly dished out to his distressed clients: *Take care of your health and go and see a GP.* He was referred to a psychologist and ended up taking medication in order to sleep. Despite the clear imprint this experience has left on him, Bornstein is quick to point out that as cyberhate targets go he remained in an 'extremely rare and privileged' position. 'I had enormous support. I called in favours from politicians, from people I knew in the police force,' he says. 'I had a team at [his law firm] Maurice Blackburn working on this feverishly to try and fend this off.'

'The female cyberhate victims who are writing to me are, essentially, alone,' I say.

'Correct,' he replies.

#

Consumed with curiosity about the strange fake accounts, Potaka found MoonMetropolis on Twitter and started to chat with him. Following her journalistic instincts, she asked him all kinds of polite questions: *Who are you? Why are you impersonating jihadists? What's your interest in Junaid Thorne? Why did you set up a fake account?*

'But in the back of my mind, I was like, "I am going to find out who you are",' she says. She was far closer to the truth than she realised. In fact, she had already stumbled across the troll's real name. But her assumption was: *A troll partaking in such complex mimicry would surely cover his tracks. Whatever game he's playing, he wouldn't use his real name.*

As Potaka probed further, she noticed MoonMetropolis kept mentioning the Twitter user Australi Witness as the supposed 'TOP Australia-based ISIS Twitter account'. She quickly figured out MoonMetropolis was somehow connected to the Australi Witness Twitter account.

Another Twitter user sent Potaka a collation of screenshots linking MoonMetropolis to the Bornstein hoax[6]. One of those screenshots showed MoonMetropolis was the very first Twitter user to draw attention to the *Times of Israel* article. This tidbit seemed to be a dead giveaway.

'He [the hoaxer] was really not being that careful about what he was doing. The clues were all there in his tweets,' Potaka says. Given how dangerous the troll turned out to be, she's at a loss to explain why authorities didn't pick up on the evidence: 'There were all these red flags, but they were just being overlooked.'

As an investigative journalist, Potaka wondered if there might be a story in all this but realised she couldn't find the person behind the MoonMetropolis account by herself. She needed the assistance of someone with technical skills, someone who understood the murky water beneath the ice. She reached out to someone Bornstein describes as 'Australia's number-one troll hunter'. His name is Luke McMahon. The trolls aren't even sure whether he's a real person. But he is.

#

McMahon meets me at Melbourne University's Law School wearing a black t-shirt and worn-out jeans. He's got a five o'clock shadow and a resonant voice. Within seconds we're chatting as if we've met dozens of times before. He leads me up a few floors and past a library jammed with legal books and a creepy modern painting of a judge with deep-set eyes. The mock court on this floor, where law students practise their future profession, is empty. We sit down.

'Do you see yourself as a troll hunter?' I ask.

'No, not really,' he says, fidgeting in his chair, 'although other people might.'

In an email McMahon had already obliterated any presumptions. 'I have really very little interest in trolling,' he wrote.

> My main area of interest is the law. I just like solving complex puzzles and I really don't like bullies. At the end of the day it boils down to a different way of looking at complex information and finding small details, or patterns, being obsessive, technically proficient and having a good understanding of human psychology. I don't consider myself especially skilled.

To be precise, because troll hunting isn't really a profession, McMahon is a journalist with a legal background.

'How do you find somebody?' I ask.

'What I'm looking for are things like giveaways. I'm looking for associations. I'm looking at *what's their motivation?*' McMahon says. 'Human beings are habitual. It's a big problem for them because it makes finding them a lot easier.' For example, he explains, if someone uses a handle on one platform they may well use the same handle in another location. Just like MoonMetropolis on Facebook and Twitter.

When McMahon read Potaka's first detailed email explaining why she thought MoonMetropolis and Australi Witness were the same person, he knew straight away her analysis was sound. 'For me it's an intuition thing,' he says, although he's careful to explain that proving your intuition is an altogether different matter.

He was hooked. McMahon started sitting up until four or five in the morning for days and days, trying to solve the MoonMetropolis puzzle. 'I mapped it out,' he says. 'Trawling through tweets, through Facebook stuff, through everything, going through individual photos, eliminating profiles. People think hacking is some mystical skill … Actually it's not. A lot of it's social engineering stuff, like going through people's garbage bins, a company's garbage bins, looking for passwords and that kind of stuff.' McMahon is constantly in motion. He keeps leaning back and I have to repeatedly gesture to him: *Come closer to the microphone.*

The troll McMahon and Potaka were hunting had numerous aliases on numerous platforms. 'He would publish an article, like, under the name Tanya Cohen, which was one of his aliases, and it would get mad outrage. And then he'd tweet [about the article] from all his different accounts,' McMahon says. Then he'd also tweet numerous journalists about his articles, nagging them, 'Have you seen this?'

Like Potaka, McMahon was determined to track the hoaxer down: 'I was like, "If we're going to get this guy, I'm going to confront him".'

McMahon jumped right in. He started direct-messaging Moon Metropolis on Twitter, using the Twitter handle Media Direct. 'I said to him, "How long are you going to keep this up?" I opened with a bang.'

Over many months, he developed a relationship of sorts with MoonMetropolis and gradually drew out information. 'So originally I thought I was dealing with a Neo-Nazi because I knew that Michael Slay was his pseudonym on the Daily Stormer,' McMahon says. The Daily Stormer is the prominent Neo-Nazi website run by notorious internet troll weev, or Andrew Auernheimer, and Andrew Anglin.

But the troll then admitted to also being behind the fake ISIS Twitter account Australi Witness. He was a chameleon, constantly changing colour to suit the issue of the day. 'He was trolling all through the night and he never left his house. He told me he lived with his parents … [and] he never had any sort of social contacts with anyone,' McMahon says.

This lonely fact was confirmed by law enforcement later in the year as they surveilled the house where MoonMetropolis lived. Officers repeatedly 'observed the shadow of a person moving around the inside of the residence ... [and] were unable to observe anything beyond the shadow'.[7]

'His thing was free speech,' McMahon says. 'That's why he targeted Josh Bornstein because Josh had written something about it and ... was seen as anti–free speech.'

Free speech absolutism is something trolls of all stripes express repeatedly – with the irony being that their actions often result in the liberties of others being impeded. In her book *Hate Crimes in Cyberspace,* Danielle Keats Citron notes that the 'absolutist, almost religious devotion to free speech' should be weighed against 'important interests that cyber harassment jeopardises'.

'Because the Internet serves as people's workplaces, professional networks, résumés, social clubs and zones of public conversation, it deserves the same protection as off-line speech. No more, no less,' she writes. She goes on to say it is possible to regulate speech that harms people and doesn't make a valuable contribution to public debate.[8]

#

Paid social media ads have become a favourite tactic of trolls all over the world to hurt their targets. The strategy made international headlines when the media revealed Russian trolls had purchased more than 3000 Facebook and Instagram ads during the 2016 US presidential election. The ads were designed to sow discord and division, peddling messages that were anti-Clinton, anti-Muslim and anti-immigration.[9] Amid a deluge of social media bots and fake news – also largely planted by non-US parties – some experts started questioning whether the democratic process had been imperilled.[10]

The US Office of the Director of National Intelligence provided a report to the president in January 2017 addressing the same issue, predicting: 'Moscow will apply lessons learned from its Putin-ordered campaign aimed at the US presidential election to future influence efforts worldwide, including against US allies and their election processes.'[11]

Twitter and Facebook have moved to quell the problems of fake accounts and the purchase of advertisements – both of which are frequently used for predator trolling. A Facebook spokeswoman said, 'We look at different signals to see if an account is fake and these are constantly evolving. To prevent bad actors from gaming the system, we do not share specific details on how we identify fake accounts, but it's a constant arms race and we are committed to stop it happening.' She did elaborate a bit, noting that while 'there are still certain types of content, for example hate speech and bullying, that require human review to understand context', the platform was increasingly using artificial intelligence and automation tools to identify spam, fake accounts, nudity and terrorist propaganda. When it comes to advertisements, Facebook says these are reviewed against the company's relevant policies. The company has recently tightened those rules but we're yet to see how effective these measures are in stopping cyberhate.[12]

Twitter has taken a similar approach, including using machine learning to proactively identify 'problematic accounts and behaviour rather than waiting until we receive a report'. The platform claims it has reduced the visibility of suspicious accounts and content in people's timelines and improved the sign-up process. It has also mass-audited existing accounts.[13] (But the success of this is disputed.[14]) Just like Facebook, Twitter says all ads must adhere to their rules and 'we have never allowed advertisements that propagate hate'. It must be noted that whether or not something is allowed does not stop trolls.

According to well-known Australian internet researcher and academic Kate Crawford, trolling in politics isn't just limited to the buying of Facebook ads; it's bigger than that. In an extensive Pew Center report about trolling and the future of free speech, she was quoted as saying: 'Distrust and trolling is happening at the highest levels of political debate, and the lowest.'

Crawford, who now lives in the United States, says in the last few years, 'We have heard presidential candidates speak of banning Muslims from entering the country, asking foreign powers to hack former White House officials, retweeting Neo-Nazis. Trolling is a mainstream form of political discourse.'[15] And US President Donald Trump is idolised by trolls; he's seen as a kindred spirit. Alt-right trolls, in particular, seem to admire Trump's hyperbole and ability to be disruptive. Sadly, there's some indication the affection goes both ways. In May 2016, a CNN reporter asked Trump about abuse incited by the Daily Stormer's so-called 'troll army' against journalist Julia Ioffe the previous month, and he replied: 'I don't have a message to the fans.' The Stormer's owner, Andrew Anglin, interpreted this as an endorsement.[16]

The troll hunter explains to me that MoonMetropolis had learned to use paid social media ads from the troll weev. 'I have logged conversations where weev discusses his imminent ban from Twitter and where MoonMetropolis requests advice about running Twitter ads to troll people,' McMahon says.

The impact of these ads only becomes obvious to me later, when I start to understand the harm MoonMetropolis caused not just online, but in real life. weev played a crucial part in this harm by teaching MoonMetropolis skills that he used to great and damaging effect.

McMahon sends me some of the screenshots: weev is indeed coaching MoonMetropolis on how to get around Twitter's rules for paid ads, advising him, 'You're going to have to be very subtle.' There are also publicly accessible tweets sent from the MoonMetropolis Twitter account to weev's now-defunct Twitter handle rabite, asking questions such as 'What platforms don't check ads?' and 'How much does Facebook charge for ads?'

MoonMetropolis invited McMahon onto weev's private chat server, which had the name NAQDI.[17] McMahon sat there for months watching and listening. 'What I was trying to ascertain or interpret was, *who is this guy?*,' he says, about MoonMetropolis. 'Is he one of the crew? For a while I thought he might be weev or Andrew Anglin.'

When I spoke to weev on Skype in January 2018, he initially denied knowing MoonMetropolis but after a while conceded he was aware of him under a different name associated with the Daily Stormer. Still, weev wouldn't admit to being in an IRC chat room with MoonMetropolis or having any specific conversations with him. In answer to my repeated questions, he retorted: 'How many bullshit claims do I have to talk about?'

Meanwhile, McMahon tracked MoonMetropolis through various IRC chatrooms and acted as a fellow troll and troublemaker, while Potaka played good cop. She pretended to be the 'naive journalist' who was simply 'keeping in contact with him about things he posts'. The journalists were in constant contact with each other, spending hours on the phone and sharing information online so they could, in turn, elicit more information from MoonMetropolis. They were inching closer and closer.

#

Potaka had been investigating MoonMetropolis for about a month when, on 3 May 2015, two men wearing body armour attacked a security officer and a police officer outside the Curtis Culwell Center in Garland, Texas. The centre was showing an art exhibition that featured images of the prophet Muhammad. Shortly afterwards, the attackers, Elton Simpson and Nadir Soofi, were shot dead.[18]

The attackers' motivations could only be guessed at until, months later, in September 2015, the FBI filed a criminal complaint with the United States District Court, revealing Australi Witness had posted a map of the centre before the incident, urging anyone in the area to attack 'with your weapons, bombs, or knives'. Simpson had used his own Twitter handle to retweet Australi Witness' message. According to Special Agent William J. Berry, who lodged the criminal complaint, Australi Witness used a second Twitter handle to tweet, 'I'M BACK KUFFAR! DIE IN YOUR RAGE!' *Kuffar* is a derogatory Arabic term used by Islamic extremists to refer to non-Muslims or non-believers.

Point 13 of the thirty-four-page document publishes, in full, a rant written by Australi Witness on the link-sharing website JustPaste.it a month after the Garland attack. In the post, he takes responsibility for 'inspiring the attacks in Garland, Texas'. In part it reads:

> My biggest inspiration was the Australian Muslim human rights
> activist Mariam Veiszadeh, who has worked tirelessly and diligently
> to outlaw blasphemy against Islam in Australia ... All who defame

the Prophet (PBUH) [peace be upon him] must be crushed. [Cartoonists] Bill Leak and Larry Pickering will soon meet their demise, as will Josh Bornstein.

Recently, I have met two mujahideen online – one in Los Angeles and one in Melbourne – and I have successfully encouraged them to carry out jihad in their respective cities. Both of these mujahideen will, using guns, shoot up local synagogues when the maximum amount of Jews are praying. The entire thing was my idea, and I helped them every step of the way. I gave them the idea in the first place, I pointed them to local synagogues, I provided them with copious amounts of encouragement, and I helped them coordinate the attacks. All of this was done over the Internet.

After claiming he lives in the Australian city of Perth, Australi Witness goes on to attack the Australian government and Jews as 'filthy cockroaches'. He finishes his 700-word diatribe by saying:

I have a vast network of mujahideen around the world, and I will continue to inspire and coordinate jihad attacks around the world. There is absolutely nothing that you can do to stop me. I am an expert in computer security who uses multiple proxies, and I am also an expert in Australian law due to my extensive work with human rights organisations. Chase me all you want, but you will never find me, and you will also never stop the wrath of Allah (SWT) on the decadent West.[19]

Perish in your rage, kuffar!

Back in May 2015, when the Garland attack occurred, the Australian Federal Police (AFP) had only just started investigating Australi Witness. The two people who knew the most about Australi Witness were journalists Elise Potaka and Luke McMahon. As in so many stories about predator trolling and law enforcement, the police seemed baffled and missing in action. But with this case, their confusion and inaction seemed to increase acutely.

Meanwhile, the journalists were gathering intelligence at a rapid pace. Even so, it wasn't enough: 'We still didn't know who he was,' Potaka says. 'All we knew was that Australi Witness was possibly MoonMetropolis, but we didn't … have enough information to know in the real world who was behind this and who orchestrated it.'

Finally, in June 2015, MoonMetropolis admitted to McMahon that he was Australi Witness. From that moment, the journalists' investigation moved fast. Their project started to take on a sense of urgency: with the events in Garland still fresh, they started to wonder if he'd incite more terrorist attacks.

One night McMahon found a thread on Reddit: Australi Witness was discussing the flag of Orange Park, a town in Clay County, Florida. It clicked into place: *This is where MoonMetropolis/Australi Witness lives.* Then he uncovered an old dating profile on the website OkCupid belonging to the troll. It included a tiny photo and confirmed that he was located in Orange Park, Florida. Thereafter, he stumbled upon the piece of information he describes as 'the tweet that got him'.

To anyone else, the Twitter exchange might have seemed innocuous. McMahon is not anyone else; he's a troll hunter. He tells me what he found that day – and why it mattered: 'He messaged somebody using his MoonMetropolis Twitter account. She'd made a comment that she was fat. He responded, "You're not that fat." And she said, "Oh, no. Trust me. You haven't seen me in a while."' For McMahon, this was the vital piece of the puzzle. *He actually knows this person in real life,* he realised.

His next step was to comb through the woman's social media: 'After probably a month of … looking at all her social media and going through all her photos … I eventually got onto the sister [of MoonMetropolis].'

Meanwhile, Potaka had narrowed her search down to the same person, and the same location. 'So, while Luke was tracing him down through the friend and located the sister's profile – with a family photo that we could compare with his OkCupid photo – I looked up the electoral roll,' she says. She found the whole family's US voter registrations. MoonMetropolis was a registered Democrat. Once they'd age-matched all the information about each family member, they had

MoonMetropolis' name and home address. Using Google Earth, Potaka and McMahon could even see the family's backyard pool.

The terrorist troll was a Jewish-American man called Joshua Ryne Goldberg. At the time, he was twenty years old.

'Maybe this is kind of the troll in me,' McMahon says. 'I wanted to let him know that I knew who he was because right up until the end, he was keeping it from me. And I wanted to see how he would react to it once I told him.'

In classic troll style, he confronted Goldberg by making a meme. 'He would use the word "wigga" a lot, which is like white nigger. So I got a photo from his sister's Twitter account of her graduation and … the whole family [was] together and he was there in that photo. And it's probably one of the only times he'd been out of the house [in recent years]. And I cropped him, and I wrote, "Surprise wigga" onto the image – one word above and the other below – and I sent it to him and I just waited for his reaction.'

In the first instance, Goldberg ignored McMahon's meme and went right on chatting. Then he denied his identity. McMahon responded by prodding him: 'You're in Florida, man. Go outside. Your parents have got a pool. Do you swim in the pool? Can I come over and swim in your pool?'

Once Goldberg realised McMahon had an iron grip on who he was in the real world, he changed tack. Instead of hiding information, Goldberg began sharing it in spades.

'I think that he trusted me, bizarrely,' McMahon says. 'It was only after he was actually arrested that I realised that everything he told me was the truth.'

On separate occasions, Goldberg told Potaka and McMahon that an Australian terrorist attack – and perhaps another American one – was imminent and the two journalists became increasingly worried. 'He started telling me that he had people in Melbourne,' McMahon says, 'and they were going to organise an attack on a synagogue.'

And Potaka recounts, 'To Luke, he would say stuff like, "Oh, yeah, I'm talking to this kid in Melbourne. He's an idiot. I sent him instructions on how to make a bomb." He had also emailed me as Australi Witness and written, "These brothers are going to carry out an attack in Melbourne and Los Angeles."'

Potaka and McMahon had planned to write up the MoonMetropolis story as a piece of investigative journalism for their respective news outlets. But then MoonMetropolis metamorphosed from 'just a troll' into someone who was potentially going to cause serious real-world harm. The events that transpired in Garland, Texas, a month earlier underscored the threat. Potaka recalls thinking, 'Okay, you know, it's a shit-hot story, but I don't think we can sit on it anymore. I don't think we can be comfortable within ourselves to not go to the police with this.'

With McMahon's agreement, Potaka emailed a contact of hers in the media office at the AFP. The way she tells it, the police response was tepid: 'We know that Australi Witness is a troll. We don't know who he is, but we think he's either in Melbourne or Perth. It's probably just some kid in his bedroom.'

'The cops were very sort of blasé about it,' Potaka says.

The AFP didn't put forward someone to interview, but provided detailed written answers to my questions. In their response, the AFP denies that they were blasé, claiming they did take the matter seriously and saw the Australi Witness persona as a 'potential threat', and that this was 'evidenced by the allocation of the matter to AFP Counter Terrorism investigators'.

#

McMahon says he also contacted the AFP on 17 July 2015 and gave them the fact-checked brief he'd prepared for his editors at Fairfax who intended to publish the story. He provided them with screenshots of his conversations with Goldberg, using his various aliases.

'They sent people down from Canberra from the terrorism team,' he says. 'So I went down to the Federal Police Centre in the city here and met with them.'

He describes the meeting – which took place on 22 July, at a big round table with half-a-dozen AFP officers – as bizarre. 'I went through the material with them, why I thought it was him [Goldberg],' he says.

'The reaction I got was one of scepticism. I found the whole experience simultaneously perplexing and surreal. They all just stared at me and didn't say anything.'

From the AFP's perspective, this is standard procedure. 'Investigators are trained to test and question all information when conducting an investigation. To some people, this may be perceived as scepticism.'

A week after the meeting, McMahon received a phone call from an AFP officer in the counter terrorism team, who said: 'We think he's trolling you. We don't think he's Joshua Goldberg.'

With the threat of an Australian terrorist attack front of mind – and no clear indication Goldberg was going to be apprehended any time soon – McMahon urgently wanted the police to intervene. He confesses to 'freaking out'. 'I think I said, "Listen, motherfucker! Do I have to walk you guys through this shit again? This is him. I tracked him. You're not getting it. I tracked this guy independently. This is him." And he's like, "All right. We'll get back to you." Blah, blah, blah. I just think they looked at it all and it was just all too confusing for them.'

The days ticked by. Keen for information, both McMahon and Potaka kept contacting the AFP, trying to get answers. Their primary concern was that more terrorism might be on the horizon. After all, this was what Goldberg was telling them. McMahon asked police how he should be interacting with Goldberg. 'They're just like, "Behave like everything's normal. Don't do anything unusual",' McMahon says.

Potaka recalls the AFP's response was generally along the lines of, 'Oh, I can't say too much, you know, but there are things underway.' As a seasoned journalist, she understands police have procedures to follow but she is nevertheless critical of the AFP's responses during this period.

'We had no idea what was going on,' she says flatly. 'I just had an uncomfortable feeling in the pit of my stomach during that time … I just was hoping that a terrorist attack wasn't going to happen.'

Despite their apparent scepticism and lack of communication, the AFP did tell McMahon that they had put in a mutual assistance request with the FBI. McMahon believes contact with the FBI, who then began their investigation into Goldberg, triggered a sudden change in the AFP's behaviour. Australian police requested he come in and make a statement. On 2 October 2015, McMahon went in to give his statement at the AFP headquarters in Melbourne.

Special Agent Berry's lengthy criminal complaint against Goldberg, submitted to the US District Court in September 2015, repeatedly refers to McMahon as 'L.M.' and seems to imply the information he supplied to the AFP may not be credible. (The AFP refused to be drawn on this matter, telling me they do not 'comment on the credibility of Australian-based witnesses'.)

The troll hunter interprets Berry's written comments about him in a different way to me. He explains that under the US Fourth Amendment, the information he'd provided to the AFP couldn't be used to obtain a warrant. 'The FBI couldn't admit to using my evidence because it could have resulted in all the evidence being thrown out. The FBI would need to follow their own legal protocols, which meant entrapping Goldberg by having him engage with a confidential [FBI] informant. Once that process was complete, the FBI were then able to take that information to a judge and apply for warrants to search his house.'

Until now, I've been struggling to understand how the US authorities have put this case together. It seems to be missing most of the information that Australians have told me about Goldberg and his online behaviour. Yet when McMahon tells me this, I read the criminal complaint again, for the fifth time. Amid the fog of names and dates and facts, it becomes clear just how much weight the FBI gave their informant and the terrorism-related evidence he gathered while messaging with Goldberg. To them, the predator trolling was just noise, worthy of only the briefest mention.

#

On 9 September 2015, Joshua Ryne Goldberg was arrested at his parents' home in Orange Park, Florida. They had no idea what he'd been doing online.

He was days away from a planned pressure-cooker bomb attack in Kansas City. In online discussions with a man the troll believed to be a jihadi, Goldberg talked about detonating the weapon at a memorial event where Kansas firefighters honoured first responders killed in the terrorist attacks of 11 September 2001.

The 'jihadi' Goldberg had been communicating with was an FBI informant codenamed 'CHS' in all official documents. During the month of August, Goldberg gave CHS detailed instructions about how to make the bomb.

'Be careful, brother,' Goldberg wrote. 'Don't buy all the materials at once or the kuffar will know you're up to something. Buy them at different stores.' He told the informant to fill the pressure-cooker bomb with metal and nails. 'If you can, dip the screws and other shrapnel in rat poison before putting them in [the bomb]. That way the kuffar who get hit by them will be more likely to die.'

The official version of how Goldberg was apprehended – with the clever work of an FBI informant and international policing cooperation – is quite different from the accounts of Bornstein, Potaka and McMahon.[20] When Goldberg was arrested, Potaka and McMahon reported the story for Fairfax, quoting a statement from police: 'Investigations by the AFP in June 2015 established no initial threat to the Australian community. When investigations determined it was likely the person responsible for these threats was based in the United States, the investigation became the jurisdiction of the FBI, with the AFP in a support role.'[21]

The AFP was confident there was no threat to the public. However, Goldberg repeatedly spoke about having contact with jihadists in Melbourne who were going to destroy a synagogue. How could the AFP be so sure this wasn't going to happen? It's logical to assume that the Australian police knew there was no imminent threat because Goldberg was actually conversing with undercover AFP operatives online, instead of jihadists. Excerpts from private conversations between Goldberg and at least two different AFP federal agents prove this was the case. (These conversations, which occurred on Twitter, Facebook and other platforms such as Kik Messenger, were submitted to the court as evidence by the AFP during Goldberg's US trial. We'll talk about that shortly.)

Even though the AFP was confident that the Melbourne attack was not going to occur, does it follow that the threat to the public was eliminated? I put this question to McMahon in an email. He says:

'Based on what I know – he [Goldberg] was in multiple conversations in different jurisdictions. He mentioned being in conversation with someone based in Sydney and [is] suspected of speaking to at least two more young people in Melbourne. [A]s long as Goldberg was online and talking to people, coupled with his fixation on Australia, a threat existed.'

In the same police statement, the AFP's then Acting Deputy Commissioner for National Security, Neil Gaughan, went on to praise law enforcement's ability to carry out policing investigations into matters that are online and 'use our long-established partnerships to work with overseas agencies to bring people to account for their actions'.[22]

After Goldberg's arrest, he 'voluntarily waived his [constitutional] rights and spoke to law enforcement', according to Special Agent Berry's account of events. While Goldberg initially denied involvement in plotting the Kansas attack, he then confessed to being Australi Witness and made it clear he also 'believed the information would create a genuine bomb'.

> JOSHUA GOLDBERG made varying statements in an attempt to explain his actions in providing bomb making information to the individual.
>
> In general, JOSHUA GOLDBERG claimed that he intended for the individual to either kill himself creating the bomb or, if not, that he intended to alert law enforcement just prior to the individual detonating the bomb, resulting in JOSHUA GOLDBERG to receive credit for stopping the attack.[23]

This statement contradicts what Goldberg had told McMahon four months earlier in an IRC chatroom. McMahon asked him if he was at all concerned by the fact that some of these 'jihadi nutcases' might actually kill someone at his behest. Goldberg replied, 'These guys are pussy keyboard warriors.'

Goldberg was eventually found competent to stand trial during his fourth and final psychological evaluation in March 2017. His lawyer, Paul Shorstein, restarted negotiations with the government, which led to a plea agreement just before Christmas the same year, with sentencing to come. On Monday, 25 June 2018, Joshua Ryne Goldberg, now twenty-three, was sentenced to ten years in federal prison, to be followed by a lifetime of supervised release, for 'attempted malicious damage and destruction by an explosive of a building'.

Although the US Federal Justice Department put out a press release, there was surprisingly little media coverage.[24] Local Florida station News4Jax aired a short story on the day of the sentencing, at the end of which journalist Ashley Spicer told viewers, 'Before the Goldbergs left the court room his [Joshua's] mother, Rebecca, approached Goldberg and said, "I love you," and he said, "I love you too."'[25]

Looking at the sea of papers on my desk and office floor – the articles about Goldberg, the court documents, interview transcripts, the emails from his victims – one question remains. Why did he face just one charge: attempting to damage and destroy a building by means of an explosive? The damage he did to his numerous trolling victims seeps out from the piles of printed type like an unheard and destructive song. The AFP spokesperson who answers my numerous questions notes the length of the jail term and says: 'The sentencing judge took into account Goldberg's actions in Australia and how his actions affected the Australian community.' But to me, the pain that individuals suffered as a result of Goldberg's actions online is absent from the official record.

Shorstein says that when the US Federal Government is making a case against you, 'it's not really about taking what you did and fashioning a case that accurately depicts what you've done. It's more, "We're going to do what we need to do to get you to do what we want, which is enter a guilty plea".

'What they want is to strongarm you and they want to make it really difficult for you to fight them,' he continues, explaining that the authorities do this by charging people with 'crimes that come with these massive penalties' such as terrorism. And in comparison, 'Who cares about the cyber stalking or the cyberhate … It's been ignored because it's just not really effective for them.'

Like me, Potaka finds it strange that Goldberg's severe and damaging trolling was overlooked by the justice system. 'I think it was fair for him to be charged with terrorism on the one hand,' she says, 'but I also think they took this approach as they don't know how to deal with trolls, or maybe it's harder to find a fitting charge. They took the easy route.'

From Potaka's vantage point, the two investigative journalists are like disappearing ink on a page. 'The FBI has tried to erase our hand in it. They basically claimed that it was their informant who got him. [But] they would not have known about him unless we had informed the AFP, who then informed them.'

According to the AFP, police started investigating Australi Witness and was trying to find the person behind the Twitter account 'after becoming aware of several concerning tweets' posted by that Twitter handle; McMahon and Potaka didn't trigger their inquiries. However, the statement provided to me by the AFP does say police are grateful for the help provided to investigators by numerous journalists, including McMahon.

Potaka believes the AFP 'really failed to identify this person' who, contrary to their public statement, 'ended up posing a serious risk'. Even after the two journalists had handed over all their information to the AFP, it was still a few months before he was apprehended in the United States.

We've been talking for a long time and Potaka seems done, so I switch my tape recorder off. But, as often happens when an interview appears to be over, she suddenly relaxes and is struck by something important. What she really wants to say. I press the record button again.

In a rapid-fire volley of words, Potaka says, 'The frustrating thing about Goldberg is none of this was hidden. It was all out there, and it was all publicly available. You know, I'm a layperson and I could look at all his Twitter accounts and put things together. There were clues … all over his social media pages. And if the police or anyone in a position of power looking into him had just sat down in front of a computer and opened his Twitter account, they would have had a pretty good idea that he was linked to Australi Witness and all these other aliases. It's not like this stuff is happening on the dark web or in IRC.

'Trying to expose these people doesn't … necessarily require any particular dark web skills. We did it through old-fashioned journalism, which was spending hours and hours and hours trawling through his public social media profiles and putting two and two together. And I think the cops could have done that, but they didn't.'

Now it's all done and dusted and Goldberg is in prison, there's no sense of triumph. Looking at his case, police were slow to respond and seemed baffled by its complexity. Police claim they were all over the Goldberg case like a rash. But were they really? What would have happened if Potaka and McMahon weren't so persistent?

As other commentators have already suggested, the combination of law enforcement being unwilling to take online issues as seriously as terrestrial crimes and simultaneously lacking technical skills means cases are falling by the wayside. Even once US authorities took over, they refused to connect the dots. Instead, the FBI chose to focus only on the heaviest charges they could lay against a lost young man who was, by all accounts, extremely isolated and mentally unwell.

It's been three years now. Looking back, Potaka sees Goldberg as 'one messed-up young guy, who couldn't function in the physical world and so inflated himself up into a monster online'. McMahon thinks of the terrorist troll 'as quite a sad figure'. 'There were moments where I reflected and felt a lot of sympathy for him and his situation, even though he'd done horrible things,' he says, adding, 'I'm glad he's not behind a computer anymore.'

Surprisingly, McMahon says now that Goldberg has been sentenced, he's planning to write to him. The troll hunter wants to meet the troll face to face: 'I want him to know what happened, why it happened, so that he's confronted with the reality. I think that's part of trolling – the ease with which you can fuck with people's lives and never, ever have to face those people.'

13

The internet was my parent

A S ELISE POTAKA suggested – and many others too – law enforcement is sadly lacking when it comes to cyberhate. And yet we
know the harm trolls can do.

On Safer Internet Day in early February 2018, I attend an event at
Parliament House in Canberra. All the big wigs are there, including
then–Prime Minister Malcolm Turnbull. He gives a brief speech,
declaring he shares with UK Prime Minister Theresa May a concern
'that the coarser and more abusive discourse that you far too often see
online is also reaching back into traditional forms of communication
and discourse, whether it is in the playground or in politics or in a
newspaper and coarsening that as well.[1']

With Joshua Ryne Goldberg on my mind, Turnbull's comments seem
facile. The internet did not create the hatred. It's just the vehicle. And in
fact, plenty of the trolls are emboldened by the bigotry and hate speech
of leaders. It's a green light.

My questions are: How many other damaged young men is the
system failing? For how many of them is trolling effectively a canary in
the coal mine?

When I spot former policeman and internet safety expert Nigel Phair
in the crowd, this is what we immediately start talking about. I tell him
about Goldberg. About how the trolls aren't just trolling, they are cutting

deep wounds into our offline lives. How the police can't connect these dots and how even our leaders – the likes of Theresa May and Malcolm Turnbull – blame the internet, which is only the vehicle, instead of looking at this as a deep-rooted human behaviour.

Phair gives me the wry smile of a cop who has been on this beat a long time and says: 'After spending twenty-one years in the police it doesn't surprise me that they [the trolls] aren't just ratbags doing one sort of nasty behaviour, like trolling, but they are engaged in other criminal activities too.'

These questions about failures in the system – not just law enforcement, but how some mentally ill individuals aren't given help until it's too late – don't flit past like some others do. They weigh heavily, and lead me back to Goldberg's story – to try to understand who he is. How he got to that terrible place where he rarely left the house and spent up to twenty hours a day on the internet, often using it to hurt other people.[2]

It's hard to say definitively how Goldberg saw the world or what he really believed. But the paper trail leaves some significant clues. At the request of his lawyer, Goldberg undertook a mental evaluation by a forensic psychologist at the Federal Detention Center in Miami, Florida, a few months after his arrest. Shorstein had spent enough time with his client to know 'he was in pretty bad shape mentally' and suspected he wasn't competent to stand trial.

'No defendant is supposed to make any decisions in court, or have to defend himself from any charges or prepare his case for trial or sentencing, unless it's clear he is mentally competent to do so,' Shorstein explains in an email. 'I also thought there was a possibility that he could be found not guilty by reason of insanity, and I wanted the doctors to evaluate that and give an opinion. That obviously didn't work out.'

Under First Amendment rights, Goldberg's mental evaluation was released three months later, in January 2016, with a small percentage redacted.[3] Within the evaluation, the psychologist repeatedly refers to Goldberg's 'incoherent' and 'tangential thought processes with strained logic'. Goldberg's thinking, the psychologist writes, was marked by 'grandiosity and paranoid delusions, including delusions of persecution'. He had 'an exaggerated notion of his importance, power, or identity'.

He didn't have insight into his own mental health or legal problems, and 'his judgement as to cause and effect relations was poor'.

Perhaps, then, Goldberg didn't hold consistent trains of thought in relation to his actions. Perhaps this is why he didn't – or couldn't – cover his tracks and left 'red flags' everywhere. Why he said one thing and then contradicted himself, his muddled statements a window into a confused – albeit dangerous – mind.

The psychologist writes of Goldberg's 'poor eye contact' and his 'significant social deficits, and poor interactions with others'. She notes his numerous previous mental health diagnoses, 'ranging from Anxiety Disorders to Schizophrenia'. Using the bible of mental disorders, DSM-5, she diagnoses Goldberg as having 'Unspecified Schizophrenia Spectrum and Other Psychotic Disorder'. She concludes her report by recommending 'that Mr Goldberg be found incompetent to Stand Trial [sic] and that he undergo mandatory competency restoration treatment at a more appropriate setting, such as a medical facility'.

This was indeed how events unfolded. After being deemed incompetent to stand trial in November 2015, he was transferred to the Federal Medical Center, Butner, in North Carolina.

Reading the mental evaluation, I'm drowned in the same involuntary grief for Joshua Goldberg – and his family – that I felt for the Aztec High School shooter, William Atchison. This strange, deluded man did so much damage. But he *was* so damaged. I wake up at 2 am with phrases from the psych evaluation running through my mind like a stuck vinyl record. The needle scraping around and around. 'Mr Goldberg's prognosis is poor … he has an extensive documented history of mental health treatment which has reported to be unsuccessful.' He stayed indoors for so long that many neighbours didn't even know he lived in the Orange Park home with his parents and siblings.

The time difference between Canberra and Jacksonville is tricky. Before getting up in the cold and dark early morning to speak to Shorstein about Goldberg, I read the sentencing memorandum he submitted to the US District Court on Goldberg's behalf in March 2018. Then I read it again, scrawling notes in the margins and highlighting various phrases.

The creeping sadness is back, lapping at my door. The document paints a devastating picture of Goldberg as a young man, with severe and misdiagnosed mental health issues who 'is terrified by most human interactions'. 'He had one kid in the neighbourhood with whom he played video games,' Shorstein writes in the memo, and this 'was the closest Joshua ever came to having a real friend. That relationship ended at age ten … He has never had one meaningful relationship of any kind with a member of the opposite sex.'[4]

The first time Shorstein met Joshua Goldberg was at jail in Baker County, Florida, shortly after his arrest. 'He was in pretty bad shape mentally,' Shorstein says down the scratchy phone line, recalling his client as 'really anxious' and struggling to focus. 'It was hard for me to get information from him … I did the best I could.'

Shorstein occasionally tries to make jokes with his clients to break the ice and lessen the stress of facing court. With Goldberg this was impossible. His demeanour was 'really literal' and 'just very nervous, he's very anxious, he worries about everything … doesn't have different facets to his personality like most people do'.

Once he was incarcerated, Shorstein explains, Goldberg's problems relating to others 'caused him a lot of problems' including 'a lot of disciplinary action' and being isolated from other inmates. 'He has a hard time coping with different personalities, and a hard time just being a functioning adult with different people who have a different way of communicating.'

In the memorandum, Shorstein writes that, growing up, Goldberg was incorrectly diagnosed with a spate of issues including ADHD, ODD, mood disorder, major depressive disorder, OCD, anxiety disorder and schizoaffective disorder. 'There was no recognition of his autism. On the contrary, he was misdiagnosed with schizophrenia.' His 'autism characteristics were misclassified as psychosis'. This meant that 'for many years … Joshua was not taking the proper medication and was not getting proper treatment'.

In April 2016, while he was incarcerated at FMC Butner, Goldberg was finally diagnosed with autism spectrum disorder and 'major depression' by experts from a specialist program at the University of North Carolina.

Shorstein believes Goldberg's mental illnesses 'are the most critical and relevant factor in this entire case'. In the sentencing memorandum he expands on this in tragic detail: 'If Joshua did not have these impairments, he would not have committed any crime … How do we treat the mentally ill in the criminal justice system, and how much should we punish them for conduct that is the direct result of those mental illnesses?'

And then later in the same document:

> He knew at an early age that he would have a very hard time becoming a functioning member of society. He feared becoming a burden to his family for the rest of his life. The evidence … establishes that Joshua devised a plan to address this problem that consumed him and fed his depression.[5]

Picking up on this thread in our telephone conversation, the lawyer expresses a desire to 'help him and treat him, rather than punish him'.

I bring up the attack in Garland, which Goldberg claimed credit for inspiring, and also the damage he did to those Australians who became his cyberhate victims. 'The question I'm really asking is where compassion ends when a person is causing real-life harm?'

Although the lawyer doesn't directly answer my question, he does acknowledge that while plenty of antisocial behaviour online is harmless, some of it isn't and this can lead to 'the materialisation of actual violence'.

While making it plain he's not defending Goldberg's actions, Shorstein is deeply scathing about the way society deals with an offender like his client who 'can barely sit still and talk to me for ten minutes' and is up against the full force of the US Federal Government. 'That's our justice system, when you've got one side with every resource and dollar they want, against me and my client, who can barely understand what's going on. That's not fair by any means but it is what it is.'

As I said, Goldberg was finally found competent in March 2017. I ask whether the issue of competency was a tactic Shorstein used in his client's defence. He diverts the discussion to the meaning of the word and asks me to think carefully about what it really implies. 'I want to stress the importance of the difference between being legally competent and being actually competent. There is a big difference,' he says. 'You could be legally competent, but really not competent in any other sense of the word.'

Competency is 'a very low standard in criminal courts in this country', Shorstein says. 'And even if you are found incompetent, they just send the defendant to a hospital, drug the defendant up until some doctor says he's now competent. And then they ship him back to court, legally competent, but not well equipped to … defend himself.'

With this in mind, Shorstein explains, he had no choice but to enter plea negotiations with the federal government because his client couldn't manage being cross-examined on the witness stand. 'That would be a complete disaster. There's no way he'd be able to hold up in a situation like that. He couldn't even go to school with people his age because he couldn't fit in the classroom environment.'

The memo goes into some detail about how, concerned about his future, Goldberg hatched a 'flawed' and 'fantastical' plan to become a reporter and was using the alias Australi Witness/AusWitness to do this. 'Starting arguments, causing chaos, getting attention – these were his only methods of social interaction and feeling important,' Shorstein writes. 'He planned to discover and acquaint himself with real extremists over the internet, get them to reveal plans of attacks, memorialize them with screenshots, and then expose them and write about them to become a journalist.'[6]

I'm coming to this case with wide-open eyes and a heart to match. And I have some sympathy for the terrorist troll and some insight into his crumbling mental health. But it still seems like a stretch to claim he did all that damage in the name of journalism. Not to mention that his predator trolling is missing from the narrative.

Shorstein believes that when Twitter user Media Direct (aka Luke McMahon) confronted Goldberg with his true identity, he freaked out. 'It cannot be understated how much this terrified, intimidated and rattled Joshua,' he writes. According to Shorstein, not only was Goldberg concerned about being exposed as a fake to dangerous real-world terrorists, but he was scared his dreams of becoming a journalist would be destroyed.

'Joshua responded to Media Direct's implicit threats by putting more energy and authenticity into this Australi Witness and related alias accounts.'[7] Reflecting on this aspect of the case, the lawyer adds, 'That doesn't mean we wouldn't still be here if not for Media Direct, but yeah. I'm not a real big fan of the way that was handled.'

Luke McMahon scoffs at this interpretation of events, telling me in an email that he believes the lawyer was out of his depth: 'Shorstein's memo is … completely at odds with reality. It's also factually wrong on many grounds.'

I ask about Shorstein's theory that McMahon's communications with Goldberg put more pressure on the troll and served to magnify his aberrant behaviour. McMahon replies that this is 'a truly laughable and desperate attempt to divert attention away from Goldberg's conduct'.

On the one hand, it is hard to understand why so much about the Goldberg story is missing in official documents written by both his own lawyer and by the FBI. On the other hand, it's hard to disagree with Shorstein's view that his client's catastrophic mental illness and questionable grip on reality led him to offend. There are so many 'what ifs' in Goldberg's case. What if he had received high-quality, ongoing mental health treatment *before* he ended up in prison? Would he have ever toyed with terrorism?

#

One of the most interesting things about the troll Meepsheep is that, despite being idolised by younger trolls, he still partially sees himself as belonging to this category of marginalised young white men. In a trollish fashion, he describes himself to me as 'southwestern white trash'. Putting that aside for a moment, if you can, there is a key difference that distinguishes him from some of his trolling counterparts and makes him especially valuable to talk to. This difference is insight.

Meepsheep is studying psychology at college. He thinks a lot about how people – including trolls – think, what they think and why they think it. Sometimes the things he makes me consider are deep and wide. At other times, it's simpler than that. He's teaching me how to interact online and this, in turn, helps me to talk to and understand trolls.

Meepsheep's online messages are full of acronyms.

IDK
KK l8r
IDR
W/E
G2G or GTG
CP
RLY
IDC
BBL

Trying to keep up is an effort and Google repeatedly catches me off guard. The acronyms are so polite:

YW: You're welcome.
TY: Thank you.
GTG TTYL SRY: Got to go. Talk to you later. Sorry.

The first time we actually talk with voices, Meepsheep doesn't want to switch on Skype's video. Or, to be precise, he says he doesn't have video. His Colorado accent rings out of my laptop, disembodied and disconcerting, into my family's home halfway across the world.

'To some degree, my sense of humour has kind of always been dry humour and pranks and stuff like that. So the minute I started using the internet, I started using it for trolling,' he says. Meepsheep was eleven years old and his pranks were those of a young kid. For example, he recalls jumping onto Yahoo Answers to 'give someone bad advice [or] write something stupid'.

This is a pattern I've observed with trolls. At some point in every interview they will usually say to me something along the lines of: no one paid me any attention, and from age eleven (somewhere between eleven and sixteen) I was just on 4chan (or maybe Tumblr) alone. For hours. Every day.

In other words: the internet was my parent.

When I suggest to Meepsheep in one of our long messaging conversations this is a kind of radicalisation into trolling – where individuals become hardened into the ideology – he surprises me by agreeing. After pondering the idea for a moment, he clarifies. 'When I say radicalization, I mean more like a radical turn in favour of self-expression.'

For criminologist Dr Clarke Jones, an expert in radicalisation, connecting the concept with trolling doesn't seem far-fetched in the least. 'If there's something wrong, a child or a young person's behaviour will manifest out in some way,' he says, and there are often 'trigger events in a young person's life … that can cause a behavioural change'. He says in order to understand the radicalisation of young people – of which internet trolling is arguably one form – we need to consider the child's makeup and how they were parented.

'What were the boundaries set in their upbringing?' Dr Jones asks, echoing the concepts psychologist Dr Williams explored as he reviewed Mark's video. Dr Williams has suggested that trolls aren't born harassing others online. Their behaviours are learned and therefore must mirror facets of our communities in one way or another.

Meepsheep believes young white men are at risk of isolation and disenfranchisement. 'I think that people have the sense that because white men are so "privileged" they don't need help. You get cases like [high school shooter] William Atchison. He just fits the category of somewhat intelligent young white men who are marginalized and discouraged and also suffering from some kind of mental illness that nobody is paying attention to.

'In the same way the criminal justice system here [in the United States] can be unfair to young black men, I think the education system and mental health system within it is unfair to young white men,' he says.

When I try to point out that surely as a group young black men have it harder, he responds by telling me it's ridiculous to try to 'quantify how "unfair" something is'. By doing so, I'm effectively saying: 'Your problems aren't as important as "X" group, so they don't matter.'

Meepsheep isn't alone in the belief that young men are struggling. Controversial University of Toronto psychologist Dr Jordan Peterson has a huge and loyal following, and firmly believes that it's men and boys who are falling behind socially and economically.[8] Speaking on Rupert Murdoch's Fox News, Dr Peterson told viewers that masculinity is under attack:

> If you're made out to be a potential manifestation of rape culture, if you're part of toxic masculinity, if your competitive drive is regarded as part of a tyrannical impulse, if the heritage to which you belong is regarded as an oppressive patriarchy, then how in the world are you going to step forward with confidence and shoulder that burden? Why would you? Why wouldn't you step aside and retreat, which is exactly what's happening?[9]

For a feminist fighting the construct of white men being at the centre of things and holding the power, the notion that these same men are marginalised and struggling is disconcerting. I spend plenty of my time – writing, speaking and volunteering – in the service of equality. Hoping that one day men and women will be treated the same. Hoping that one day sexual and domestic violence against women won't exist. Hoping that the gender pay gap will be closed. Hoping that my daughters won't be discriminated against at work, like I was, when they have children themselves. Hoping that in every facet of life, across the world, our opportunities to thrive will one day equal those of our male counterparts. Naively, I assumed that in this fight, young men would be on our side. And perhaps some are. But it's horrifying to consider that, among the alt-right in particular, the opposite may be true. Feminism has left them behind. Instead of questioning society's complex structures of power control – and understanding how inequality becomes entrenched – these young men take the more simplistic (and well-worn) route of blaming women for their problems.

In the case of trolls, instead of retreating, as Dr Peterson contends, they are manifesting their hurt and anger in a different way. Meepsheep describes the young men around him as steeped in 'emotional poverty'.

This draws them towards trolling: 'When the world makes you feel like you're worth absolutely nothing and it tears you up inside for years, and then you find an outlet with people who understand and agree, and it's also the only place you've ever found that, it does become something that consumes you,' he says, bringing Goldberg firmly back to mind. 'And then you realize that you collectively have the power to get back at the world – or at least think you're doing that.'

In a consideration of marginalised young men, the late Junaid Hussain, known as TriCk to his online buddies, is a standout example. Although he wasn't white like so many other trolls I speak to, Hussain is someone who became radicalised and, in the end, his extremist ideologies killed him. The trolls knew TriCk when he was an affable guy from TeaMp0isoN (Team Poison) – a pro-Palestinian syndicate that sometimes worked alongside Anonymous and Rustle League.

However, by early August 2015, the young British-Pakistani man was listed by the Pentagon as the third most wanted person on their kill list.[10] Hussain had traded Team Poison for ISIS and the so-called 'Cyber Caliphate'. According to *The New York Times*, he had become 'a central figure in the Islamic State militant group's online recruitment campaign'.

By the end of that month, he was dead – reportedly killed in an airstrike outside Raqqa, Syria.[11] Perplexed by a strange web of pieces that don't seem to fit together, I find a *Vanity Fair* article by Lorraine Murphy. Her article about TriCk is compelling – and not just because it's well written:

> Hussain was Team Poison's best outreach agent, a personable fellow keenly attuned to the zeitgeist who had a way with 140 characters. A gifted writer as well as coder, with a knack for quotable epigrams, he was also a passionate and outspoken enemy of racism, prejudice, and marginalization in any form. And he was my friend. We met on Twitter.

What changed TriCk from this guy – who couldn't stand prejudice or marginalisation – to someone fighting a cyber war on behalf of ISIS?

Murphy, who specialises in hactivism, writes that in 2012 Hussain spent six months in prison for hacking the online address book of the personal assistant of former British prime minister Tony Blair and also for causing more than 100 nuisance calls to the UK antiterrorism reporting hotline. 'After his sojourn in prison, he seemed to have become a weaponized nihilist, avoiding his old friends completely.'

She goes on to quote McGill University anthropologist Gabriella Coleman: 'The Trick story is such a fascinating one and an important one to tell, especially the jail experience. It changes you.'[12]

This brings weev to mind. In March 2013 weev was sentenced to forty-one months in federal prison for his part in revealing the email addresses of more than 100,000 AT&T iPad users.[13] After some legal wrangling, he was released in April the following year. His trolling buddies draw a line between who he was before the stint in prison and after it. (Though I should say, he categorically denies jail changed him or his ideology.) Yet I can't help wondering, *What role did the state play in hardening these men and their extremist ideologies? How will prison affect someone as socially inept and mentally unwell as Joshua Goldberg?*

All this is percolating at a time when my kids and I are staying with my mother on the New South Wales coast during the school holidays. The idea is that they get a break and hang out with their grandmother while I crack on and work on edits to the book. (There's a limit to how much frozen pizza I can distractedly feed them in aid of getting writing done.) This area is in drought and, suddenly, it's pouring rain.

I stare out the window, watching the water dropping onto the parched grass. Almost without thinking, I mentally tally the times in an ordinary day when my children ask me a question. When we chat. Drop. Drop. Drop. Perhaps another kid is mean or hurts them. I talk to them about not responding with violence. How we are all human. About being kind, even when others aren't. Drop. Drop. When they get hurt and need a hug. Drop. Drip. Drop. Then, I think about all the kids like Meepsheep who are left alone to grow up online, surrounded by echo chambers of hate. No adult there to talk to them or hug them. Once, when we were talking about why so many young men seem to hate women, he said to me: *It's so hard to figure this stuff out on your own. When you don't have help.*

Right then I know in my core, in my spine, that perhaps more than anything else the story of trolling is one about parenting.

14

White men at the centre

MEEPSHEEP IS PRESIDENT of the offensively named trolling syndicate the Gay Nigger Association of America (GNAA). Previous presidents include weev and the troll and hacker Jaime Cochran, aka asshurtmacfags. Although GNAA is not a big syndicate like some of the others, they have pulled off some high-profile stunts. One of the most well known attacks occurred in November 2016 during the US presidential campaign. Meepsheep vandalised a number of Wikipedia pages, including those of Hillary and Bill Clinton. His attack included 'a huge tiled background of some chick's naked butt' alongside a message:

> Reminder that voting for Hillary Clinton this Novmeber [sic] means proving how much of a spineless, boring cuck you are. Nuclear war will be inevitable, as will be Bill Clinton raping more women and children. Save the America you know and love by voting for Donald Trump. Also girls send ass pics to @Meepysheepy.
>
> This message has been brought to you by Meepsheep and the Gay Nigger Association of America. Thank you for your time.[1]

(The word 'cuck', short for 'cuckold', is frequently used online to refer to blokes who are sexually inadequate.[2]) This Wikipedia attack, I quickly learn, sits within a category of trolling known as 'media fuckery'. US academic Whitney Phillips defines it as 'the ability to turn the media against itself … by either amplifying or outright inventing a news item too sensational for media outlets to pass up'.[3] Even as a member of the media myself, it's easy to see that sometimes media fuckery – and trolling in general – is downright hilarious. At other times, though, the way trolls appropriate racial and gender stereotypes and employ dehumanising language effectively ends up amplifying those pernicious tropes.

Recalling the Clinton/Wikipedia attack, Meepsheep says, 'The purpose wasn't that I was actually trying to rally support. It was just to get a reaction out of people, and politics is an easy way to do that. I'm not a die-hard Trump supporter or anything,' he continues, but 'I will play one on the internet sometimes to get a rise out of people.

'For me personally,' Meepsheep says, 'trolling has always been a bit more about kind of confusing people and getting a laugh out of causing confusion, or bad advice or whatever, as opposed to just being inflammatory and trying to make someone upset by saying something racist or something like that.'

Another of the GNAA's most 'successful' campaigns – if you can legitimately use this word in this context – has gone down in the annals of trolling history. It's known by the hashtag #sandylootcrew. During Hurricane Sandy in October 2012, Meepsheep explains, members of the GNAA pretended to be a horde of black looters by making 'all these accounts on Twitter, pretending to be a bunch of black dudes in New Jersey and … posting that we're going to go around looting and robbing and whatever during the hurricane. We used the tag #sandylootcrew and just through that, it attracted a lot of media attention. We were saying totally ridiculous things.'

Meepsheep isn't kidding about either the ludicrousness of the tweets or the massive amount of media attention the prank generated. Many media outlets seemed to genuinely believe an army of black people were looting everything from shirts to cats. The GNAA's website lists articles by nine different media outlets, including outrage from US radio host Alex Jones and coverage by the *Daily Mail* about 'brazen thugs' who 'have robbed their neighbours'.[4,5] While there was some post-Sandy looting on Coney Island, the GNAA's tweets were explicitly and obviously fake.[6]

The posts contained racial stereotypes exaggerated to the extent that the messages became implausible. This fits neatly with Whitney Phillips' view of media fuckery: as a 'grotesque pantomime' fashioned from existing cultural material for the purpose of undermining 'the existing moral order'.[7]

Some media outlets quickly realised #sandylootcrew was a trolling campaign and quoted a member of the GNAA calling himself Leon Kaiser saying: 'Anyone who takes "NIGGA I JUST STOLE A CAT OUTTA SUM1S HOUSE GET ON MY LEVEL" at face value probably shouldn't be working in the news industry.'[8]

Meepsheep agrees with this take. 'That is kind of where some of the value of trolling comes from, that it can point out some of these flaws,' he says. 'It is a way of intellectually fighting, almost debating with someone. And then there's just some kind of satisfaction out of making someone look like an obvious fool when they're kind of already doing it to themselves.'

Once I start looking, media fuckery is everywhere. In her book *This Is Why We Can't Have Nice Things*, Phillips documents numerous media outlets swallowing the trolling bait, hook, line and sinker. The academic notes trolls get laughs and exposure while the media gets what it desperately craves – a 'hot' (albeit entirely fabricated) story.[9]

As a journalist, I'm self-consciously aware that trolls seem to understand the media and its deficiencies (and also that the media doesn't realise trolls have this insight). This seems to be why trolls can be so good at manipulating news coverage.

Trolls, limited only by imagination, can screw with the media in other ways, too. In 2014, Australian developers Dan Nolan, Ben Taylor and Matt Kelsh released a browser extension called 'STOP TONY MEOW (STM)'. The extension 'replaces photos of Tony Abbott with pictures of cute kittens' as you view articles online.[10] Essentially, STM messes with the message, altering how readers consume news stories away from the journalist's intention. Three years later, this plug-in caused me to accidentally troll myself.

As prime minister, Tony Abbott was constantly in the news. And as a news junkie, I was constantly looking at his mug on my computer screen. The browser extension seemed like the perfect solution. On my own laptop, STM worked hard replacing Abbott's picture with kittens. Every. Single. Time. I was surprised and delighted. The glee never wore off. But then the following year, in 2015, Tony Abbott was ousted. He quickly faded from the headlines; I forgot about STM altogether.

More than two years later, I was researching a story and had to look up a list of Australia's prime ministers. There they were, one after the other in chronological order, alongside black-and-white portraits and the years spent in office. Sandwiched between images of Julia Gillard and Malcolm Turnbull was a cute tabby kitten labelled 'Tony Abbott'. It was so out of the blue I took a minute to realise that STM had waited quietly, all this time, for another chance to pounce. I wasn't the only one taken by surprise by STM while beavering away at my desk. The browser extension affected Australia's highest offices. A *Sydney Morning Herald* article from 2014 reported that Dan Nolan had put in a Freedom of Information request and discovered that staff at the Department of Prime Minister and Cabinet had used up 137 pages of correspondence talking about STM. *One hundred and thirty-seven pages.* (Because the government wished to charge Nolan $720.30 to access the documents, he never actually saw them.[11])

When I consider these two bits of media fuckery – STOP TONY MEOW and #sandylootcrew – side by side, the first seems hilarious while the second irks me. What if, in exploiting the community's entrenched prejudices for caricature, you unwittingly create actual racism?

'I just don't see that as being the case, I guess,' Meepsheep says when I put this to him. 'The GNAA is not a white power group. It's the intention of the GNAA to offend people. But not specifically black people, so that [offense] would just be a by-product.'

I ask, 'If you're trolling using misogynist or racist or violent language, the person on the receiving end of that trolling doesn't necessarily care about the intention of the troll. What I'm asking is, does the intention matter if the outcome is the same?'

He thinks about this for a moment, then says: 'The intent behind GNAA and a lot of associated trolling is to either cause confusion, exploit social issues in the tech community, or manipulate media. It never gets down to the level of wanting to harm a specific individual.'

In essence, Meepsheep believes #sandylootcrew played into but also exposed deep-seated racial stereotypes that are 'already there in our culture'. And this gets us back to the GNAA's name, which is apparently not racist or homophobic but is 'intended to sow disruption on the internet and challenge social norms'.[12]

When the intensity of my conversation with Meepsheep eases off a bit, he says, 'I think part of it is that you're missing the culture of the internet a little. Nobody cares if you say nigger or faggot online, really. And so those words don't have the same weight.'

Approaching the same quandary from a different angle, one journalist, writing about trolling on Vice's Motherboard, says, 'They're using symbols like the swastika and words like "nigger" or "fag" because they're charged phrases sure to offend anyone who's not a part of the community. React with outrage and you become the victim.'[13]

To me, this explanation is reminiscent of the way women were treated decades ago when they complained about sexual harassment at work: *Can't you take a joke, love?* As though using offensive language is where the 'joke' ends. As though it can't harm. As though dehumanisation of specific groups in society can't incite real-world aggression.

Remember in the schoolyard, kids would love to chant, *Sticks and stones may break my bones but words will never hurt me.* In fact, it's not true. There's good evidence to show dehumanising speech can lead to sticks and stones. Writing on The Conversation website, psychology researcher Allison Skinner points to numerous academic studies that show dehumanisation is 'associated with an increased willingness to perpetrate violence'.

'At its most extreme, dehumanizing messages and propaganda can facilitate support for war and genocide,' Skinner writes. 'It's long been used to justify violence and destruction of minorities. We famously saw it in the Holocaust, when Nazi propaganda referred to Jewish people as vermin, and we saw it during the Rwandan genocide, when the Tutsi people were referred to as cockroaches.'[14]

As I've found out by talking to so many predator-trolling targets over many years, they are frequently dehumanised with hate speech online before becoming victims of offline violence. Just think about the person who gave Sherele Moody's dog acid. The violence started with words.

Predictably, Meepsheep doesn't agree with the notion that speech can damage a victim; he tells me – a number of times – that words on the internet never hurt anyone. 'You can't cause harm through the internet and that's why it goes back to being a freedom of speech issue because it's not like the internet presents any kind of new paradigm – as if it can actually be used as a weapon or something.

'[It's] like the old saying, I don't think that guns kill people. I think that people kill people and people choose to use guns to harm people. So what I think the ethical issue is, is someone making the choice to harm someone else, regardless of the medium.'

This is untrue in a number of ways. First, trolls wouldn't use speech if it didn't have the power to shock, offend and hurt others. Second, we like to treat the internet as if it's an impassive machine. As if it's neutral. But it was never neutral. (Even if the father of the internet, Vint Cerf, likes to claim it is.[15]) The web was made by humans and its meaning comes from our interactions with it. Many thinkers have pondered this notion including philosopher Don Ihde who, in 1979, wrote that 'particular tools unavoidably select, amplify and reduce aspects of experience in various ways'. Three years earlier computer scientist Abbe Mowshowitz similarly proposed that 'tools insist on being used in particular ways'. (These ideas were synthesised by British visual semiotician Daniel Chandler in his essay 'Technological or Media Determinism'.[16])

Just take the so-called 'online disinhibition effect'. This is where people behave differently on the internet than they would in face-to-face interactions. It's caused by factors such as a person's anonymity and a reduction in empathy because the feedback is non-verbal (and therefore doesn't seem real).[17] For better and for worse, people who interact with the internet bring along their flesh and blood, their human strengths and failings. Plus, the unique characteristics of the internet itself influence them too.

I've spent long enough now imbibing trolling texts – those weird words, phrases and memes – that, where initially their meaning might have been elusive, now the fog has cleared from the lingo and patterns of discourse emerge. The racism, misogyny, sexual violence and anti-Semitism are constant and psychologically corrosive. The discourse positions all these groups as the 'other' and white men as the norm.

'Whether or not trolls believe the things they write,' I say to Meepsheep, 'trolling has the effect of policing discourse, with white men at the centre.'[18]

He disagrees, writing, 'ED is a surprisingly diverse place.' ED stands for Encyclopedia Dramatica, one of trolling's central online hubs. On the surface, ED is a satirical and infamous not-safe-for-work wiki, documenting drama on the internet. However, in the context of trolling it's a cultural juggernaut. Every troll I've ever met has – or has had – some connection to it.

'IDK [I don't know] if I mentioned it but IRC, and also being in the GNAA specifically, has definitely made me a more open and empathetic person,' he says. Meepsheep grew up in a conservative, rural community and 'never knew any trans people or Muslim people before trolling'. 'You meet people from all backgrounds across the world and everyone is just united in the goal of being an asshole online,' he says, 'so it's a pretty interesting way of bringing people together.'

Right from when I first talk to Meepsheep, in December 2017, he wants me to understand the trolling universe isn't just made up of one type of person, despite how it may appear to me. He suggests asshurtmacfags as a great person to consider, or IRL (in real life), transgender woman Jaime Cochran. She was president of the GNAA and also a former member of Rustle League (RL), a group most well known for trolling and hacking Anonymous.

Writing for Vice back in 2013, journalist Fruzsina Eordogh made RL sound like a bunch of huggable tricksters: 'What makes Rustle League interesting is that they aren't pricks. They retain a sense of mischief rather than menace, and they're not trying to change the world either, like Anonymous appear to be doing right now.'[19]

Not everybody sees it like that, of course. Illinois lawyer Sue Basko has been persistently attacked by members of RL and ED. In one blog post she wrote: 'I have been stalked, terrorized, denigrated, endangered, defamed, traumatized – and had mocking, belligerent young sadists tell me this is "fun."'[20] And, in a subsequent post: 'These attackers have harmed me deeply and in ways that will never be repaired. They have stolen nearly two years of my life. They have harmed my health beyond repair.'[21]

At the start of 2018, Meepsheep plans to contact Cochran on my behalf to see if she'd like to talk. I'm keen to hear from her. As someone who isn't a young white man, how does she feel about her friends' ideas on trolling and diversity? Fingers crossed. She's spoken to the media before. In 2012 she appeared in an SBS segment alongside weev. He admitted on air to abusing 'a grown woman' by calling her fat and autistic. Adhering to the now-familiar trolling doctrine of free speech absolutism, Cochran noted she wouldn't say things like that herself but said, 'I respect his right to do so.'[22] She clarified for viewers, 'I draw the line ethically for myself, like, I'm not a malicious person … I like to say things that are just. I have a sardonic wit but I don't attack people.'

Even so, Meepsheep tells me she's 'likely different' from him in her trolling style: 'Probably more extreme in some ways lol, she tends to say a lot more offensive shit than I do.' For a few days, he waits for her to come online. Then sends another message: 'asshurtmacfags was found dead yesterday so I doubt you'd be able to contact her now.'

At first glance this sentence reads as if it's lighthearted. It isn't. She was his friend. He travelled a long way to be at her memorial service in Oakland, California. He met her family and says, 'I'm glad I did, for closure.'

The Facebook page for her memorial – held on 13 January 2018 – is still live.[23] There's a photo of Cochran's angular face nearly smiling as she snaps a selfie in the mirror. Below the image, her friends and family have written: *Jaime Cochran: Memorial of a Psychedelic Hackress.*

In a scratchy video of the speeches made that day, her friends pour out their love and laughter. One by one they take the microphone, mostly introducing themselves using their online aliases. They recall the times she helped them. Times when they needed a friend and she was there. Over and over her friends say: *She was so funny.*

A lean blonde woman dressed in black and wearing sunglasses says: 'Every single second that I spent with her ... was probably some of the best fucking time I've ever spent doing anything.'

Another guy speaks. His voice cracks as he reads a heartfelt letter, which finishes by thanking her family: 'Thank you from the bottom of my heart for giving us a genuinely wonderful and amazing human being. Please know she was truly and sincerely a gift to the world and that she used her life to enrich so many others.'

The pink-haired MC, a work colleague of Cochran's, says sometimes people would google her and be shocked by her trolling exploits. But, the woman says, 'She was a great girl. She wasn't just a troll on the internet.'

Months later, when quite a few trolls are trying to mess with me, I tell Meepsheep about their strange and sometimes spiteful antics. He says, 'IDK, I wish you could have met Jaime. She was someone else that I think was pretty easy to talk to no matter who you were.'

'Yes,' I reply, 'I would have really liked to meet her. I've thought about that too. Also kind of irrelevant but I just liked the look of her face.'

In direct contrast to Meepsheep's views on both diversity and the policing of discourse, Amnesty International's *Toxic Twitter* report details the particular ways in which people who are *not* white men get attacked online:

> In the case of online violence and abuse, women of colour, religious or ethnic minority women, lesbian, bisexual, transgender or intersex (LBTI) women, women with disabilities, or non-binary individuals who do not conform to traditional gender norms of male and female, will often experience abuse that targets them in a unique or compounded way.[24]

By way of example, the report quotes US journalist Imani Gandy:

> I get harassment as a woman and I get the extra harassment because of race and being a black woman. They will call white women a 'c*nt' and they'll call me a 'n*gger c*nt'. Whatever identity they can pick

they will pick it and use it against you. Whatever slur they can come up with for a marginalized group – they use.

The general consensus, not just from Amnesty but from social media users who represent minorities, is that the way speech is policed online has the effect of driving marginalised voices offline. Whether this is a deliberate tactic, or just a kind of collateral damage, it's hard to know.

One person who has experienced this firsthand is 36-year-old appearance activist Carly Findlay. Her story is one of triumph, though, not retreat. She has a facial difference caused by the skin condition ichthyosis and considers herself disabled. Her skin is red and often shiny. As well as being a fashionista and an activist, she's a keen blogger.

While analysing her blog statistics early one morning in December 2013, Findlay discovered something was amiss. Despite there being no new posts for a while, there was loads of new traffic. 'I saw the traffic source and I'm like, "Shit, it's Reddit,"' she recalls. If you've never stumbled across Reddit, it's a social content aggregation site where people can rate posts. It has a history of hosting creepy content, including child porn, hate speech and sexualised pictures of unconsenting women.[25]

As her heart pounded, she wondered, *What have they said about me? Do I want to look?* Her photo had been posted and ridiculed on a Reddit message board titled 'WTF'.

Findlay acknowledges something most of us have experienced – and it's especially pertinent to trolling; there's a kind of magnetic draw when people are talking about us, even if they aren't being kind. We have to know what's being said. 'You can't not look,' she says, 'it's so weird.'

Looking at the post, she saw a picture of herself smiling and holding a glass of bubbles at the premiere of the TV series *Rush*, in 2009. Underneath Reddit users were writing comments such as:

What does your vagina look like?
WTF is that? Looks like something that was partially digested by my dog.
Lobster.
Kill it with fire!!

One commenter claimed it made them 'uncomfortable' to look at her and went on to say she had a 'dead-eye mouth-smile'.

Reading the 200-odd comments, Findlay says, 'It was almost like there was a whole heap of people in the playground just taunting me from [with]in a circle. Yelling from all angles.' She didn't respond to the online abuse like most people would have. She didn't go offline or bite back in fury. Instead she wrote back with extraordinary grace, taking the opportunity to explain, educate and even thank some of the more supportive commenters. Underneath her photograph on Reddit she wrote that for many years she didn't share her photos online, and this exact pile-on scenario was why:

> But now, after gaining confidence and support through years of blogging, I couldn't care whether they call me a lobster or silly putty. The love I have around me and success I have had through telling my own story to break down stigma like these Reddit threads is stronger than any of those words.
>
> Yes I have Ichthyosis. Yes that picture is me. Don't fear it and don't criticise it. I am proud of the way I look, what I have achieved and for telling my story.
>
> FYI: I have two forms of Ichthyosis – a mix of Netherton's syndrome and erythroderma. My skin is shiny because I use paraffin. My body is less red than my face as it's not exposed to the elements, but it is generally more painful. Ichthyosis is survivable – I have lived a very full life.

Findlay urged those who wanted to learn about 'the real me rather than through the speculation on this thread', to go back to her blog. And, just like that, the conversation turned right around. The original poster gave a backhanded apology and people started thanking Findlay for educating them. Others chimed in with messages of support and questions about her condition, which Findlay diligently answered.

Some, like redatheist, shared their own difficult health and appearance experiences:

I've got psoriasis, until recently it was really bad, although with the last few months of treatment it is under control for now.

I've had times when I've felt terrible because of my skin, and sometimes I feel very depressed and hopeless. But reading your blog makes me feel better. Seeing how happy you are gives me hope that I might be as happy sometime too.

Thank you :)[26]

Thousands of Redditers upvoted Findlay's post – something platform users do when they appreciate or agree with a particular comment. One bloke wrote: 'You, madam, are the strongest motherfucker I have ever HEARD of, let alone met. If you are ever in Boston, I would be honored to buy you a beer.' Media outlets credited her with 'winning the internet'.[27]

Towards the end of 2017, Findlay and I found ourselves staying in the same hotel attending a conference. It seemed like an opportune time to do an interview about the Reddit incident. She called to say her skin condition had made her sore and she'd be wearing pyjamas. It seemed only fair, then, that I wear my pyjamas too.

It unfolds like this. We sit on the bed, a glass of wine in hand, in my first face-to-face interview done in sleepwear. I ask what made her respond to the Reddit posts in this way.

'You can't contact the police because they don't do anything. The safest thing is to make it public, because it takes it out of your mind and puts it somewhere else,' she says.

Knowing Findlay has received death and rape threats and more recently has taken out an apprehended violence order against an online stalker, I ask: 'Weren't you scared you'd make it worse?'

'I don't think it could have got any worse, unless they came to my house,' she replies. She wanted 'to set them straight, because of the misdiagnosis, because of the hate speech [and] to tell them this is who I am. I'm a person. This is the impact of your words'.

Reflecting on how she transformed the conversation from a trolling field day into a communal sea of compassion, Findlay says: 'You can actually make a difference, and change things. You speaking up and telling your story, telling your truth, changes that. People will change their mind when they know that you're a person. I don't know whether they realise you're human, you know?'

This is the strangest thing to me. And something my mind comes back to again and again. Amid all this hate, flashes of humanity emerge. An unpredictable kind of troll activism. One of the most compelling stories reported by journalist Lorraine Murphy involved the story of a young schoolgirl called Kylie. She was being relentlessly bullied by her classmates on Twitter.[28]

Towards the end of 2012, Kylie tweeted:

I don't know what to do anymore. I can't get out of my room. I can't face the world. I don't want to be alive I'm done.

It's like this pain will never go away this sadness will never leave me.

One post stated she had a razor blade in her hand. She said goodbye. The tweets from her classmates in response told her to 'cut deeper'. One troll wrote, 'drink bleach.'

We hate you just die ... From Sara, Jesse, Hayley, Cat, Josh, Becca and others.

Then all of a sudden, members of Anonymous and Rustle League stepped in (which in itself is interesting, given that these two hacker syndicates are often trolling each other).

A Twitter user with the handle GonzoPhD responded to Kylie:

Hi Kylie. Me & my Friends are here to stop the bullying aimed your way. And when I say it will STOP, it will STOP.

Another member of RL or Anonymous then wrote:

Kylie. Follow and DM me. We'll see how funny these trolls think they are when we wade into the fight.

The RL and Anonymous members indicated there were hordes of them fighting on Kylie's behalf.

They threatened the bullies:

You made MANY mistakes. See you soon, kiddies.

Troll a 15 y/o girl to DEATH?? Game ON: Bitches.

RL/Anonymous told Kylie's harassers they would send the police to investigate the bullying and inform the perpetrators' parents.

Laugh now, bitch. You can cry later. Expect cops in the near future.

Fairly quickly, the school predator trolls became scared and started apologising:

I'm going to say sorry to kylie tomorrow ... I'm done this is over.

We're sorry for doing this to her. We will leave her alone forever. Promise.

Not done with schooling the bullies, GonzoPhD replied:

GOOD. NOW MAN UP, PROTECT HER & BE A FRIEND TO HER. SAVE HER LIFE BRO, DON'T HELP END IT.

Looking back six years, Murphy reflects that 'the Kylie story shows the distinction between trolls who hurt people in an amoral fashion, like the guy who jumped in and told her to drink bleach, and trolls who use their powers for good, who promptly doxed the hell out of him'. 'Rustle League was always against "moral fagging" Anonymous-style, but when push comes to shove and someone's telling a teenager to drink bleach, they stopped that shit cold.' ('Moral fagging' is a derogatory term used to denote someone who is using emotions rather than logic in order to win an argument.)

Without knowing more about GonzoPhD and the other trolls who defended Kylie in 2012, and the nature of their usual online activities, it's impossible to know whether this assessment is accurate.

Yet it's interesting to consider whether bullying speech was harming Kylie while other types of speech possibly helped save her. Online and especially in the world of trolling, the contradictions never end. Perhaps because, after all, behind those keyboards are humans. And we are complex, changeable creatures.

On the one hand, Meepsheep tells me words on the internet never hurt anyone. On the other hand, he says, 'At around age sixteen, I did do a lot of stuff that I now regret that I know had real-life impacts on people.' When I ask for a specific example, he recounts a chain of events that relate to a kid we'll call Andy. A quick bit of backstory first. In addition to his involvement in GNAA, Meepsheep is enmeshed in ED as an administrator and has been since 2008. Seven years ago the platform had a serial pest – a young kid who kept posting child porn: Andy.

'He [Andy] tried to fit in with the trolling scene on there and at some point, he uploaded a picture of some naked kids. So I banned him, removed the picture and whatever and then he came back, and he did the same thing.' Along with other ED users, Meepsheep found out Andy's real name, his home address and his school, and mounted a campaign against him. The pranks included contacting his parents, sending pizzas to his school and 'drunk Russian plumbers' and the local sheriff to his home.

'He was never heard from on the internet again,' Meepsheep says. 'At the end of the day, I'm sure that's not something that destroyed his life, but I still feel guilty for being such an asshole to this kid.'

Almost simultaneously, we both wonder: *What happened to Andy? Could we find him?*

A few weeks down the track, Meepsheep sends me a screenshot of an online conversation. He's found Andy. (Andy knows I've got the screenshot and is happy to participate in telling this story.) The correspondence starts with Meepsheep explaining why he's getting in touch – I'm writing a book. He then recalls the trollish chain of events back in 2011 and writes:

I promise you we're not trying to fuck with you, this is for legitimate research purposes and I've grown past wanting to ruin random people's days on the internet. Let me know what you think and I can put you in touch with her. I'm sure it was strange to get this out of nowhere so I apologize for that. While I'm at it, I'd also like to apologize for sending all those people to your house and calling your parents when we did.

Astoundingly, Andy doesn't seem to care that his former online buddies turned on him all those years ago and seems oddly happy to hear from Meepsheep. Nor does he seem fazed by Meepsheep's repeated apology. His response is airy:

Hey, it's the Internet. Taught me a good lesson.

He doesn't explain what exactly the lesson was. However, he does say that after the trolling incident, his parents put the computer in the kitchen for a year and 'severely limited' his internet access. He became a 'normie', which is internet slang for a 'normal person'. He got a girlfriend, finished high school and went to college. Now he has a union job.

This all seems like a neat, satisfying and even quite friendly ending to Andy's public shaming. The thing that's noticeable to me, though, is his parents' intervention. All of a sudden they knew what their kid was doing online. They monitored him. And he turned into a 'normie'. Could that be a coincidence?

As a kid, Meepsheep moved fairly quickly from upsetting people on Yahoo Answers to other platforms. 'I got into trolling Wikipedia,' he says, and it has 'become my biggest target throughout my trolling career'. As someone who regularly uses Wikipedia, I find it hard to understand why a source of public knowledge could raise and hold his ire for more than a decade. Yes. Here we are, back at media fuckery.

'It is very liberally biased,' he says. 'The people who administer the site tend to kind of be assholes and for the most part, a lot of them tend to be pretty egotistical, pseudo-intellectual, self-congratulatory. I also think that Wikipedia … has too much of an influence over information on the internet.'

According to Meepsheep, his 'personal vendetta' against Wikipedia has led the GNAA to 'hit them from all angles'. 'We have exploited the software. We caused disruptive vandalism. We've held on to longstanding accounts and gotten into the community and provoked the community using its own rules,' he says.

It takes the Wikimedia Foundation's press office nearly a month of me nagging them to respond. For the most part, they don't directly address my specific questions about the GNAA's vandalism of Wikipedia and Meepsheep's justifications for doing so. Like Facebook and Twitter, they're keen to provide a bland statement. The email from Samantha Lien, communications manager at the Wikimedia Foundation, says, 'Wikipedia aims to provide neutral, reliable information across a wide array of subjects.' When edits are made that 'go against Wikipedia's intended purpose … volunteer editors have created tools and systems to address them' and 'most vandalism on the site is removed quickly, often within minutes'.

Curiously, Wikipedia's entry on the GNAA seems incredibly vague in parts: 'The group is run by a president, but little else is known about its internal structure.' Meepsheep says this is because 'the only people who contribute to it are us [GNAA members] trying to talk up the group and Wikipedia admins trying to get as much as possible removed from the page'.

It's not especially hard to find out about GNAA's structure – and, uncomfortably, this makes me wonder about how much truth lies in trolls' criticisms of the media. Maybe overall, the media is left-leaning. Maybe as a group, journalists aren't self-critical or self-reflective enough. Maybe we're not asking the right questions, not listening hard enough. And media fuckery is how people are talking back.

Meepsheep will answer anything I ask him; he tells me there are about eleven core GNAA members and others come and go. There's a vice president and 'other members get random titles like CFO as we feel like assigning them'. Presidents, Meepsheep says, are elected 'maybe once every two years' and this happens live on air via the IRC call-in podcast, L0de Radio Hour (LRH).

According to its Patreon page, LRH is a long-running weekly show 'broadcasting from the darkest pits of Internet Relay Chat'. Among other things, it delves into troll culture.[29] (Although I honestly tried to listen to LRH a few times, I couldn't get past the host's terrible radio technique or the rambling, abusive content. The show seemed to mainly consist of people calling each other 'gay nigger Jews' and baselessly accusing each other of being paedophiles.)

When it comes to the GNAA's presidency vote, generally several people vie for the spot. 'The entire show that night will be centred around a debate,' Meepsheep explains. 'There is usually one clear-cut winner from the start, and then there will be two to three other people, random retards from IRC trying to get attention … But it usually ends up just being people swearing at each other, and repeating memes, and stuff like that. People call in, and they tell [the host] L0de who they're voting for. L0de acts as a judge,' he says. 'It's only done for the president, it's not done for any of the other roles.'

Over many months, my conversations with Meepsheep meander all over the place. Like all conversations about trolling with a person who identifies as a troll, they inevitably circle back to what he describes as 'my free speech bullshit'. With two exceptions, Meepsheep believes in absolute free speech as defined in the US Constitution under the First Amendment. While he acknowledges that some types of content on the internet – namely child exploitation material and direct threats of violence – can be harmful, he says outside of those things 'speech alone has no effect, other than how people choose to interpret it and choose to react to it'.

'I very passionately believe that freedom of speech is necessary for a society to function to its best ability. And I think that it's necessary for individuals to function to their own best personal ability,' he says. 'Freedom of speech is a component of freedom of expression. Generally speaking, the ways in which freedom of speech are limited are a mixture of unnecessary and potentially harmful to the collective good of the society and culture.'

What's striking to me, though, is that we don't have absolute freedom of speech in other parts of our lives or in other public places. We couldn't say anything we like to anyone we like in the supermarket or on the street. And in workplaces our speech is certainly limited. This is why there's an endless stream of people who are fired from their jobs after mouthing off on social media. So what makes us think we can expect absolute free speech online – especially when it harms other people?

In no uncertain terms, lawyer Josh Bornstein says we shouldn't expect it: 'There has never been a free-for-all on speech and there never should be a free-for-all on speech. If speech causes harm, then there needs to be regulation.' He says there are reams of laws, covering everything from intellectual property, copyright, bullying, sexual harassment, assault, nuisance and parliamentary laws regulating conduct in parliament, that curtail free speech.

'Employers control free speech [too]. Social media policies regulate free speech very, very severely so that if you contravene a social media policy, you lose your job … So, you tell me,' he asks, 'what is this nonsense about there being some unfettered right to free speech?'

In fact there's good evidence to suggest that cyberhate is chilling free speech. PEN America, an organisation that defends free expression and fosters international literacy, launched their *Online Harassment Field Manual* in April 2018. Not only does the manual provide practical advice about cyberhate for writers, employers of writers and their allies, but it directly addresses how free speech and democracy are being harmed by predator trolling. To be clear, this is the exact opposite of what trolls think they are doing, which is championing and defending free speech. (A little like what the social media companies say they are also doing.)

'Online harassment directly harms the free flow of information by deterring participation in public discourse. People are targeted not only for what they write and publish online but often simply for being an outspoken member of a particular group,' PEN states. '[T]his problem is at its worst when people are trying to engage with the most complex, controversial, and urgent questions facing our society: questions about politics, race, religion, public policy, the rights of marginalized groups, and social norms.'[30]

We're losing the ability to have nuanced, complex conversations about things that matter and are instead driving out alternative, diverse views. Take the case of Australian lawyer and outspoken advocate against Islamophobia, Mariam Veiszadeh. Towards the end of 2014, she publicly voiced her outrage that a Woolworths supermarket in Cairns was selling singlets printed with the Australian flag alongside the tagline, 'If you don't love it, LEAVE'.

Three months after her tweet, the far-right anti-Islam group The Australian Defence League posted her tweet to their Facebook page. From there, it was picked up by the alt-right Daily Stormer website. The Daily Stormer post about Veiszadeh, written under the byline Michael Slay, demanded of its thousands of followers: 'Stormer Troll Army ... assemble!' 'We need to flood this towelhead subhuman vermin with as much racial and religious abuse as we possibly can,' the spite-filled post reads. And further on, 'We need to be as hurtful as possible when abusing her, and we need to offend her Moslem [sic] sensibilities too (make sure to send her insulting pictures of the pedophile Muhammed [sic]).'[31]

The text included all of Veiszadeh's electronic and phone contact details and her place of work.

By way of an excuse for inciting the trolls to attack, Slay referred to the arrest of a 22-year-old Ipswich woman by Queensland Police. The woman, who had sent Veiszadeh racial vilification and threats, was charged with 'using a carriage service to menace, harass or cause offence'.[32] Without a bean of irony, Slay's verbal tirade harped on and on about protecting free speech.

The call to arms worked. The troll army hunted Veiszadeh down. Among other things, she received a photoshopped image depicting her cuddling a decapitated pig's head. It was accompanied with a message stating the trolls would behead both her and her mother and bury them with pigs. Another image depicted her dead after being stoned to death. Rocks surrounded her corpse and blood was dripping down her cheeks. The police notified Veiszadeh that the bomb squad had opened a suspicious package addressed to her. The parcel, sent to her former home address, turned out to be bacon.

To give an idea of just how much this predator trolling personally impacted Veiszadeh, I need to relay something that might not seem significant, but speaks to the trauma suffered by victims. Veiszadeh agreed to do an interview with me and then she cancelled. We arranged a new time. Then she cancelled again. Eventually Veiszadeh sent a stream of text messages that were raw and alarming. They were also dreadfully familiar.

'The truth is, I just can't put myself through this right now. It will affect me for days to come and I end up the worst version of myself without even realising why. I am already anxious and experience vicarious trauma every time I speak about these issues. I subconsciously kept delaying doing this interview for this precise reason. I want to speak about my experiences but it hurts so much when I do. I have tears flowing down my cheeks as I type this. I'm really sorry.'

In the end, Veiszadeh sends me an email to replace the interview. Reflecting on the 2015 attack, she tells me it caused her to suffer from prolonged anxiety, paranoia, dizziness and vertigo. She took time off work and 'narrowed [her] circle of trust'. 'What people don't realise is the long-lasting impact this has on you and how much it changes your life.'

Later in 2015 Luke McMahon and Elise Potaka reported in Fairfax newspapers that Michael Slay turned out to be not one person, but two.[33] One of those two men was Joshua Goldberg, whose main trolling preoccupation was preserving freedom of speech. As the troll hunter explained earlier, this was how he ended up choosing targets such as Josh Bornstein.

'The idea that what trolls are doing by tormenting strangers is fighting for "free speech" is absurd and might itself be an act of trolling,' US academic Whitney Phillips says. She notes that trolls imagine themselves as patriots and delight in wrapping 'trolling in the American flag'. Instead, she believes, they are calling 'attention to the ugly side of free speech which is so often cited by people whose speech has always been the most free – namely straight white cisgendered men … to justify hateful behaviours towards marginalised groups.'

Phillips believes this is less about respecting the First Amendment 'and more about not wanting to be told what to do, particularly by individuals whose perspective one doesn't respect.[34]'

Back with Meepsheep, I'm pressing him about why trolls are so dogged on this issue: *Is someone threatening the free speech of young white men?*

'It feels that way in America, at least,' he says. 'Free speech does not exist in the schools or universities [and] having any beliefs that contradict what is either the norm or what the liberal professors say is likely to get you literally bullied irl [in real life]. The collective ideals that they [liberal professors] are subscribing to are hindering freedom of speech. I can identify with some of the grievances of the alt-right in this regard.'

Where Meepsheep takes a nuanced view of most issues and is prepared to engage in genuine discussion, the notorious troll weev – aka Andrew Auernheimer – is not. When it comes to free speech, he takes a particularly extreme view.

'If you take away people's human right to free speech, then all they have left is violence. That's a fact. That's a fact and anybody who interferes with the right to free speech deserves to die,' weev rants during our Skype interview in January 2018.

'That's a fact' is a phrase he uses regularly. He says it – and repeats it – when what he's talking about is not a fact at all. This often has the unintended effect of drawing attention to the flaws in his claims.

Between torrents of speech, I say, 'Some people would argue, though, weev, that your actions – like when you're doxing other people – are infringing their liberties.'

This seems to enrage him. 'This is a ludicrous assertion that I'm taking anybody's rights away … if you don't like it, you should turn off your computer.'

Here again is the suggestion that any harassment predator-trolling victims attract is their own fault. Only this time it comes not from law enforcement or the media, but from a powerful troll. He has freedom of speech and you have no right to take it away. Yet he can take your freedom of speech any time he likes. And if he does, you're to blame. What are you doing online, anyway?

It's not just US trolls who are worried about freedom of speech. Mark is Australian and, when prompted about his views on free speech, says, 'Governments and corporations want everyone to think the way they want them to think, and the only way to do that is to try to shut down and ban the type of speech they think is bad.'

He gives the example of social media platforms like Facebook and Twitter, which he believes use censorship against trolls like him by either slapping a three-day ban on them or removing their profiles altogether. To Mark, this sends the message: 'Hey, if you don't want to be cut off from everyone … and don't want it to happen again, how about from now on you don't express these opinions?'

'Even [billionaire investor and philanthropist] George Soros is calling them out for it and saying that Facebook and Google have too much power over how people think and act and need to be shut down,' Mark says. He's referring to comments Soros made in January 2018 suggesting 'social media companies influence how people think and behave without them even being aware of it. This has far-reaching adverse consequences on the functioning of democracy, particularly on the integrity of elections.'

'The internet monopolies have neither the will nor the inclination to protect society against the consequences of their actions. That turns them into a menace and it falls to the regulatory authorities to protect society against them,' the billionaire said at the World Economic Forum in Davos.[35] This is the point Bornstein made about social media companies having too much power and effectively acting as monopolies. Like Soros, Bornstein proposed legislation as a solution. Whether we can regulate our way out of this, as Germany has tried to do, remains to be seen. But what is clear is that despite all noises to the contrary, social media platforms are failing to protect us and our free speech, as evidenced by Leslie Jones, the only black member of an all-female *Ghostbusters* cast, being temporarily forced off Twitter after particularly vile and racist harassment in 2016[36] – one example among many. The internet isn't a welcoming place for women or minorities of any kind. Having the luxury of free speech depends entirely on who you are.

Just like any other social group, trolls have their allies and foes. They all seem to know and form judgements about each other, some of them quite brutal. Meepsheep points out some of the people I'm interviewing might be trolling me. 'They probably give you a lot of bullshit and then tell each other what they told you and laugh about it.'

'Sometimes I troll them back,' I reply.

I flick him a screenshot. It's an email I received after publishing an opinion piece about the incessant trolling of young Australian Indigenous poet Ellen van Neerven by Australian high school students in October 2017. 'Subhuman cunt. This is a good description of you,' reads the email. 'Kill yourself.'

The fabulous Australian feminist academic Susan Carland taught me a troll-busting trick that I employed in response. I sent the 'subhuman cunt' guy a *Mean Girls* GIF showing Regina George's character saying, 'Whatever, I'm getting cheese fries.'

'Hahaha,' Meepsheep writes back when he reads about my response. 'Tbh [to be honest] it would probably piss them off ... that they're getting anything other than some outrageous reaction.'

Then after further consideration: 'I guess it [the email] doesn't exactly meet my definition of trolling either. I think real "trolling" requires some degree of wit or at least a punchline.'

This is the strange thing about Meepsheep. There's an ideological chasm that, by rights, should block our communication. Then there's the characteristically offensive trollish words and phrases that tumble out when he types: *Retards. Bitches. Faggots.* Perhaps when he forgets it's me, that I'm not from the internet. Or when he's just having a dig and seeing if he'll get a rise.

If I can manage to treat this like a cultural issue (some days I'm better at this than others) and shove my disquiet into a box, something else comes with these conversations. An alien freedom because societal norms don't apply. We're not following the usual moral code. Trolling culture allows a person to say almost anything. Ask almost anything. For a journalist, it's a kind of gift. And at the same time, the ease in talking to him is hard for me to accept. The truth is, it reminds me of being at university. Staying up all night talking with your mates and sparring intellectually just for the fun of it. He's well read and can usually argue the toss. Still, I wonder if he thinks I'm being too earnest about trolling and taking the internet too seriously. Just not 'getting it'.

'Thanks for answering all my questions,' I write to him one evening. 'Hope I'm not boring you to death.'

He disappears for some days and then, unexplained, comes back online.

A message pops up:

BTW [by the way] you're not boring me since I think about these same questions all the time.

15

A professional racist

WHEN I'M TALKING to and about trolls, all roads lead back to weev, supposedly 'the world's most notorious Internet troll'.[1] In the trolling world, everyone knows him and knows about him. They know his exploits and have plenty of opinions ranging from admiration to scorn. I have never spoken to him before and yet when we talk in a video call, he hurls a litany of abuse my way:

You're a lying whore. That's what you are.

You fucking kike media shills.

You just hate white people.

You're just ignorant.

Are you retarded? Serious question.

You're clearly a waste of time.

Our interaction is so beyond the spectrum of normal human communication, I burst out laughing. Rapidly, though, the laughter dissipates. Another thought enters my mind: *Is it actually ethical to interview him? He seems insane.* Then I remember who is. What he's done, what he believes, who he's hurt. And make a split-second decision to press on.

(Some days later, I bring up weev's abuse and ranting with Mark. How weird the whole interaction was. He suggests that weev 'may have been purposely acting retarded. I spoke to him a couple of months ago and he seemed his normal self.')

weev is an example of trolling taken to its greatest extreme, of the anger and hatred in one lost young white man becoming toxic to himself and to others. Of free speech absolutism taken to its furthest point, where it can lead to real-life violence. Where humans are hurt. When I speak to weev, he's the embodiment of the worst parts of trolling culture, without any of the usual associated humour or flashes of humanity. He continually disavows violence, while simultaneously and repeatedly calling *for* violence. This is a way of gaming the US First Amendment and using it as a shield – most probably imprecisely. Trolls think they are safe in its arms; the experts say they aren't. Before we get to that, though, let's wind back the clock a little bit.

weev didn't spring out of nowhere. As an enfant terrible, his rise to notoriety seemed to start when a *New York Times* article on trolling appeared in 2008. 'I hack, I ruin, I make piles of money,' he boasted to the reporter. 'I make people afraid for their lives.'

Even back then, he was talking about the evils of Jews – in spite of his own Jewish ancestry – and putting bloggers 'in the oven'.[2] For many years this incessant bigotry and big-noting did nothing to quell the affection for him among journalists. If anything, his apparent gumption did the opposite. In 2012, right before he went to jail for revealing the personal data of thousands of AT&T customers, the blog Gawker headlined him as 'The Internet's Best Terrible Person'. Perhaps they should have asked a few more questions.

In the article, Adrian Chen writes, 'In person, he exudes a downhome country charm that is so disarming you may not realize he's been expounding very loudly about Jewish-controlled banks and armed revolution against the U.S.'[3] A year later Chen describes him as 'an endlessly charming, unrepentant asshole.'[4]

A website set up in weev's defence after the charges were laid, Freeweev, describes him as follows: 'He never takes anything seriously and generally treats life as a piece of performance art. He's undisciplined and lazy … but he's very charming and funny at a dinner party. That doesn't really change how gigantic of a jackass he is.' Sections of the media, like Vice's Motherboard, picked up on this characterisation of him and ran with it.[5]

Like many celebrities – for that's really what he's become – journalists scramble to cover anything and everything about weev: his supposed motives, his swastika tattoo, his obsession with Norse mythology, his drug-taking history, his adopted black siblings, his mother, his disputed Jewishness. The time he hacked unprotected printers across the United States in March 2016, commanding them to produce thousands of swastika-adorned flyers. The damage he's incited against individuals such as game developer and programming instructor Kathy Sierra. Doxing. Smearing. Rape threats. Death threats. Driving her offline for six years.[6]

Taken as a whole, the press coverage seems exhaustive and exhausting. After a while, it stops being interesting and feels like being on a roundabout. Here we go again. We're back where we started. My inclination is: *leave weev's tired story alone.*

It's the trolls who change my mind. In their offhand comments is the whisper of something unheard; it's as if weev is their exiled, fallen god. It's like a signpost telling me to go back to his story again. Turn it around and around in the sunlight. Take Dr Williams' advice. Listen hard and think hard.

Since being released from prison in 2014, weev has been living overseas in various locations. Initially his choice of a new home was Lebanon, because the country has no extradition treaty with the United States.[7] In a 4chan chat from May 2015 he explained his decision to go into exile:

I was hassled up until the minute I left United States soil ...
I realized that if I stayed on US soil, I would be financially strangled to death. I hadn't been able to find work in years. I left the country and now I have income again. Beyond all that there is no way I want to contribute to a fucking kike economy. Leaving the USA is the only moral thing to do until the day we can return with an army to kill each and every piece of Jew shit out there.

He tells me twice in Russian – a language I don't speak – that he's currently living in 'Pridnestrovskaya Moldavskaya Respublika'. This is the self-declared state of Transnistria, once part of the USSR. It is not recognised by the United Nations. Just like Lebanon, it has no extradition treaty with the United States.[8] (Whether this is actually where he's living is anyone's guess; even his friends don't seem to know his whereabouts with any confidence.)

Early on in my research, one of the trolls shoots me a warning about weev: 'He lies.' Mark later repeats this sentiment, telling me, 'He lies. His entire image is fake. And he lives his entire life off his internet image. I've never seen someone say the amount of delusional bullshit, which is why he keeps having to move to different internet communities, as each one gets sick of putting up with it and tells him to shut the fuck up.'

Luke McMahon, the troll hunter, says it too: *weev lies*.

'Partly, I think this is a defensive mechanism should the [US] State choose to prosecute him at some point,' McMahon writes in one of many emails to me. 'weev has what some may call "rat cunning". It is my strong view that weev fits the classic definition of a sociopath. He lacks empathy for his victims, he is manipulative, callous, hostile to anyone who dares confront him with his actions; in that regard he is deceitful, and he refuses to take responsibility for the harm he causes.'

And yet it's neither weev's complex, changeable facade nor the lying that seems to bother his trolling cohort. (Hackers and trolls can lie.) What bothers them is how he's changed, especially since he came out of prison in 2014. One troll, who asked not to be identified, told me:

We just want him to go back to his old fun self, before he was a neo-Nazi. We like to tease weev a lot because it's just a way of expressing that we wish he'd go back to his old self.

He's basically created his entire life around internet trolling [and has] reached a point where he's really trapped in his troll persona. At the end of the day I think there is a genuine and kind person inside of weev somewhere … in private convo you can get him to drop it [the facade] sometimes.

As always, this response is not what I expect. They're affectionate and nostalgic about him. They miss who he used to be.

Journalists research people. They gather a body of evidence about a person or an issue and build a picture. Yet the more the trolls tell me about weev, the more of an enigma he becomes. There's only one thing I'm sure of: no one is using the word 'charm' anymore.

In a reflective mood one evening, a troll I regularly chat with says, 'I think he just needs love.'

'WHAT?' I reply. And then, 'Are you trolling me?!'

The troll finds this very funny and says no, he's not trolling me; he really thinks that. It could be true. It could be untrue. Or partly true. It could be the troll trolling weev through me. Take your pick.

Before my interview with weev I'm told he'll try to 'fuck with me'. After years as a journalist, I know this kind of attack dog. Or think I do. But I'm unprepared.

weev gets on Skype. He's got dark eyes planted in a long, pale face. He removes and replaces his glasses every so often and leans into the camera. His ginger beard is unkempt, verging on disordered. A physical sign hinting at the diatribe that's about to come out of his mouth. I ask for his name and title as he'd like it to appear in the book.

He says, 'I am a professional racist and my name is Andrew Auernheimer.' He immediately launches into the notion of polemic, in rapid-fire speech. 'The world "polemic" comes from the Greek "Polemos". Polemos means war, of course. So, the history of this sort of rhetorical combat …' He moves on to how it ties into Scandinavian history. How the Saxons employed polemic. How the Norse used 'senna' as a type of insult-trading. He keeps going, seemingly without drawing breath:

> In ancient times, the precursor to actual physical combat would be this sort of rhetorical poetic combat, known as senna, and that's what I do.
>
> I think it's a very valuable part of white European history. And I strive to live my life … [and] follow old gods and I follow old ways … And the internet has seen a rebirth of this kind of attitude – we highly value this kind of hashing-out of differences, this airing of

grievances. It's a very valuable part of the human experience that has been suppressed by governments for about a century and a half.

There's no easing in or slow start. It's just *game on*. As Chen insightfully noted about weev back in 2012:

Auernheimer deploys a peculiar rhetorical strategy that he's learned to work to his advantage: he peppers his conversation with bizarre but true facts and historical references – he has an encyclopedic knowledge of ancient Greek history, world religions and contemporary U.S. anti-government extremists, among other things – then hits you with dubious details about his own life. The idea is that the overwhelming strangeness of the world will make you more receptive to the relatively banal stuff Auernheimer makes up about himself.[9]

Despite the Southern Poverty Law Center's verdict that he's a Neo-Nazi, and his fellow trolls consistently reinforcing this, not to mention his role as a webmaster for the Neo-Nazi website Daily Stormer, weev denies it: 'I've never identified as a Neo-Nazi. That term has no meaning. I've always been a racist.'

To me this is a moot point, made simply for the purpose of being contrary. He holds Neo-Nazi views. He has a swastika tattoo and believes 'Hitler was perfectly morally justified on every level'.[10] (As the saying goes, if it looks like a duck, swims like a duck, and quacks like a duck, then it probably *is* a duck.)

weev also denies the notion that his thirteen-month prison term from March 2013 to April 2014 hardened his white supremacist views. 'You can check my work far before prison,' he says. 'My opinions of race have not changed.'

He flicks me a link to a blog post dating back to January 2008. It's headlined 'Dear white people' and goes on to disparage all Jews – 'who took your print and broadcast technologies from you last century' – and all people of Africa: 'When will white Americans stand up for themselves? When will you demand White living space and White-owned media – the only option to having a safe and stable nation (One which does not slavishly fight the Jews' wars)? You will soon be minority [sic].'[11] Just his willingness to point me towards a piece of writing so embarrassingly flawed is a statement in itself.

weev's ability to spout Jewish conspiracies seems to know no bounds. He says the word 'Jew' thirty-eight times in our fifty-nine-minute conversation. He says that, while his communication techniques 'have evolved', his political ideas are the same as they always were: 'I got a feel for what the truth is, through learned experience, through actual going out and living in the world versus being indoctrinated from the liberal-controlled, the Jewish-controlled colleges.'

Yes, those liberal professors again. Ruining the world. But the Jews. They are even worse:

The Jewish are the establishment in the West and they've abused their position of power. They took over the banks and they made all these financial bubbles. They took over the media and they promoted absolute degeneracy. Pornography is an explicitly Jewish industry and they brag about it … These people deserve to be punished. They are wicked.

Some minutes later he returns to this hobbyhorse:

The Jews are controlling every country in the world. Isn't that funny? Isn't that funny? There's only a very few number of them where they don't control. There's Iran, there's Syria. You know, all these countries we supposedly want to bomb, for some reason, they all happen to be countries without Jewish influence. Hm. I wonder what's going on here, you know.

Yet weev has Jewish blood running in his veins. His mother confirmed it – for the second time – to *Newsweek* in January 2018.[12] As you'd expect, he does his best to minimise this: 'I had a great-great Jewish grandparent. That's not exactly a lot of Jewish blood. That's a fraction, a modicum. Under the Nuremberg laws, I would be not Jewish at all.'

I say, 'You've called for the killing of Jewish children.'

Combative, he replies, 'Quote me where I told people to go kill Jewish children. It didn't happen.' When weev printed 50,000 white supremacist flyers for college campuses in March 2016, and again in August of that year, some of them read,

> I unequivocally support the killing of children … We will not relent until the cries of their infants are silenced by boots stomping their brains out onto the pavement. I believe that our enemies need such a level of atrocity inflicted upon them and their homes that they are afraid to ever threaten the white race with genocide again.[13]

The flyers went on to name 'enemies' including Jewish people, black people and federal agents. He repeated a similar sentiment in early 2018, on a podcast: 'If you don't let us dissent peacefully, then our only option is to murder you. To kill your children.'[14]

I press the point about his actions and hate speech infringing the civil liberties of other people. He's irate. 'No. Nobody's actions, nobody's posts on the internet infringe the civil liberties of others. You're a lying whore. That's what you are,' he says.

I try to move the dialogue from hurling abuse back to holding him to account for his views, especially when it comes to his calls for the slaughter of Jewish kids. Eventually, in sentences split up by his ranting, I manage to relate one of his own direct quotes about this back to him.

On my mind – and in my heart – is this. My grandmother's older sister, Elizabet, had a baby who was murdered at Auschwitz by the Nazis in World War II. We never even knew his name.

'You fucking kike media shills will take everything out of context,' weev says. 'You take one fucking quote that does not call for violence, period, and claim that I'm calling for violence. Why? Because you're a liar. Because you're a shill. Because you just hate white people.'

'I don't even know what a shill is. Is that an American word?' I say calmly.

'No. That's an English word. You're just ignorant.'

In fact, shill is a North American term that means 'an accomplice of a confidence trickster or swindler who poses as a genuine customer to entice or encourage others'.[15]

weev says he sees both Oklahoma City bomber Timothy McVeigh, who killed 168 people, and Norwegian mass murderer Anders Breivik, who killed seventy-seven people, as 'patriots' because '[T]hey are martyrs. They sacrificed their own lives.' Of Breivik he says, 'I don't think people should go out and commit acts of violence … but he was willing to sacrifice his own life and his own happiness, striving for the future of his fellow citizens, and that part is an admirable thing.'

'He killed children,' I say.

'They were fucking like sixteen years old,' weev replies, 'and they were at a political, a Marxist political, elite camp. Come on. Come on. That was the next generation of the people that were plotting to undermine his nation, flood it with Muslims. That's a fact.'

Astoundingly, weev tries to wriggle out of his violent rhetoric by claiming context. But discussion of violence and speech that calls for real-life violence against particular people or communities are hallmarks of his story.

'I didn't tell people to kill people. I said, "If you take away people's right to dissent, then violence is the only answer." That's contextualised by the fact that the Daily Stormer, on its sidebar, has a disclaimer on every single page against violence.' He's obviously touchy about this subject. 'On my last podcast episode … we had about a forty-five-minute conversation about why violence is wrong and ineffective. We consistently tell people that we're acting peacefully and we tell them to send lawful criticism.'

This description of the conversation is wildly inaccurate. Among other topics, weev and podcast guests Mike Enoch and Christopher Cantwell – also white supremacists – offer support to 37-year-old Dennis Lloyd Mothersbaugh. This man pleaded guilty to assault charges after punching two people during the 2017 Charlottesville riots. Underneath the podcast episode, posted on YouTube, the text says: 'This is a festive podcast. It is not intended to condone or encourage hate or violence or elicit any kind of feeling other than coziness.'

This is a tactic used by predator trolls from the United States. On the one hand they will seemingly incite violence. On the other, they explicitly say they don't condone violence. If you look back to the archived Daily Stormer post about Mariam Veiszadeh, you can see that despite doxing her and using dehumanising language to its greatest extreme, the post also states in bold:

DO NOT THREATEN THIS MOSLEM [sic] WHORE. THE DAILY STORMER DOES NOT CONDONE VIOLENCE OR THREATS OF VIOLENCE. FLOOD HER WITH RACIAL AND RELIGIOUS ABUSE, NOT WITH THREATS OF VIOLENCE.

Once I've seen this more than a dozen times in numerous different trolling contexts, I have the light-bulb moment. Surely this isn't an accident. It must mean something. But what?

On the day I email Mark D. Rasch, a cybersecurity and privacy attorney based in the Washington, D.C., area, he replies, 'You're the third Daily Stormer victim I worked with this week.' I'm not a direct victim of weev and Andrew Anglin, but there are plenty who are, it would seem.

'The tactic of both promoting and apparently disavowing violence is common in the online community in general and on the Daily Stormer website in particular,' Rasch confirms. He explains that under US federal law, a so-called 'true threat' can, in principle, be prosecuted. In legal terms, this is 'any communication containing any threat to kidnap any person or any threat to injure the person of another'.[16]

It's not that straightforward, though. The US Supreme Court, Rasch says, has previously found, in the case of Elonis v. United States that it 'was insufficient that the target of the threats felt threatened, or even that such a feeling was objectively reasonable, the government had to prove that it was the INTENT of the poster to threaten'.

Coming back to the Daily Stormer, Rasch told me, 'This is probably why posters of threatening, harassing or intimidating materials online disavow their own intent to threaten or to violate the law. Of course, I cannot claim to speak for these individuals. However, when these threats are reported to federal, state or local law enforcement, many of the police agencies (or prosecutors) may look at the language explicitly disavowing violence and decline to investigate or prosecute these actions as "true threats".'

Rasch goes on to explain that website operators are essentially trying to distance themselves 'from the violence advocated by its users'. The likes of weev and Andrew Anglin may believe they are covered under Section 230 of the US *Communications Decency Act*, but this assumption isn't set in stone and, Rasch suggests, would need to be tested in court.[17]

'It seems that the disavowal, by this site and others, is done with a wink and a nod: "I would NEVER recommend that someone be harassed at home, but here is the target's home phone number ..." A court would likely find both to be harassment, threats, intimidation and actionable,' Rasch says.

When it comes to online harassment, one of the world's most well-known opinions is that of Dr Mary Anne Franks, Professor of Law at the University of Miami and Vice-President of the Cyber Civil Rights Initiative. Like Rasch, she believes this trolling manoeuvre is purposeful.

'My read is that this is a tactic intended to go right up to the edge of what is permissible under the First Amendment but not cross it,' she says. 'Even the least well-informed "free speech absolutist" is aware that the First Amendment does not protect all speech and that engaging in certain forms of expression can lead to lawsuits or even criminal sentences. The Daily Stormer trolls are apparently under the impression that the only speech that crosses that line are threats of violence, and so they explicitly warn their followers to avoid making those. They are not right about this, but they are probably right that they will never face consequences for their actions under US law,' she explains.

Dr Franks – who is writing about the Daily Stormer in her own forth-coming book – says the website operators' 'understanding of what is and is not protected by the First Amendment is pretty muddled'. 'One reason for that is that they don't seem to be particularly constitutionally literate; another is that American free speech jurisprudence is inconsistent, vague, and often unprincipled.'

Aside from 'true threats', she points to several other types of speech the First Amendment does not protect. There's the so-called 'fighting words' doctrine, which prevents words which 'by their very utterance, inflict injury or tend to incite an immediate breach of the peace'.[18] (Dr Franks notes this category 'has virtually been unused in recent decades'.) Another liability may be incitement, but she says the US legal standard is very stringent. 'In other words, US courts are unlikely to find that hateful speech, even if it calls for physical violence, qualifies as incitement unless the lawless action it calls for is likely to occur very soon after the speech is expressed.'

That's not the end of the story, though. Dr Franks points to another possible law that may have the potential to make websites publishing cyberhate, such as the Daily Stormer, liable.

> There is a federal criminal statute (18 U.S. Code § 2261A) prohibiting what is sometimes referred to as 'cyber stalking'. That statute … makes it illegal to engage in a course of conduct against a person that could be reasonably expected to cause substantial distress to that person, if done with the 'intent to kill, injure, harass, intimidate, or place under surveillance with intent to kill, injure, harass, or intimidate another person'.

Adding to the legal complexity of online harassment in the United States is the fact that, as in Australia, civil wrongs (as opposed to criminal ones) can arise from speech.

'Defamation … actions can follow false and harmful speech,' Rasch explains. 'Many US states also support civil lawsuits for things like invasion of privacy, false light, as well as harassment and threats. More modern statutes may also either punish or provide a civil remedy for things like revenge porn or doxing.

'Having a right to say something does not mean that you are insulated from the consequences of what you say,' he says, adding that under US law a person who threatens harm is presumed to mean it and a court would likely view it in this way.

In short, when online harassers invoke the First Amendment as a coverall for predator trolling that causes real-life harm, they are playing with fire. It might burn other people. It might burn them. Not only do the best legal minds question whether trolls understand the First Amendment, they point to numerous other US laws that may make their actions illegal.

Why does it matter whether trolls use violent speech and game the First Amendment? It matters because, as the Nazis knew all too well, speech goes beyond words. It dehumanises others and can lead to real-life violence. With this in mind, I try to ask weev about how much responsibility the Daily Stormer should take for the violence – and death – at the Charlottesville 'Unite the Right' rally in August 2017.

In the lead-up to the event the Neo-Nazi publication strongly promoted the rally, dishing out instructions on how to get there and telling readers to bring pepper spray and torches:

> You absolutely must attend this event. Take a few days off work, reschedule appointments, do whatever you must do BUT GET YOURSELF THERE!
>
> You didn't spend all this time shitposting and debating crime stats and IQ charts, while making dank memes and trolling cucks and leftists alike, just to stay home when the rubber really hits the road, now did you?

Someone using the handle Azzmador co-wrote the pre-Charlottesville post with Daily Stormer publisher Andrew Anglin, further stating:

> We are there for a very fundamental reason: We must secure the existence of our people and a future for White children![19]

weev refuses to concede the publication he works for is in any way responsible for the Charlottesville violence: 'Now you're saying Charlottesville is attributed to content on the Daily Stormer when we didn't organise that rally … you have no arguments here. You have nothing.'

The day after the rally Anglin published a post describing Heather Heyer, the woman who was rammed and killed by a vehicle during the rally, as a 'Fat, Childless 32-Year-Old Slut'. Ohio man James Alex Fields

Jr, a Neo-Nazi sympathiser, was charged with second-degree murder. His trial is set for 26 November 2018. As this book went to press, there was not yet an outcome for this trial.

Within two days of the Charlottesville riots coming to a close, the web-hosting company and domain registrar GoDaddy Inc. unceremoniously dumped the Daily Stormer, stating: 'Given the Daily Stormer's latest article comes on the immediate heels of a violent act, we believe this type of article could incite additional violence, which violates our terms of service.'[20]

The Daily Stormer moved to Google, which also dumped it. The publication was then forced to move to the dark web, temporarily making it inaccessible through normal browsers.[21] When I try to broach this with weev – that these companies clearly thought the Daily Stormer did bear some responsibility for incitement of violence at Charlottesville – he attempts to deflect the issue: 'Our hosting has been uninterrupted … It's almost as if the media don't know what they're talking about, about anything.'

Ignoring his questions about whether I'm bright enough to use a search engine, I ask, 'Why do you think it kept getting bumped after Charlottesville?'

'Because the Jews have exerted illegal control over the entire world … [and] are making false narratives in their media to try to justify the violation of other people's human rights. That's the fact of it,' he replies.

Three days after the rally, screenshots posted by right-wing internet personality and activist Laura Loomer appear to show weev trying to find out the location of the dead woman's funeral in order to harass mourners. In the deleted tweets he wrote:

I want to get people on the ground there.[23]

As if it wasn't awful enough that a woman who was simply expressing her democratic right to protest had been killed, he wanted to cause further harm and pain – and possibly violence – to those grieving her death. These are not the actions of someone disavowing violence. weev suggests that just turning off our computers can stop us from becoming cyberhate victims. *Words on the internet never hurt anyone,* the trolls say. But neither of these things are true for Heather Heyer – or for those who loved her.

On Twitter and in his articles, journalist Michael Edison Hayden has repeatedly pointed to the increasing violence in weev's rhetoric.[24] He's not the only one to notice. Lorraine Murphy and I are in a message chat one night soon after my Skype call with weev. She writes, 'I think he has changed. He's more hardline, the fun and mischief is all gone. He's enraged now … [and] he's deliberately looking for ways to hurt the US.'

She's right: weev's cohesive arguments about trolling as 'a way of expressing working class discontent' are gone.[25] Only one thing is left in the ashes of weev's razed house: unadulterated anger.

This babbling rage is what I cop during our conversation: 'Guess what? You guys determined the way that this works. We're playing by the rules that your team set.'

'Who is "you guys"?' I ask.

'You, you, you, you liberals, you leftists, you media types, right. All of you collectively, all of you collectively set the rules that people live by.'

'Come on. That is ridiculous.'

I can't see how it follows, but he then names some people involved with the AT&T prosecution, saying, 'They literally had me kidnapped. They had me tortured. I was starved. I was beaten. I was thrown in solitary confinement at the behest of these people on false charges. That's a reality and this is the reality of anybody who holds our political viewpoint in America and the rules have been set by you, by you, by your team.' He throws in 'that's a fact' for good measure.

'Where are you saying that this happened?'

Like many of weev's responses, this one is big on hyperbole and short on detail: 'All over several US incarceration facilities. All over.'

When I change the subject and ask if he's working in Transnistria, he's equally vague. 'I'm just, uh, chilling out. You know … it doesn't take a lot of money to live here.'

'You're living off donations?'

'Uh, no. No, I'm not living off of donations. I get some donations, but it's not my primary source of revenue, I guess.'

'Well, what is?'

'Uh, you know, just um, uh, whatever, whatever … Stuff.'

Right at the end of our conversation I say, 'Okay. Thank you very much for your time.'

As if we've been chatting about the weather or talking about gardening, he pleasantly says, 'Yeah, you too. Have a good one.'

I think back to weev's notion that he's somehow a devotee of the Socratic method, asking his 'students' endless questions until contradictions are exposed. This strikes me as the polar opposite of the way weev behaves. He appears to be unable to ask questions. Or if he does, has no intention of letting the other person answer. He only wants to talk and have others listen.

When I mention this to Mark, he muses that perhaps weev isn't accustomed to being taken to task on his beliefs. 'I think that he is so used to people buying what he says at this point that when someone doesn't, he's not quite sure what to do,' Mark muses.

'It's pretty unusual to shout at someone you've never met for an hour and scream about killing Jewish kids,' I say.

'Yes, he's very insecure about his Jewishness at the moment.'

The effects of aggression on the human brain are a subject of current research, and of particular interest when it comes to trolls and their targets. During my conversation with weev I found myself uncharacteristically lost for words. The shouting didn't rile me. I stayed calm, just like the troll hunter told me to. But it was hard to think straight with such persistent noise. Yes, weev uses Socrates to justify his aggressive trolling tactics. However during the interview I couldn't, for the life of me, spit out Socrates' name. It's as if my brain was locked. On the edge of drawing out words that just wouldn't come. It bothered me. And not just in the moment, but later too. I wanted to know more about why this had happened.

On the day Associate Professor Tom Denson calls me back, he's insanely busy. With students and grant applications and manuscripts.

This must be what happens to someone who diligently and passionately researches aggression and the brain. Everyone wants to hear what you have to say.

Denson is not surprised that words evaded me while I was being shouted at by weev. Although he can't comment on my individual brain, he sees this as a fairly straightforward equation. A person's prefrontal cortex, he explains, is the 'part of the brain involved in regulating your emotions, staying calm, staying cool, which is, I imagine, what you were trying to do, rather than flying off the handle, even though it sounds like this person was saying some pretty provoking things to you.

'That's effortful and it takes a lot of energy and it's very hard to do. And so that may be one reason why you found it difficult, then, to come up with a good question or even think clearly when this person was in your face,' he says.

'The conscious brain is slow and can really only do one thing at a time. And the most important thing to do in that situation is to control yourself. We're not computers. We can't run multiple conscious processes in parallel at the same time.'

weev's anti-Semitism. The relentless violence in his speech. The hate. The baby without a name.

I ask Denson: 'When you're being shouted at, does it matter what the content is?'

Indeed, it does. Denson points to another part of the brain called the dorsal anterior cingulate cortex, located in the midline. Its role is conflict detection. 'We know from our research that the larger the response you get in that conflict detection centre, the more effort you're going to put into controlling your anger. If it's more insulting to you, more provocative … that's a bigger discrepancy between how you want to be treated and how you are being treated. And so you will try harder to control yourself. Your brain's going to be working harder,' Denson explains.

For three days after the interview with weev, I'm flattened. Lethargic and dark. I can't see the point of the book. Or anything, really. Lying in bed with the blinds drawn and staring at the fan going around and around seems like the best option.

'One of the functions of anger, if you think about it from an evolutionary perspective, is to get people to do what you want them to do. And one of those things that people often want people to do when they're angry is to go away,' Denson says.

However, he's quick to add a caveat: 'We don't know everything about human behaviour and the brain. There are a lot of individual differences in how people respond to these things.'

Thankfully, the blackness doesn't last. And for that, at least, I'm grateful. The dramatic effect that weev's unexpected – albeit short-lived – aggression has on me and my ability to function puts the suffering of cyberhate targets into razor-sharp focus. What does this kind of hatred and anger, especially if it's sustained, really do to our brains?

The late Charlotte Dawson admitted she was unable to stop checking and stop responding: 'I know that I shouldn't respond, and in most cases I don't, but sometimes, particularly on Twitter, when a heinous comment is directed right at my "handle", I just can't let it go.'[26]

Her friend Megan Hustwaite points out that Dawson didn't just defend herself – she defended numerous others online too. 'I would always like her to be remembered as someone that stood up for others … She would be just as affected by someone else being trolled or bullied.'

The way Dawson responded to the trolls is something people continually asked her about. 'Charlotte, why did you keep reading it?' asked veteran *60 Minutes* reporter Tara Brown in the morally questionable post–suicide attempt segment back in 2012.[27]

Personally, I know this behaviour well. The constant, anxious checking when you are the target of a vicious and continuing cyberhate attack. The blood pounding in your ears. Your heart racing. And clicking and clicking: *What are they saying about me now?* A train wreck that is impossible to turn away from.

Once I start looking, it becomes clear that plenty of predator-trolling victims experience the pull of vicious online commentary. Appearance activist Carly Findlay mentioned that during the Reddit incident she couldn't stop looking. Likewise, British columnist Laurie Penny, who has written and spoken extensively about cybersexism, makes mention of this seemingly irrational behaviour too.[28] As a kind of straw poll,

I ask two other women who've been subjected to sustained cyberhate: *Did you constantly check the foul messages too?* 'Absolutely,' both of them reply.

This leads me to Adam Alter. Aside from being an Australian expatriate, Alter is an associate professor of marketing at New York University's Stern School of Business. He's an expert in technology and addiction, and just the person to ask about this subject.

While he cautions that 'what you're asking about doesn't have a single simple answer', he is prepared to offer some enlightening pointers.

> Even if you're ninety-nine per cent sure the feedback will be negative, there's a slim chance it won't be. That slim chance of reward is akin to hitting a jackpot on a slot machine. It's addictive. People prefer some feedback to no feedback at all, even if that feedback is generally negative with a slim chance of being neutral or positive. In general, humans prefer negative feedback to being ignored or not discussed.
>
> If you know people are discussing you, it's hard to ignore – the same way it's hard to stop a movie halfway through, or to know a paper at uni has been graded and not to check the grade. Even if you know you didn't do well on the paper or you aren't interested in the movie, people tend to be completionists. We need to close the loop, to know the answer. That explains the rubbernecking you see when people pass accidents. They don't wish harm on anyone, and they admit often that what they're about to see will be disturbing, but they can't look away. They need to know.

In short, Dawson behaved just like the rest of us when we're being talked about by other people; she simply wanted to know what folk were saying – even if it hurt her.

As part of our now-regular banter, I relate parts of the conversation with weev to the troll hunter.

McMahon messages back, 'That's his intent. To rattle you. But see through it, and what's left?'

'The devil is in the detail,' I reply. 'And he wouldn't give me any detail.'

'He understands the situation he's in [and] walks a fine line. He knows he can end up back in prison.' Then he adds, 'He will go after you, by the way.'

Considering my unwieldy digital footprint – something the troll hunter explicitly avoids himself – and everything I've written over the years that remains online, I say: 'I'm an open book if they come after me. That's a problem.'

'Just gotta go to the AFP,' McMahon replies. And then, a few seconds later: 'LOL.'

#

There are so many questions about weev's story no one is asking. Maybe it's possible to map out events in his life and understand how they're connected to his endless fountain of hate. As Dr Williams notes, trolls weren't minted that way. They develop their habits over time. Was weev, like so many other trolls, left alone to grow up online? Or were other factors at play?

Over many months, I try to contact his parents, Alyse and Mark Auernheimer. His father's internet footprint is small. His mother, on the other hand, isn't hard to find. In the photos, her dark eyes and pale face are weev's eyes and face. News stories online mention her charity work.[29] She seems passionate about helping the community. And it's hard not to wonder what she thinks of this son who talks constantly about violence and war and killing children. (For weev's part, he believes: 'My parents are perfect examples of how secular liberalism destroys families and will rot out the foundations of our very civilization.'[30])

When I finish my email to Alyse Auernheimer, my finger hovers above the send key for a second. *What would it be like to get an email like this?*

She doesn't answer. Not my email, not the letter that I post her, the Facebook messages or my phone calls. Instead, one of the trolls sends me an email Alyse Auernheimer wrote back in 2009.[31] While I believe this email to be authentic, I'm unable to say that this is the case with

100 per cent certainty. (And in fact this is the legacy not just of weev's story but of trolling more broadly. The truth is hazy.) I do, however, spend hours trying to verify whether Auernheimer wrote the email or not. I contact the host of the website where the email is publicly archived. He doesn't know for sure. I ask several of the trolls. They tell me the content rings true but still can't confirm the document is genuine. Neither weev nor his parents respond to my questions on this. In the end the tone of Auernheimer's email, and some of the personal details contained within it convinces me.

It's not entirely clear who she's writing to. However, what is clear is that her family has been doxed.

She's asking for their photos and personal information to be taken offline. She's worried about the safety of her children and mentions that one poster expresses 'a desire to rape me'.

Auernheimer writes from the heart to the person who has doxed her:[32]

We too are victims of Andrew. The hardest part for all of us is that he used to be normal. He loved us and was sweet and kind to his siblings. Several years ago he developed a relationship with a girl with a serious drug problem. He began by using xtc [ecstasy] regularly and eventually graduated to LSD and heroin. About three years ago he had a mental breakdown and began hearing voices and talking to himself. He vanished from our lives … There are references to his lavish lifestyle on this thread but the sad truth is he is paranoid schizophrenic and has been homeless a number of times. I am not excusing his pathetic behavior.

In the lengthy correspondence, she goes on to say:

Andrew was never abused or neglected. When he lived with us he was a totally different person, prior to his substance abuse issues. He became a different person in Cal [California].

He had to get as far away from us as he could to participate in this kind of behavior because we would have called the cops and kicked his ass to the curb. From his postings he is deranged and a drug addict.

This seems to be as close as we'll ever get to understanding, from his parents' viewpoint, how he was raised, although the detail is still missing. Further on in the email chain, Alyse Auernheimer writes about feeling 'physically sick' to see some of the things weev has posted online and says: 'I don't cry over Andrew anymore.'

Truthfully, until about a year ago we didn't even know about this ugly, racist rhetoric because we weren't wasting our days looking. Many years ago he was online railing against [conservative commentator] Bill O'Reilly and the far right and saying anything to inflame. He used to be a radical liberal.

Her despair over her son seems to increase as the correspondence continues:

[T]he irony is we are a multi-racial family. My great grandparents were Czech, Jewish immigrants, and I am native American. As the white parents of black kids [weev's adopted siblings] living in the south you can be sure we know about racism. The world is a small place and we are all one. Andrew and his victims are but one of the many sad, dark consequences of drug addiction, internet addiction, and the internet itself. I am so so sorry for your suffering. We too are suffering. This is a nightmare. We feel like hostages.

One after the other, she's peeling back layers and layers of grief:

Many of the postings referred to our family as nice. This is accurate. Our other children are everything Andrew rejected, kind, smart, hard-working, dedicated to making a difference through public service, and we have left Andrew behind ... Don't get me wrong we will always love Andrew and our hearts will forever be broken where he is concerned but what else can we do but move on. It's like the Andrew we knew died long ago. Hope does spring eternal and sometimes I dream the real Andrew is home and we are all together.

As a mother myself, the correspondence is crushing to read. All that love and pain with nowhere to go. That hopelessness. That longing. While it remains unclear to me whether – or precisely how – weev's upbringing affected who he became, what is clear is that he hasn't just harmed strangers; his family is suffering too.

Later, on Skype messenger, I seek to follow up a few things with weev.

'Tell me something,' I write. 'You say you're living in the Pridnestrovskaya Moldavskaya Respublika. This is a territory where freedom of speech and assembly is limited. And yet you're a champion of the First Amendment. How does this work?'

'As long as you don't say it in Russian nobody cares,' he says. 'And I'm out to fix America, not somebody else's country.'

'You're going to fix it remotely?'

'Are you retarded? Serious question. Seriously, what do you do for a living? You make media. Do you personally deliver the copies of the media you make to every member of the audience?'

'I do write stuff on the internet, sure,' I reply. 'But I'm not trying to "fix" a country of 323 million people remotely from a non-country in the former USSR.'

'Well, I believe in the Constitution. And I expect anyone that might hurt it to either leave my country or die horribly.'

'Your mom said you're shitting on the First Amendment.' (To be clear, this isn't exactly what she said. Her 2014 quote was: 'Free speech is the cornerstone of democracy, but I think if you love free speech you don't take a shit on it.'[33])

He snaps back, 'I am sure my mom is an authority on First Amendment jurisprudence.' Then, a few seconds later, 'You're clearly a waste of time. If you'd like to use my time further you can arrange for the payment of my retainer.'

Not long afterwards, he stops answering my messages altogether. Aside from the journalist in me wanting further answers and clarifications, the human in me is relieved to be out of his poisonous orbit. All that anger, violence and misogyny makes me feel dirty – like I need to take a shower and scrub myself raw. Even reading the transcript of his interview long enough to write this section takes unprecedented effort. His hate. His mother's unrelenting grief. His extremist adulation of his own free speech to the exclusion of all other factors, including the free speech of just about anyone else. His disingenuous disavowal of violence while purposefully inciting it. His scorn for victims like the late Heather Heyer. Yes. We can kid ourselves that turning off our computers helps. Or that words don't have power. But words incite actions, and actions can kill us.

Notes in the margins
The hardest conversation of all

I N THE SEA OF communication with all the trolls, Mark starts questioning me about my writing. 'Do you think you've gone a bit too deep?' I try to brush him off but he's insistent. 'I'm asking if you realise how desensitised you are now. A couple of years ago you were getting upset over rape jokes. Now you're not fazed by me laughing about how my ISIS friends were drone-striked.'

The hairs are prickling on my arms: defensive.

'It's not that I'm desensitised,' I say. 'It's that I know, or have more of an idea, what's coming. Does that make sense? But, sure, there are days it's getting to me. In regard to you. I'm mostly used to you.'

As usual, Mark wants me to know he's manipulating me. 'You stopped questioning me a long time ago and now it's friendly chats. You probably even think I'm an OK person, in a way,' he writes in the messenger app.

I can't help myself: I rise to the bait. 'You don't know what I think. You think you do, but you don't. There are hard bits in the book. I'm still the same person. I get upset. It's all in there. It's like pulling all the drawers out and dumping the clothes on the carpet.'

For once I'm glad it's online. He can't hear my voice. This feeling again. The sense that I'm losing my footing and my clarity about what's right and wrong. *Am I saying I'm not desensitised because I want it to be true? Or because it is true?*

#

The truth is that the trolling did more damage to my family than I've ever been prepared to admit. The proof lies with my husband. It takes him weeks to agree to an interview with me. He says yes. Then he says no: 'I feel uncomfortable.' Then he says, 'Okay, yes.'

The clock ticks around to when we're meant to sit down together and record. 'Not tonight,' he says.

Finally, days later, the children are in bed and we're sitting on the red couch together. His face looks taut and he's much stiller than usual. He looks straight ahead, and not at me.

The red record button. An easy question to start with: 'If you think back to 2013, before cyberhate affected us personally, what did you know about trolling?'

'Prior to what happened to us, I thought trolling was a fairly innocuous social phenomenon. Until you really experience it firsthand, you don't realise how bad it can be and how threatening it can be. That particular event, what happened to us back in 2013, has caused great anxiety in my life. In our lives,' he says.

After a brief pause, he continues: 'The mere fact that you're writing a book about trolling, which may herald another year of focus on you and our family, makes me extremely anxious.'

It's hard to dwell on this thought – I'm making my family's life harder and keeping us within something dark and dangerous. To try to get past this point, I push the conversation forward. Or back to June 2013, when the child sex offender Mark Newton was sentenced.

'What do you remember about that time?' I ask.

'It was pretty bad, of course,' Don says, before faltering and trailing off. He's visibly upset and, truth be told, so am I. We stop the recorder for a few minutes.

'It's hard,' I say into the quiet of our lounge room. 'I know it's hard. I'm finding it tough too.'

Then we start again. We're a journalist and an interviewee. We're also a husband and wife having one of those wrenching conversations that, in different circumstances, might be better avoided.

'I remember you getting the news that they [Newton and Truong] were being investigated,' Don says. 'And I just thought, "Oh, God, that poor boy." Then it dawned on me that these guys effectively fooled you, and I then thought, "How will this affect your media career?"

'And then, when they were convicted, and the full story came out and the trolling began, and it was quite unrelenting for a while, I just remember being so overwhelmed by your reaction to it all. You were profoundly upset about the attacks on you.

'You weren't sleeping. Both of us weren't sleeping. We were up all night, looking at our phones, looking at your Twitter feed. I remember, through your own stress and my anxiety around the situation, the household was functioning at a very bare minimum. And, yes, you were pretty crabby as well.

'The attacks were extremely unjust because you are one of the most compassionate people that I know. And for the trolls to say these awful things about you – that you supported paedophilia, which was an awful accusation – and also the way these trolls linked the child abuse and paedophilia with your staunch defence of the gay community, it was extreme, right-wing commentary. It was so offensive.'

There's a strangeness and a humiliation in suddenly seeing the image of yourself being attacked by a mob with pitchforks – vulnerable and in harm's way – through the eyes of the man who is closest to you.

'I noticed that you were extremely distracted. You were not getting any support from your workplace. They did not know what to do.' Don's critical of how ABC management handled the situation, recalling that my bosses simply suggested I call the Employee Assistance Program to get psychological support. 'There was no security element to it. That led to you, and particularly me, feeling quite lost and anxious.'

I say, 'You keep using the word "anxiety". And just now we had to stop the conversation. So obviously this still affects you.'

He confirms, 'I think it's fear. Seeing our family photo – you and me with our daughter, Elsa, and you pregnant with Kitty, in a happy family photo posted on a fascist website, I found that extremely distressing and it affects me to this day.

'From that moment I always thought, is your career placing our family in danger? If you're reporting on tough stories or if you get trolled on a particular issue, what does that mean for our family? Even just the retelling of this story, it has made me really worried. I am already quite a shy person in most social situations, but following that event, it makes me even more reluctant to join you in public-facing events. I feel like we're constantly being judged now.

'I'm a person of colour. I'm in a minority. I'm married to someone with Jewish roots. That doesn't play well in the fascist rhetoric, or the extreme right rhetoric.'

'Do you mean, we're like a double minority?' I ask.

'Yes,' he replies.

We discuss the moment he found the photo on the Nazi website and how, at the same moment, he realised all my tweets had geolocation data attached to them; anyone could find our house.

'It was at that moment I understood how the boundaries between the virtual and the physical were blurred. Until then I had never even contemplated that using such technology could have compromised our physical security,' he says.

'Do you remember the tweet that said, "Your life is over"?' I ask.

'Yes,' he replies. 'And I did not know how to take that. Was it a threat against your career? Was it a threat against your life?'

'I think I'm a pretty gutsy person,' I say, 'and I think I'm a pretty tough person, but I have never felt so afraid as that moment. I was really scared about the kids. It's easy to find out where we live. And there was no way to gauge the level of the danger.'

Don nods and continues, 'I'm already a helicopter parent and I'm an anxious parent and you know that. And after that event, it has made that particular aspect of me even more acute. It's had a lasting effect on me. In this modern age, the safety of my children feels more precarious.

'There's an underlying fear still. It's murmuring in the background. It's not as intense as it was then, of course. But I feel that there is a constant shadow following us. It's just this thing in the back of my mind that I know exists and I'm just waiting for it to show itself again.'

'Given everything you've said, what did you think a couple of years later when I went out to interview trolls and to write about them? Did you feel as if I was being bloody-minded and putting you and our kids and even myself at risk?'

'Yes, I did.' After a short pause, he says, 'I was pretty angry. I thought to myself, "Why is she doing this? Why is she exposing herself? Why is she making herself accessible to these people?" I felt as though it was a topic that we should have moved on from, but I knew that you wouldn't. Sometimes you don't realise how driven you are.'

As he says this, it's like one of those dreams when you suddenly find yourself partially clothed or naked in public. And you run and run. Is he right? Did I – do I – charge ahead no matter what? No matter who stands in the way? This is another kind of shame, one I've brought upon myself.

'But despite my fears and my concerns, it went well for you,' Don pivots. 'That period in which you built your writing around your involvement with trolls and trolling was a defining moment in your career.'

'I didn't do it for my career,' I say quietly.

'That's not what I'm saying,' he replies. 'I had my concerns ... but over time, it's gotten easier to deal with because I see the professional success that's resulted and also the strength that I've seen develop in you over that period. Seeing you grow has made it easier for me to cope with.'

Defensive, I try to explain. 'For me, it was a social justice thing. I felt like there was no choice but to investigate this story. Other women I knew were being attacked and the technology-enabled abuse was relentless. It was ruining their lives and nobody was helping. Nobody cared. It seemed like an emergency. To be honest, it still does seem like that to me. Also because of the way I am and my curiosity about the world, I really wanted to know: Who are these guys? Why do they do it?'

Even as I say these idealistic things, they feel feeble next to the cocoon I'm supposed to have built, and stood guard over, for my children.

'I remember you saying to me at one point, "Can't you just leave it alone?" And I know that you were worried about [the troll] Mark in particular and the fact that he has stayed in touch with me regardless of when I've tried not to be in touch with him.'

I want him to respond to this. To be soothing and say the mistakes I've made are okay. He does not say that. Instead, he changes tack. 'I think it has affected the way I interact with your work as well. I took a step back. Maybe that was wrong of me, but I needed some space from your work.'

'I totally understand that maybe you feel like I put our family at risk,' I say, trying to resolve it in my own mind, 'but I hope that you can also see I was trying to make good come out of something so awful – and not just an awful thing that happened to me, but is happening to other people every day.'

'That's something that you say, and I hear you saying, and I don't doubt that. But you have to understand from where I sit, it's an issue of security and also dealing with the personal ramifications of that event,' he says. 'I'm not a social justice journalist. I love the work that you do, and I love the way you fight for other people, but in this instance, I am first and foremost concerned about you and my family.'

'Are you happy for me to write the book or would you rather I left it alone?'

'Well, we've had many arguments since 2013. I've seen you become triumphant in the way you stand up to such difficult issues. Also, perhaps the book is a way for you to get some closure in this aspect of your life,' he says.

'I'm not scared in the way I was,' I say.

'And neither am I. Trolls are horrible monsters. That's how I choose to view them, especially where they incite people to harm themselves or where they cause direct harm to people. So while technology offers society great opportunities, in this instance, trolls are undermining these freedoms. I'd be lying if I said to you I wasn't anxious at all but I know it's important for you to write about this stuff. That's what I'm trying to say,' Don says.

I press the square 'stop' button. The conversation has driven us to the boundary and we have to leave it here now.

Conclusion:
Reaching back across
the cold water

WRITING THIS BOOK has been a long, hard journey. At times I wanted to give up because it seemed overwhelming and hopeless on both sides. The cyberhate targets were often speaking to me amid the debris of their ruined lives, with help a long way out of reach. The trolls were isolated, damaged and unrelenting in their anger and hatred.

The infinite potential of the internet to lift humanity up, educate us and connect us seemed like a pot of gold at the end of a fantastical and fading rainbow. A lie we'd been sold about utopia in the face of great harm. Social media companies routinely feed us lines such as '[W]e are working to build the social infrastructure that brings us closer together and builds a global community.'[1] These platitudes cease to have meaning because when it comes to cyberhate, tech platforms are rearranging the deck chairs on the *Titanic* while the ship sinks. And all the while these big players are altering democratic processes and reaping huge profits from our personal data.

More believable are Facebook CEO Mark Zuckerberg's messages to a friend in the early days of the platform. In response to his friend's query about why people were signing up in droves with all their personal information, Zuckerberg reportedly replied: 'I don't know why. They "trust me". Dumb fucks.'[2]

Yet despite the cynical disregard for the safety of internet users displayed by everyone from the public to tech companies and law enforcement, I somehow felt – and still feel – duty-bound to dig deeper. To cling to shreds of hope and salvage something from the wreckage.

Hearing one of the fathers of the internet, Vint Cerf, speak at the Australian National University in June 2018 helped me (and maybe it'll help you too). His address was an urgent reminder of the web's great promise, taking us back to the start, when hope was strong. Cerf spoke of how, nearly fifty years ago, he worked on an early packet-switching network called ARPANET – a technology that later became the foundation of the internet. (For tech nerds, he was also the co-designer of the TCP/IP protocols, which were crucial to the modern internet.) Then, in 1977 – before the internet as we know it today was operational – Cerf was part of a team that sent 'packets' of data over a computer network to Europe from the United States and back again for the first time.

'I remember leaping around saying, "It works, it works." Like it couldn't possibly work … [T]his was a very important demonstration of the technology of the time,' Cerf said, his eyes glinting and his voice just as shiny. 'Here we are, we have this wonderful platform, which enables that kind of collaboration and sharing of information like nothing we've ever seen before. We have computers helping us find information and interpret it and maybe massage it in ways that give us new insights. All these wonderful and positive things about this new environment.'

This moment reveals the vision those men had in connecting us all. I can't help wondering, is there a way to recapture that promise?

Looking at the horror contained in these pages, promise seems distant: shootings, suicide and suicide attempts, terrorism, a woman killed and many others injured at the Unite the Right rally, indecent communication with a child, stalking, domestic violence, PTSD, mental illness, hatred and anger, limitless misogyny and racism, anti-Semitism, Moody's dead horse and poisoned dog.

This is human darkness playing out online to its fullest potential. But then there are those moments of humanity. How the trolls helped Kylie when they didn't have to. How many of them helped me. How some of them, after talking to me over many months, seemed to hate women less.

This made me understand two things. First, the seeds of promise are still there. Second, this is a human problem, with a human solution.

Let me pull this apart a bit more by zooming out slightly. More and more frequently I'm interviewed in the media as a cyberhate expert. (In truth this moniker has taken me a while to become comfortable with, although strangely even some of the trolls accept this label.) Without fail, I leave those encounters with other journalists painfully aware of how complex the problem is – and how most of us are yet to understand the issue even on its most basic level. Unfailingly, reporters ask me: *Isn't social media to blame?* No, it isn't. The internet provides a platform – or a megaphone if you like – for the spread of ideas. Those ideas were already there in society before they ever went online. As the Pew Center report states: 'It is the people using the network, not the network, that is the root of the problem.'[3]

The toxic misogyny and hatred I've seen spreading online started with us, right here in our bedrooms and lounge rooms, our schools, supermarkets and boardrooms. It might fester online, but it was born offline. eSafety commissioner Julie Inman Grant sums it up this way: 'Social media does surface the reality of the human condition.' She goes on to say the ugliness we witness online 'obviously exists underneath the surface' and so 'we need to tackle some of these social issues, but also have higher standards for the kind of digital civility that we need to see online'.

That's exactly right. The #MeToo movement may have started it, but it's time for big, ongoing conversations about the values we hold as a community. Are we truly willing to tolerate extreme hatred, bigotry, polarisation and misogyny that leads to real-life violence? Or will we, like New Zealand Prime Minister Jacinda Ardern suggested at the United Nations General Assembly, barrack for kindness and tolerance and inclusiveness?[4] As so many great leaders have asked over the decades, will we judge ourselves not just by how the most privileged in the community are treated, but by how we treat those who are marginalised?

And if we did the latter, how would things change? At the start of 2017, company director Dr Kirstin Ferguson (now the Australian Broadcasting Corporation's acting chairwoman) found herself frustrated by the hatred and misogyny online and decided to do something about it. Her pledge was to celebrate 'two women from anywhere in the world and from all walks of life, every single day in 2017'. By year's end she'd 'celebrated 757 women from 37 countries around the world'.[5] Her #celebratingwomen posts were viewed by millions of people. The campaign lifted women up and, interestingly, attracted no trolling. Just like that, in a not-so-small way, she changed the conversation. Another example is the relatively new platform Kialo, which has been designed to promote thoughtful, non-abusive discussion and help users engage with alternative viewpoints. The jury is out as to whether it's working. Still, it was designed for civilised conversation right from the start, which is an improvement.

These examples point to something both the eSafety commissioner and Cerf have suggested, which we all instinctively know: social norms are important online. Trolling begets trolling.[6] In the same vein, social pressures and norms can work wonders when it comes to making people behave. This is why people generally don't swear, spit, fart loudly or abuse each other at weddings or funerals.

Despite working for Google and positioning himself as the internet's 'chief evangelist', Cerf still says his biggest disappointment is that people use the web for harm. One of his solutions – predictably – is a technical one. He calls it 'traceability by design'. 'I would like it to be the case that while people should be able to appear to be anonymous to most of the general public, it should be possible to find out who somebody is in the event that they're doing something harmful. This is not too different than the licence plates on your cars. For the most part we don't know who is attached to the licence plate,' Cerf explains, but in the event a crime is committed authorities would be able to track the culprit.

The issue of anonymity is raised over and over again as the big solution for online hatred. It is seen as a tool that allows trolls to attack others with impunity online. A logical solution might therefore be to remove anonymity. But this is simplistic and overlooks a glaring flaw in the argument. Anonymity can be helpful for some of the most vulnerable members of society who are seeking support. For example, young people who self-harm or have eating disorders or are LGBTIQ+ often seek out support groups online. Likewise, adults who have gambling or drug addictions, or find themselves in domestic violence situations. Are we really going to take these crucial support networks away by insisting people use their real identities?

Author and academic Dr Emma Jane suggests that giving up anonymity has advantages. She proposes that when people are creating new accounts, they should have to 'provide enough evidence of who they are as real, flesh-and-blood humans. These are the sorts of details that could then be used by authorities to track down offenders even if these offenders abandon their accounts after committing abuse'.

One of my bugbears in this discussion is the oft-repeated but untrue claim that the human-made and human-utilised internet is a 'neutral platform'. Cerf asserts this notion of neutrality too.[7] It's not neutral and shouldn't pretend to be. In supporting this, Dr Jane suggests technology needs 'an ethical upgrade'. '[E]thics should also be taught to engineering and design students: not merely as a soft subject or "politically correct" inconvenience, but as a way of "baking in" ethical functionality into software and platforms,' she says, neatly melding the human and the tech together and looping back to the idea of making things safe from the start.

As for legal solutions, legislation only takes us so far. It may be part of the solution – but not the whole solution. Case in point: in Australia we have a federal law that makes it illegal to menace or harass someone online; it's been around for more than ten years. While it's positive that victims have a means of legal redress, we can't honestly say this law is stopping people from engaging in sustained predator trolling. There are simply too many victims to make that claim.

Layering more legislation on top of existing laws isn't always the answer, especially when other facets of society remain the same. We may wish to hold perpetrators to account. But new legislation is unlikely to help when police responses are patchy. Given all the victims who have reported to me that they were unable to get sufficient help from police, this is a key part of the problem – and where we need to look for solutions too. Law enforcement must be willing to investigate and prosecute offenders. They must be trained and resourced to do this.

Now think back to Germany's strict law that requires social media companies to take down hate speech within twenty-four hours or face the possibility of a 50-million-euro fine. Some dubious critics, like Human Rights Watch, have said it leads to 'overbroad censorship' and privatises enforcement of the law.[8] Ultimately, there's a fine balancing act when it comes to legislating. Joe McNamee, executive director at European Digital Rights, concurs and takes the point a step further: 'This privatisation of regulation of free speech ... raises existential questions for the functioning of healthy democracies.'[9]

Those questions are complex and confronting. If we're so willing to put decisions about enforcement of free speech, the law and all our personal data into the hands of companies like Facebook and Twitter, can we really claim to be amazed when those companies influence democratic elections? Or won't hand over crucial information to police so they can progress criminal investigations? Or decide not to take down predator trolling that influences someone's decision to commit suicide because it 'doesn't violate our policies'?

The success of Australia's eSafety office suggests an independent statutory body, working with social media companies but simultaneously holding legal clout, may be a decent halfway point. (It was created by an act of Parliament – so this is partly a legal solution.) It doesn't create unnecessary and under-utilised laws. And it stops the balance of power constantly swinging away from individuals – and even away from police – and towards the powerful tech companies.

Sometimes we forget that in historical terms, the internet as we know it has only been around for the blink of an eye. Therefore, when it comes to cyberhate, as with many things, time may be the great healer. Before online discourse reaches total paralysis, innovators will inevitably come up with solutions – as they have already. In an attempt to discover how online discourse would be shaped by trolls over the next decade, and what a more civilised discourse might look like, the Pew Research Center canvassed 1537 tech experts in business, academia and government. The resulting report suggests that in the future, hate speech and trolling may simply be filtered out, much in the way spam is today.

Still, we need to be real about this too. As with new laws, this may create a new set of problems. A number of experts quoted in the document predict the online environment will splinter 'into segmented, controlled social zones with the help of artificial intelligence'.[10]

If this isn't the case already, will this then create an internet that is the opposite of what most of us would hope for? Imagine the internet as a place littered with walled-off communities where we're constantly surveilled and censored. In those communities, we're no longer exposed to diverse ideas. We change our sharing behaviours because of the atmosphere and restrictions therein.[11] How does freedom of expression look then?

The great irony will be that trolls – who as a cohort consistently defend their right to say absolutely anything to anyone – might be responsible for a global chilling of free speech online. (Arguably, this is happening already, especially when it comes to minorities.)

It's unlikely trolls and hackers, who already feel disenfranchised, will accept an increasingly restrictive online environment. And therefore, we'll likely see a continual and escalating arms race as they fight back against any perceived constraints.[12] From a trolling perspective, Meepsheep agrees with this take: 'Restrictions like that are always going to cause self-righteous groups like [hacker collective] Anonymous to fight back in whatever ways they come up with. Other people are going to find out how to bypass technological barriers, like how they've never actually been able to stop online piracy.'

There are signs things are changing. Back when I was first trolled in 2013 it was almost as if Australia hadn't yet woken up to the harm that could be caused online. At the time a local policeman told me to 'Stay off the internet, love'. One of my then bosses told me to stop carrying on and speaking out about cyberhate, in case people viewed me as a 'victim'.[13]

Five years later, the landscape – and the public conversation – is rapidly shifting. Increasingly people are aware that being online isn't a choice. It's a necessity for living, working and staying connected to those we love. Of the 7.5 billion people on this planet, approximately 3.6 billion are currently connected to the internet. Within the next decade, there will be a billion more people online.[14]

We know that approximately four in ten Americans (41 per cent) have experienced at least one type of online abuse.[15] The national polling done by the Australia Institute shows an extremely similar pattern here in Australia, with more than one third of us (39 per cent) having experienced harassment via the internet. Cyberhate is something that affects all of us. If we haven't been abused online ourselves, someone we know has. And they are suffering because of it.

For many years, cyberhate has been a sleeping giant. As a community we've been unwilling to examine the scope and depth of predator trolling and its catastrophic and expensive impacts. In the name of innovation, the tech companies have been allowed to ignore the harm they're doing on multiple fronts. Perhaps the giant is waking. As US Senator Ron Wyden said recently, the platforms had better take action otherwise it'll be out of their hands.[16] We may well see, as Josh Bornstein has proposed, the breaking up of those monopolies and/or a legislated duty of care.

In some ways, the social media companies have preferred to fade into the background at this point, conveniently claiming they are not publishers. Inconveniently, this is not the case. Social media companies must stop bleating about taking online harassment seriously – which they've been doing for more than a decade now – and implement decisive and large-scale change to protect their users. Our trust is fast eroding. Stop giving us platitudes and *show us* that we're safe in the spaces you've created.

As Julie Inman Grant suggests, this is a critical point in time, when we've reached a 'tipping point' of public anger and 'our expectations are for our technology leaders to do better'. The Pew Research Center report echoes this sentiment and also posits we've reached 'peak troll'.[17] Victims are getting tired and angry and our voices are getting louder. Just a few days ago, I contacted domestic violence survivor Eva to fact-check something in her story. I apologised for the endless questions and for making her relive her harrowing predator-trolling story. She replied, 'At least someone is finally listening.'

She's right. It's taken a long time, but people are starting to listen. Not just the public, but the media too. Editors are more willing to publish stories about predator trolling and its resultant carnage. Thankfully, that news coverage is increasing in frequency and complexity. (Although as I've written in opinion pieces, it often focuses on the harm done to children, while completely ignoring adult victims – something I'd like to change.)

We know trolls love to claim the cost of cyberhate is just 'hurt feelings'. Words on the internet can't harm anyone, they say. Stop being a snowflake. We only have to remember all the people who have died to know this isn't true. Predator trolls are wrecking people's lives. Thanks to the Australia Institute, cyberhate now has a dollar figure attached to it. Australia alone is somewhere between $330 million and $3.7 billion poorer because of predator trolling and online harassment.

One of the most profound – and easy to understand – answers to the question of how we tackle cyberhate comes from Nigel Phair, director of the Centre for Internet Safety at the University of Canberra. He draws an analogy to the way the community has reduced trauma on the roads – through safer car and road design, better law enforcement and changing social norms around damaging behaviours, such as speeding and drink driving. 'In terms of cyberhate, the whole ecosystem needs to respond via technical and non-technical means,' he says.[18]

#

As I set down these final paragraphs, I'm in shreds – as a person and a writer. I never dreamed writing this book would be so harrowing or dark. If I knew what was coming, perhaps I would have done more self-care in these last months. Been kinder to myself. Hidden the red wine. Not shouted at my kids or cried as much. In many ways, I've learned the most about trolling (and about myself) from the trolls themselves. Yet my strange and enduring relationships with some of them have come at a great cost. At times that price was my own mental health.

Meepsheep knows I drink wine. Right before the book's first draft was due, he was ribbing me about it being 'feminine'. He admitted to trying to piss me off. I told him not to – especially not right now. I said, 'The same thing that makes me good to talk to also makes me easy to hurt.'

As the book deadline bore down on me, I asked him to stop talking to me for a week. 'I hope you understand,' I wrote. 'I have to get the book finished before it finishes me.' It was a kind of troll joke. But one of the ones we'd usually tag with #jokingnotjoking.

At other points on this road, it was my journalistic objectivity that was forsaken. In return, I gained insights into the trolls' lives that could come no other way. I owe a debt of gratitude to Meepsheep. After building up trust over many months, he was willing to take me to what lay beyond the seemingly endless quest for 'lulz'.

'You're after that [lulz] because everything else in your life sucks,' he told me. 'Realistically a lot of these people [trolls] are suffering in some way and this is how they cope.'

This brings us back to something clinical psychologist Dr Williams said, which struck me as a kind of revelation. He suggested trolls didn't fall out of the sky. They weren't born trolls; they became trolls.

'If the flowers are growing a certain way, what's happening in the soil?' he asked. He urged me to think harder and look harder. The soil in this case seems to be dysfunctional parenting and the increasingly isolating and fractured mess of society. As minors aged somewhere between eleven and sixteen, a number of the trolls explained they were left alone online for years, imbibing vile and extreme content with no supervision. People didn't parent them. They had little to no human guidance. Instead, the internet parented them – badly.

Inman Grant agrees it's crucial for adults to be involved in the digital lives of their children. 'Parents have to be educated about what their kids are doing online, who they're talking to, what they're doing. They have to start the conversations early and often. They have to let kids know that they're going to be engaged in their online lives the way they are in their everyday lives. There's just no getting around that,' she says.

When society discusses online bullying, we talk about how parents need to know what their kids are doing online. We're aiming this point at the bullying victims, but it also applies to the trolls.

Beyond being a journalist, I'm a mother. Every day I help my own children understand the world around them. I talk to them about understanding social cues and helping other people. About being smart and strong and trying to leave society better than you found it. About being kind and fair, even when others are unfair.

I know with my heart more than my head that we can't leave kids alone in echo chambers of online hate and then wonder why they emerge as socially isolated individuals full of rage. Why they believe the world is an inhospitable place. Why they want to hurt, isolate, damage and enrage other people – and laugh at them – the way that they've been hurt.

It's time to reach our hands back across the cold water – not just to predator-trolling victims, but to the perpetrators themselves. Because we all live in the society that made them.

Endnotes

Preface

1 Levenson, E and Diaz-Zuniga, L. 'New Mexico High School Shooter was Investigated by FBI in 2016.' *CNN*, December 9, 2017. http://edition.cnn.com/2017/12/08/us/aztec-high-school-shooting-william-atchison/index.html

2 'Kiwi Farms User Shoots Up School and Then Kills Himself.' December 12, 2017. https://kiwifarms.net/threads/kiwi-farms-user-shoots-up-school-and-then-kills-himself.37291/

3 'Full News Conference: Gunman Identified in Aztec School Shooting.' *KRQE*, December 8, 2017. https://www.krqe.com/news/aztec-high-school-gunman-identified-in-newsconference_20180305061832855/1009308950

4 Know Your Meme. 'An Hero.' https://knowyourmeme.com/memes/an-hero

PART 1: Trolls

Material used in the writing of this section was originally cited in my TEDxCanberra talk: https://www.youtube.com/watch?v=GaGIyyYW5tQ
Other parts of this text first appeared in an article I wrote for the ABC called 'A Journalist's second thoughts', http://www.abc.net.au/news/2013-07-10/gorman-second-thoughts/4809582.

1. The paedophiles, the trolls and the journalist

1 Queensland Association for Healthy Communities. 'Improving the Lives of LGBT Queenslanders: A Call to Action.' https://communitydoor.org.au/sites/default/files/Improving%20the%20Lives%20of%20LGBT%20Queenslanders.pdf

2 Ralston, N. 'Named: The Australian Paedophile Jailed for 40 Years.' *Sydney Morning Herald*, June 30, 2013. http://www.smh.com.au/national/named-the-australian-paedophile-jailed-for-40-years-20130630-2p5da.html

3 Despite spending many hours trying to find this tweet again, I've been unable to locate it. I requested from Twitter all tweets sent to my former handle @freshchilli within a two-month time period from 15 June 2013 until 15 August 2013 but was told 'no one on the team had a way to service this request'.

2. WTF is trolling?

1 Schwartz, M. 'The Trolls Among Us.' *The New York Times Magazine*, August 3, 2008. http://www.nytimes.com/2008/08/03/magazine/03trolls-t.html? pagewanted=all

2 Encyclopedia Dramatica. 'Socrates.' https://encyclopediadramatica.rs/Socrates

3 English Oxford Living Dictionaries. 'Troll.' https://en.oxforddictionaries.com/ definition/troll

4 Phillips, W. *This Is Why We Can't Have Nice Things: Mapping the Relationship between Online Trolling and Mainstream Culture.* Cambridge, Massachusetts: The MIT Press, 2015, 15.

5 Wikipedia. 'Internet Troll.' https://en.wikipedia.org/wiki/Internet_troll

6 Devine, M. 'MAFS: Sean and Jo Recap: This is TV at its Cruellest and Most Excruciating.' *The Daily Telegraph*, February 3, 2018. https://www. dailytelegraph.com.au/rendezview/this-is-tv-at-its-cruellest-and-most-excruciating/news-story/27300367266f1e629bb9cc136a321684

7 Maley, J. 'It's Starting to Feel Like Women are Being Trolled.' *The Sydney Morning Herald*, October 28, 2016. http://www.smh.com.au/comment/its-starting-to-feel-like-women-are-beingtrolled-20161028-gsctb4.html

8 Cassidy, J. 'Donald Trump Will Go Down in History as the Troll-in-Chief.' *The New Yorker*, June 29, 2017. https://www.newyorker.com/news/john-cassidy/ donald-trump-will-go-down-in-history-as-the-troll-in-chief

9 Schwartz, M. 'The Trolls Among Us.' *The New York Times Magazine*, August 3, 2008. http://www.nytimes.com/2008/08/03/magazine/03trolls-t.html? pagewanted=all

10 Quinn, Z. *Crash Override: How Gamergate (Nearly) Destroyed My Life, and How We Can Win the Fight Against Online Hate.* New York: PublicAffairs, 2017, 48.

11 Citron, D. *Hate Crimes in Cyberspace.* Cambridge, Massachusetts: Harvard University Press, 2014, 19.

12 Jane, E. 'Gendered Cyberhate as Workplace Harassment and Economic Vandalism.' *Feminist Media Studies* 18, 4 (2018). doi: 10.1080/14680777.2018. 1447344.

3. Meet the trolls

Parts of this section originally appeared in Fairfax newspapers: http://www.smh. com.au/lifestyle/news-and-views/news-features/staring-down-internet-trolls-my-disturbing-cat-and-mouse-game-20170616-gwsmld.html Permission has been given by Fairfax to use this text.

1 Grinberg, E. 'Shooting Death in Video Game Leads to a Real One in Kansas.' *CNN*, January 31, 2018. https://edition.cnn.com/2018/01/30/us/kansas-swatting-death-affidavit/index.html

2 Gorman, G. 'Interview with the trolls: "We Go After Women Because They Are Easier to Hurt."' News.com.au, February 27, 2015. https://www.news.com. au/technology/online/social/interviews-with-the-trolls-we-go-after-women-because-they-are-easier-to-hurt/news-story/c02bb2a5f8d7247d3fdd9aabe0f 3ad26

3 Sest, N and March, E. 'Constructing the Cyber-troll: Psychopathy, Sadism, and Empathy.' *Personality and Individual Differences* 119, (2017): 69-72. https://www.sciencedirect.com/science/article/pii/S0191886917304270

4 Kessler, G, Rizzo, S and Kelly, M. 'President Trump has Made 3,001 False or Misleading Claims So Far.' *The Washington Post*, May 1, 2018. https://www.washingtonpost.com/news/fact-checker/wp/2018/05/01/president-trump-has-made-3001-false-or-misleading-claims-so-far/?utm_term=.7adc068e6123

5 Gorman, G. 'Interview with the trolls: "We Go After Women Because They Are Easier to Hurt."' News.com.au, February 27, 2015. https://www.news.com.au/technology/online/social/interviews-with-the-trolls-we-go-after-women-because-they-are-easier-to-hurt/news-story/c02bb2a5f8d7247d3fdd9aabe0f3ad26

6 Mayo Clinic. 'Narcissistic Personality Disorder.' https://www.mayoclinic.org/diseases-conditions/narcissistic-personalitydisorder/symptoms-causes/syc-20366662

7 Buckels, E, Paulhus, D and Trapnell, P. 'Trolls Just Want to Have Fun.' *Personality and Individual* Differences 67, (2014): 97-102. www.researchgate.net/publication/260105036_Trolls_just_want_to_have_fun

8 Gorman, G. 'Interview with the trolls: "We Go After Women Because They Are Easier to Hurt."' News.com.au, February 27, 2015. https://www.news.com.au/technology/online/social/interviews-with-the-trolls-we-go-after-women-because-they-are-easier-to-hurt/news-story/c02bb2a5f8d7247d3fdd9aabe0f3ad26

9 Know Your Meme. '/b/.' http://knowyourmeme.com/memes/sites/b

10 Rainie, L, Anderson, J and Albright, J. 'The Future of Free Speech, Trolls, Anonymity and Fake News Online.' Pew Research Center Internet & Technology, March 29, 2017. http://www.pewinternet.org/2017/03/29/the-future-of-free-speech-trolls-anonymity-and-fake-news-online/

11 'Senate Poses Tough Hurdle for Internet Filtering Plan.' *ABC News*, February 27, 2009. http://www.abc.net.au/news/2009-02-27/senate-poses-tough-hurdle-forinternet-filtering/1603944

4. When the flowers grow funny
Parts of this section originally appeared in Fairfax newspapers: http://www.smh.com.au/lifestyle/news-and-views/news-features/staring-down-internet-trolls-my-disturbing-cat-and-mouse-game-20170616-gwsmld.html
Permission has been given by Fairfax to use this text.

1 Commonwealth Numbered Acts. CRIMES LEGISLATION AMENDMENT (TELECOMMUNICATIONS OFFENCES AND OTHER MEASURES) ACT (NO. 2) 2004 NO. 127, 2004 - SCHEDULE 1 - Telecommunications offences. http://www8.austlii.edu.au/cgi-bin/viewdoc/au/legis/cth/num_act/claoaoma22004729/sch1.html

2 Wikipedia. 'Psychopathy Checklist.' https://en.wikipedia.org/wiki/Psychopathy_Checklist

5. You are literally the enemy

1 McCain, R. 'Neutral Objective Incompetence: How Ginger Gorham Aided Pedophile Network.' *The Other McCain* blog, July 2, 2013. http://theothermccain.com/2013/07/02/neutral-objective-incompetence-how-ginger-gorham-aided-pedophile-network/

2 'Interview with RS McCain of The Other McCain.' *Jumping in Pools* blog, March 29, 2010. https://jumpinginpools.blogspot.com/2010/03/interview-with-rs-mccain-of-other.html

3 McCain, R. 'Unintentional Hilarity: Feminists Ask If Julian Assange Commited "Rape-Rape".' *The Other McCain* blog, December 6, 2010. http://theothermccain.com/2010/12/06/unintentional-hilarity-feminists-ask-if-julian-assange-committed-rape-rape/

4 McCain, R. 'Equality Über Alles.' *The Other McCain* blog, August 5, 2010. http://theothermccain.com/2010/08/05/equality-uber-alles/

5 Southern Poverty Law Center. 'Hatewatch: The League of the South's Michael Hill is Having a Bad Year.' January 20, 2017. https://www.splcenter.org/hatewatch/2017/01/20/league-souths-michael-hill-having-bad-year

6 Graham, B. 'Far-right Nationalist Blair Cottrell Copping it over Rape Tweet to Sky News Reporter.' News.com.au, August 7, 2018. https://www.news.com.au/technology/online/social/farright-nationalist-blair-cottrell-copping-it-over-rape-tweet-to-sky-news-reporter/news-story/58d98064aa1d3dc242934f0ed49e2a05

7 Harrington, E. 'Before Shooting: Southern Poverty Law Center Put Family Research Council on "Hate Map".' *CNSNews.com*, August 16, 2012. https://www.cnsnews.com/news/article/shooting-southern-poverty-law-center-put-family-research-council-hate-map

8 Stack, L. 'Attack on Alt-Right Leader has Internet Asking: Is it O.K. to Punch a Nazi?' *The New York Times*, January 21, 2017. https://www.nytimes.com/2017/01/21/us/politics/richard-spencer-punched-attack.html?_r=0

9 Southern Poverty Law Center. 'Richard Bertrand Spencer.' https://www.splcenter.org/fighting-hate/extremist-files/individual/richard-bertrand-spencer-0

Notes in the margins: What the fuck did you expect?

1 White, A. 'Ethical Ground Rules for Handling Sources.' Ethical Journalism Network, https://ethicaljournalismnetwork.org/resources/publications/ethics-in-thenews/handling-sources

2 Wahl-Jorgensen, K, Berry, M, Garcia-Blanco, I, Bennett, L and Cable, J. 'Rethinking Balance and Impartiality in Journalism? How the BBC Attempted and Failed to Change the Paradigm.' *Journalism*, 18, 7 (2017): 781-800. https://www.ncbi.nlm.nih.gov/pmc/articles/PMC5732589/

3 Edsall, T. 'One Thing Donald Trump Would Like is Freedom from the Press.' *The New York Times*, March 15, 2018. https://www.nytimes.com/2018/03/15/opinion/trump-press-freedom-fake-news.html

4 Phillips, W. *This Is Why We Can't Have Nice Things: Mapping the Relationship between Online Trolling and Mainstream Culture.* Cambridge, Massachusetts: The MIT Press, 2015, 29, 33, 35.

PART TWO: Targets

6. She was asking for it

1 Rees, A. 'Twitter Bullies Reportedly Drove Australia's Next Top Model Judge Charlotte Dawson to Attempt Suicide.' *The Cut*, August 31, 2012. https://www.thecut.com/2012/08/top-model-judge-reportedly-attempted-suicide.html

2 Staff writers. 'Charlotte Dawson: How the Cyber Trolls Beat Me.' News.com.au, September 3, 2012, https://www.news.com.au/entertainment/tv/charlotte-dawson-how-the-cyber-trolls-beat-me/news-story/b577db26528d01006ba6f238a6d482e3

3 'Charlotte Dawson Speaks Out.' YouTube Video, 3:22, posted by 'Sunriseon7,' September 2012. https://www.youtube.com/watch?v=nrwnBGsyX8o

4 Webb, S. 'Trolled to Death: Model Charlotte Dawson Bombarded with Vile Messages over Twitter.' *Daily Mail Australia*, 23 February 2014. http://www.dailymail.co.uk/tvshowbiz/article-2565903/Trolled-death-Model-Charlotte-Dawson-bombarded-vile-messages-Twitter-just-hours-death.html

5 Dawson, C and Thornely, J. *Air Kiss and Tell.* Australia: Allen & Unwin, 2012.

6 These quotes originally used in this article of mine: Gorman, G. 'How We Can Avoid Another Tragedy like Dolly.' News.com.au, May 3, 2018. http://www.news.com.au/lifestyle/real-life/news-life/how-we-can-avoid-another-tragedy-like-dolly/news-story/2b899e73b32a228c117457c4b7ec2ffb

7 Caffier, J. 'Every Insult the Right Uses to Troll Liberals Explained.' Vice, February 7, 2017. https://www.vice.com/en_au/article/mg9pvx/every-insult-the-right-uses-to-troll-liberals-explained

8 Swann, T. 'Polling – Online Harassment and Cyberhate.' The Australia Institute, April 2018. http://www.tai.org.au/content/polling-online-harassment-and-cyberhate

9 Swann, T. 'Polling – Online harassment and cyberhate.' The Australia Institute, April 2018. http://www.tai.org.au/content/polling-online-harassment-and-cyberhate

10 Duggan, M. *Online Harassment 2017.* Pew Research Center, July 2017, 14. http://assets.pewresearch.org/wp-content/uploads/sites/14/2017/07/10151519/PI_2017.07.11_Online-Harassment_FINAL.pdf

11 Duggan, M. 'Part 1: Experiencing Online Harassment.' Pew Research Center Internet & Technology, October 22, 2014. http://www.pewinternet.org/2014/10/22/part-1-experiencing-online-harassment/

12 Gorman, G. '"There is Nowhere for Us to Go": Domestic Violence Happens to Men Too.' News.com.au, June 13, 2016. https://www.news.com.au/lifestyle/real-life/news-life/there-is-nowhere-for-us-to-go-domestic-violence-happens-to-men-too/news-story/d736e990f7528ade77ef3ba69e99f53e

13 Badham, V (@vanbadham). 'I reject the Right's criticism of me on #Contrarians that I "need a good root". I just want all my roots to know: you were totally great,' Twitter, posted on March 8, 2013, 1:16 a.m., https://twitter.com/vanbadham/status/309955887706013696

14 Jane, E. 'Gendered Cyberhate as Workplace Harassment and Economic Vandalism.' *Feminist Media Studies* 18, 4 (2018): 2. doi: 10.1080/14680777.2018.1447344, 2.

15 Jane, E. *Misogyny Online: A Short (and Brutish) History.* London: SAGE Publications, 2017, 56.

16 Jane, E. 'Gendered Cyberhate as Workplace Harassment and Economic Vandalism.' *Feminist Media Studies* 18, 4 (2018): 12. doi: 10.1080/14680777.2018.1447344, 12.

17 Jane, E. *Misogyny Online: A Short (and Brutish) History.* London: SAGE Publications, 2017, 4, 63.

18 Amnesty International. 'Chapter 3 – Women's Experiences of Violence and Abuse on Twitter' in *Toxic Twitter – Women's Experiences of Violence and Abuse on Twitter.* https://www.amnesty.org/en/latest/research/2018/03/online-violence-against-women-chapter-3/#topanchor

19 United Nations Human Rights Office of the High Commissioner. 'UN Experts Call on India to Protect Journallist Rana Ayyub from Online Hate Campaign.' 24 May 2018. https://www.ohchr.org/en/NewsEvents/Pages/DisplayNews.aspx?NewsID=23126&LangID=E

20 O'Grady, S. 'An Indian Journalist has Been Trolled for Years. Now U.N. Experts Say Her Life Could be at Risk.' *The Washington Post*, May 26, 2018. https://www.washingtonpost.com/news/worldviews/wp/2018/05/26/an-indian-journalist-has-been-trolled-for-years-now-u-n-experts-say-her-life-could-be-at-risk/?utm_term=.76d26149e2b8

21 Patchin, J. 'Digital Self-Harm: The Hidden Side of Adolescent Online Aggression.' Cyberbullying Research Center, October 3, 2017. https://cyberbullying.org/digital-self-harm

22 Edwards, J. 'Users on This Web Site Have Successfully Hounded Nine Teenagers to Kill Themselves.' *Business Insider Australia*, September 17, 2013. https://www.businessinsider.com.au/askfm-and-teen-suicides-2013-9?r=US&IR=T

23 Patchin, J and Hinduja, S. 'Digital Self-Harm Among Adolescents.' *Journal of Adolescent Health* 61, 6 (2017). https://www.sciencedirect.com/science/article/pii/S1054139X17303130

24 Patchin, J and Hinduja, S. 'Digital Self-Harm Among Adolescents.' *Journal of Adolescent Health* 61, 6 (2017). https://www.sciencedirect.com/science/article/pii/S1054139X17303130

25 Davies, C. 'Hannah Smith Wrote 'Vile' Posts to Herself Before Suicide, Say Police.' *The Guardian*, May 7, 2014.https://www.theguardian.com/uk-news/2014/may/06/hannah-smith-suicide-teenager-cyber-bullying-inquests

26 Patchin, J. 'Digital Self-Harm: The Hidden Side of Adolescent Online Aggression.' Cyberbullying Research Center, October 3, 2017. https://cyberbullying.org/digital-self-harm

27 Gorman, G. 'The Confronting Truth We Need to Face Up To.' News.com.au, July 24, 2016. https://www.news.com.au/lifestyle/health/mind/the-confronting-truth-we-need-to-face-up-to/news-story/90c3282d025c37fabe020a52ba5026d3

28 Patchin, J and Hinduja, S. 'Digital Self-Harm Among Adolescents.' *Journal of Adolescent Health* 61, 6 (2017). https://www.sciencedirect.com/science/article/pii/S1054139X17303130

7. Misogyny on the internet

1 Bachelard, M. 'Blair Cottrell, Rising Anti-Islam Movement Leader, Wanted Hitler in the Classroom.' *The Sydney Morning Herald*, October 17, 2015. https://www.smh.com.au/national/blair-cottrell-leader-of-aussie-patriots-upf-wanted-hitler-in-the-classroom-20151016-gkbbvz.html

2 Gorman, G (@GingerGorman). 'Why lots of women won't go on TV #cyberhate #trolling @bairdjulia,' Twitter, August 8, 2018, 1:39 p.m., https://twitter.com/GingerGorman/status/1027293209469190144

3 Morrison, P. 'Privilege Makes Them Do It – What a Study of Internet Trolls Reveals.' *Los Angeles Times*, July 1, 2015. http://www.latimes.com/opinion/op-ed/la-oe-morrison-phillips-20150701-column.html

4 ABC The Drum (@ABCthedrum). '"It's just dangerous for me to be on @Twitter." Shen Narayanasamy says the lack of civility on Twitter and other social networks is silencing women and people of colour. Georgina Dent worries about the amount of hatred #TheDrum,' Twitter, July 12, 2018, 2:56 a.m., https://twitter.com/ABCthedrum/status/1017347075896311808

5 Reyns, BW. 'Being Pursued Online: Extent and Nature of Cyberstalking Victimization from a Lifestyle/Routine Activities Perspective,' PhD, University of Cincinnati, 2010, 96-97.

6 Penny, L. 'Who Does She Think She Is?' Longreads, March 2018. https://longreads.com/2018/03/28/who-does-she-think-she-is/

7 Amnesty International. 'Online Abuse of Women Thrives as Twitter Fails to Respect Women's Rights.' https://www.amnesty.org/en/latest/news/2018/03/toxic-twitter-online-abuse-and-violence-against-women/

8 UN Women. 'Urgent Action Needed to Combat Online Violence Against Women and Girls, Says New UN Report.' September 24, 2015. http://www.unwomen.org/en/news/stories/2015/9/cyber-violence-report-press-release

9 Amnesty International. 'Online Abuse of Women Thrives as Twitter Fails to Respect Women's Rights.' https://www.amnesty.org/en/latest/news/2018/03/toxic-twitter-online-abuse-and-violence-against-women/

10 Demos. 'Demos: Male Celebrities Receive More Abuse on Twitter than Women.' August 24, 2014. https://www.demos.co.uk/press-release/demos-male-celebrities-receive-more-abuse-on-twitter-than-women-2/

11 Amnesty International. 'Chapter 2 – Triggers of Violence and Abuse Against Women on Twitter' in *Toxic Twitter – Women's Experiences of Violence and Abuse on Twitter.* https://www.amnesty.org/en/latest/research/2018/03/online-violence-against-women-chapter-2/#topanchor

12 The Senate Legal and Constitutional Affairs References Committee. *Adequacy of Existing Offences in the Commonwealth Criminal Code and of State and Territory Criminal Laws to Capture Cyberbullying.* March 2018, 33.

13 Association for Progressive Communications (APC) and Humanist Institute for Cooperation and Developing Countries (HiVOS). *Global Information Society Watch 2013: Women's Rights, Gender and ICTs.* https://www.giswatch. org/sites/default/files/violence_gisw13.pdf

14 Facebook. *Submission to The Senate Legal and Constitutional Affairs Committee: Inquiry into the Adequacy of Existing Offences in the Commonwealth Criminal Code and of State and Territory Criminal Laws to Capture Cyberbullying.* October 18, 2017, 2. https://www.aph.gov.au/Parliamentary_Business/ Committees/Senate/Legal_and_Constitutional_Affairs/Cyberbullying/ Submissions

15 Facebook. 'Community Standards: Bullying.' https://www.facebook.com/ communitystandards/bullying

16 Facebook. 'Community Standards.' https://www.facebook.com/ communitystandards/

17 Davis, A. 'Protecting People from Bullying and Harassment.' Facebook Newsroom, October 2, 2018. https://newsroom.fb.com/news/2018/10/ protecting-people-from-bullying/

18 Moody, S. 'Why I Started the Red Heart Campaign.' Medium, December 7, 2017. https://medium.com/the-walkley-magazine/why-i-started-the-red-heartcampaign-ba798daaf091

19 Hayden, ME. 'Neo-Nazi Charged with Domestic Violence Highlights Mistreatment of Women in the Alt-Right, Analysts Say.' *Newsweek*, March 15, 2018. http://www.newsweek.com/neo-nazi-domestic-violence-women-alt-right-845764
    Eltagouri, M and Selk, A. ' How a White Nationalist's Family Came to Blows over a Trailer Tryst.' *The Washington Post*, March 14, 2018. https://www. washingtonpost.com/news/post-nation/wp/2018/03/13/white-nationalist-leader-matthew-heimbach-arrested-for-domestic-battery/?utm_term= .2ebf4fc04164

20 '2018 JG Crawford Oration: Vinton G. Cerf, The Future of the Internet.' YouTube Video, 46:50. Posted by 'ANU TV,' June 2018. https://www. youtube.com/watch?v=huUDdOpeYe8 and https://www.youtube.com/ watch?v=GtJP8RKEVU8

8. Deep in the grey

1 Pederson, T. 'Regression.' https://psychcentral.com/encyclopedia/regression/

9. Your demons are omnipresent

1 Jane, E. 'Gendered Cyberhate as Workplace Harassment and Economic Vandalism.' *Feminist Media Studies* 18, 4 (2018): 5. doi: 10.1080/14680777. 2018.1447344.

2 Jane, E. 'Gendered Cyberhate as Workplace Harassment and Economic Vandalism.' *Feminist Media Studies* 18, 4 (2018). doi: 10.1080/14680777.2018. 1447344.

3 Women's Legal Service NSW, Domestic Violence Resource Centre Victoria and WESNET. *ReCharge: Women's Technology Safety, Legal Resources, Research & Training.* 2015. http://www.smartsafe.org.au/sites/default/files/ReCharge-Womens-Technology-Safety-Report-2015.pdf

4 National Network to End Domestic Violence (NNEDV). 'Recognizing and Combating Technology-Facilitated Abuse.' October 13, 2016. https://nnedv. org/latest_update/combating-technology-facilitated-abuse/

5 Quinn, Z. *Crash Override: How Gamergate (Nearly) Destroyed My Life, and How We Can Win the Fight Against Online Hate.* New York: PublicAffairs, 2017, 69.

6 Women's Legal Service NSW, Domestic Violence Resource Centre Victoria and WESNET. *ReCharge: Women's Technology Safety, Legal Resources, Research & Training.* 2015, 11. http://www.smartsafe.org.au/sites/default/files/National-study-findings-2015.pdf

7 Women's Legal Service NSW, Domestic Violence Resource Centre Victoria and WESNET. *ReCharge: Women's Technology Safety, Legal Resources, Research & Training.* 2015, 4. http://www.smartsafe.org.au/sites/default/files/National-study-findings-2015.pdf

8 Davis, A. 'Protecting People from Bullying and Harassment.' Facebook Newsroom, October 2, 2018. https://newsroom.fb.com/news/2018/10/protecting-people-from-bullying/

9 Instagram. 'How Do I Filter Out Comments I Don't Want to Appear on My Posts?' https://help.instagram.com/700284123459336

10 Northern Territory Police Force. *Submission to The Senate Legal and Constitutional Affairs Committee: Inquiry into the Adequacy of Existing Offences in the Commonwealth Criminal Code and of State and Territory Criminal Laws to Capture Cyberbullying.* https://www.aph.gov.au/Parliamentary_Business/Committees/Senate/Legal_and_Constitutional_Affairs/Cyberbullying/Submissions

11 Al-Alosi, H. 'Technology-Facilitated Abuse: The New Breed of Domestic Violence.' The Conversation, March 27, 2017. https://theconversation.com/technology-facilitated-abuse-the-new-breed-of-domestic-violence-74683

12 La Rue, F. *Report of the Special Rapporteur on the Promotion and Protection of the Right to Freedom and Expression.* 17 April 2013. http://www2.ohchr.org/english/bodies/hrcouncil/docs/17session/A.HRC.17.27_en.pdf

13 Women's Legal Service NSW, Domestic Violence Resource Centre Victoria and WESNET. *ReCharge: Women's Technology Safety, Legal Resources, Research & Training.* 2015, 15. http://www.smartsafe.org.au/sites/default/files/National-study-findings-2015.pdf
Al-Alosi, H. 'Technology-Facilitated Abuse: The New Breed of Domestic Violence.' The Conversation, March 27, 2017. https://theconversation.com/technology-facilitated-abuse-the-new-breed-of-domestic-violence-74683

14 NSW Domestic Violence Death Review Team. *Annual Report 2013-2015*. 2015. http://www.coroners.justice.nsw.gov.au/Documents/DVDRT_2015_Final_30102015.pdf

10. Not much cop

1 Gorman, G. 'Staring Down the Trolls: How Cyberhate Spills Over into Real Life Harassment.' *The Sydney Morning Herald*, 17 June 2017. https://www.smh.com.au/lifestyle/staring-down-the-trolls-how-it-spills-over-into-real-life-harassment-20170616-gwsj8u.html

2 Citron, D. *Hate Crimes in Cyberspace*. Cambridge, Massachusetts: Harvard University Press, 2014, 21.

3 Duggan, M. *Online Harassment 2017*. Pew Research Center, July 2017, 6. http://assets.pewresearch.org/wp-content/uploads/sites/14/2017/07/10151519/PI_2017.07.11_Online-Harassment_FINAL.pdf

4 Sandoval, G. 'The End of Kindness: Weev and the Cult of The Angry Young Man.' The Verge, September 12, 2013. https://www.theverge.com/2013/9/12/4693710/the-end-of-kindness-weev-and-the-cult-of-the-angry-young-man

5 Quinn, Z. *Crash Override: How Gamergate (Nearly) Destroyed My Life, and How We Can Win the Fight Against Online Hate*. New York: PublicAffairs, 2017, 160–161.

6 Cheshire Police. 'Police Issue Social Media Warning.' August 26, 2016 https://www.cheshire.police.uk/news-and-appeals/news/police-issue-social-media-warning/

7 'Charlotte Dawson Speaks Out.' YouTube Video, 3:22, posted by 'Sunriseon7,' September 2012. https://www.youtube.com/watch?v=nrwnBGsyX8o

8 Jane, E. 'Gendered Cyberhate as Workplace Harassment and Economic Vandalism.' *Feminist Media Studies* 18, 4 (2018): 7,9,10. doi: 10.1080/14680777.2018.1447344.

9 Kontominas, B. 'Online Trolls and Cyberbullies in NSW Face Up To Five Years in Jail Under Law Change.' *ABC News*, October 7, 2018. https://mobile.abc.net.au/news/2018-10-07/online-trolls-and-cyberbullies-in-nsw-face-tougher-new-laws/10348246?pfmredir=sm

10 Olding, R. 'Online Abuse: "It's So Common It's Almost Banal".' *The Sydney Morning Herald*, June 25, 2016. https://www.smh.com.au/national/nsw/online-abuse--its-so-common-its-almost-banal-20160623-gpqhdk.html

11 The Senate Legal and Constitutional Affairs References Committee. *Adequacy of Existing Offences in the Commonwealth Criminal Code and of State and Territory Criminal Laws to Capture Cyberbullying*. March 2018, 38.

12 Gorman, G. 'How We Can Avoid Another Tragedy like Dolly.' News.com.au, May 3, 2018. http://www.news.com.au/lifestyle/real-life/news-life/how-we-can-avoid-another-tragedy-like-dolly/news-story/2b899e73b32a228c117457c4b7ec2ffb

13 NSW Police classified my questions as a commercial request, and sought to charge me $155.90 an hour, for a minimum of three hours. Paying police for answers is not something I have encountered in nearly two decades of journalism. I agreed to pay despite ethical misgivings but at this point, NSW

Police claimed that they couldn't give me the information at all. I was told I could apply for it under the Government Information (Public Access) Act 2009. My aim in putting my questions to NSW Police was to give police a fair chance to comment on allegations made against them and to gain information about what taxpayer-funded officials are doing about cyberhate on the public's behalf. Those efforts were met with extreme amounts of red tape.

14 Citron, D. *Hate Crimes in Cyberspace.* Cambridge, Massachusetts: Harvard University Press, 2014, 73–78.

15 Women's Legal Service NSW, Domestic Violence Resource Centre Victoria and WESNET. *ReCharge: Women's Technology Safety, Legal Resources, Research & Training.* 2015, 17. http://www.smartsafe.org.au/sites/default/files/National-study-findings-2015.pdf

16 Inman Grant, J. 'Australia's Approach to Keeping its Citizens Safer Online – The Risks, Challenges & Opportunities.' Speech, Barton, ACT, October 3, 2018.

17 The Senate Legal and Constitutional Affairs References Committee. *Adequacy of Existing Offences in the Commonwealth Criminal Code and of State and Territory Criminal Laws to Capture Cyberbullying.* March 2018, 38.

18 Perrin, W. 'Detoxifying Social Media Would Be Easier Than You Might Think.' *The Guardian,* May 21, 2018. https://amp.theguardian.com/commentisfree/2018/may/21/detoxifying-social-media-online-misogyny?__twitter_impression=true

19 Rainie, L, Anderson J and Albright, J. *The Future of Free Speech, Trolls, Anonymity and Fake News Online.* Pew Research Center, March 2017, 4-6, 17-19, 68-70, 76. http://assets.pewresearch.org/wp-content/uploads/sites/14/2017/03/28162208/PI_2017.03.29_Social-Climate_FINAL.pdf

11. Champions of free speech controlling the message

1 Twitter. 'We're Dedicated to Making Twitter a Safe Place for Free Expression.' https://about.twitter.com/en_us/safety.html

2 Amnesty International. 'Chapter 7 – Human Rights Responsibilities' in *Toxic Twitter – Women's Experiences of Violence and Abuse on Twitter.* https://www.amnesty.org/en/latest/research/2018/03/online-violence-against-women-chapter-7/#topanchor

3 Office of the eSafety Commissioner. 'Legislation.' https://www.esafety.gov.au/about-the-office/legislation

4 Inman Grant, J. 'We Must All Step Up to Support Young Australians to Combat Cyberbullying (And Seek Help).' *Office of the eSafety Commissioner* blog, March 1, 2018. https://www.esafety.gov.au/about-the-office/newsroom/blog/we-must-all-step-up-to-support-young-australians-to-combat-cyberbullying

5 Statista. 'Number of Monthly Active Facebook Users Worldwide as of 3rd Quarter 2018 (In Millions). https://www.statista.com/statistics/264810/number-of-monthly-active-facebook-users-worldwide/Statista. 'Number of Monthly Active Twitter Users Worldwide from 1st Quarter 2010 to 3rd Quarter 2018 (In Millions). https://www.statista.com/statistics/282087/number-of-monthly-active-twitter-users/

6 Facebook. *Submission to The Senate Legal and Constitutional Affairs Committee: Inquiry into the Adequacy of Existing Offences in the Commonwealth Criminal Code and of State and Territory Criminal Laws to Capture Cyberbullying.* October 18, 2017. https://www.aph.gov.au/Parliamentary_Business/ Committees/Senate/Legal_and_Constitutional_Affairs/Cyberbullying/ Submissions

7 Brown, T. 'Social Media and Online Platforms as Publishers.' House of Lords Library, January 8, 2018. https://researchbriefings.parliament.uk/ ResearchBriefing/Summary/LLN-2018-0003#fullreport
Australian Press Council. *Submission to the ACCC Digital Platforms Inquiry.* April 2018. https://www.accc.gov.au/system/files/Australian%20Press%20 Council%20%28April%202018%29.pdf

8 Bell, E. 'Technology Company? Publisher? The Lines Can No Longer Be Blurred.' *The Guardian*, April 2, 2017. https://www.theguardian.com/media/ 2017/apr/02/facebook-google-youtube-inappropriate-advertising-fake-news

9 Newman, N. *Overview and Key Findings of the 2017 Report.* http://www. digitalnewsreport.org/survey/2017/overview-key-findings-2017/

10 Wikipedia. 'Section 230 of the Communications Decency Act.' https:// en.wikipedia.org/wiki/Section_230_of_the_Communications_Decency_Act

11 Tiku, N. 'How a Controversial New Sex-Trafficking Law Will Change the Web.' Wired, March 22, 2018. https://www.wired.com/story/how-a-controversial- new-sex-trafficking-law-will-change-the-web/

12 Tiku, N. 'How a Controversial New Sex-Trafficking Law Will Change the Web.' Wired, March 22, 2018. https://www.wired.com/story/how-a-controversial- new-sex-trafficking-law-will-change-the-web/

13 Lecher, C. 'Sen. Ron Wyden on Breaking Up Facebook, Net Neutrality, and the Law that Built the Internet.' The Verge, July 24, 2018. https://www.theverge. com/2018/7/24/17606974/oregon-senator-ron-wyden-interview-internet- section-230-net-neutrality

14 Hines, N. 'Cambridge Analytica's Dirty Tricks Elected Trump, CEO Claims.' The Daily Beast, March 20, 2018. https://www.thedailybeast.com/cambridge- analytica-bosses-we-secretly-made-ads-for-trump-and-well-never-be-caught
Auchard, E and Ingram, D. 'Cambridge Analytica CEO Claims Influence on U.S. Election, Facebook Questioned.' *Reuters*, March 21, 2018. https://www. reuters.com/article/us-facebook-cambridge-analytica/cambridge-analytica- ceo-claims-influenceon-u-s-election-facebook-questioned-idUSKBN1GW1SG
Cadwalladr, C and Graham-Harrison, E. 'Revealed: 50 Million Facebook Profiles Harvested for Cambridge Analytica in Major Data Breach.' *The Guardian*, March 18, 2018. https://www.theguardian.com/news/2018/mar/17/ cambridge-analytica-facebook-influence-us-election

15 Facebook. 'CONTENT ITEMS SHARED: 4.75 BILLION, average number of content items shared daily as of May 2013 up from 2.45 content items daily in August 2012,' May 18, 2013, https://www.facebook.com/facebook/photos/a.101 51908376636729/10151908376716729/?type=3

Twitter Support (@TwitterSupport) '500 million Tweets are sent every day! Learn how to search through all that content: https://support.twitter.com/articles/71577,' Twitter, January 13, 2015, 11:00 a.m., https://twitter.com/twittersupport/status/555076845293432834?lang=en

16 Wyden, R. 'Floor Remarks: CDA 230 and SESTA.' Medium, March 22, 2018. https://medium.com/@RonWyden/floor-remarks-cda-230-and-sesta-32355d669a6e

17 Lecher, C. 'Sen. Ron Wyden on Breaking Up Facebook, Net Neutrality, and the Law that Built the Internet.' The Verge, July 24, 2018. https://www.theverge.com/2018/7/24/17606974/oregon-senator-ron-wyden-interview-internet-section-230-net-neutrality

18 Lecher, C. 'Sen. Ron Wyden on Breaking Up Facebook, Net Neutrality, and the Law that Built the Internet.' The Verge, July 24, 2018. https://www.theverge.com/2018/7/24/17606974/oregon-senator-ron-wyden-interview-internet-section-230-net-neutrality

19 Wagner, K. 'Mark Zuckerberg Says He's "Fundamentally Uncomfortable" Making Content Decisions for Facebook.' Recode, March 22, 2018. https://www.recode.net/2018/3/22/17150772/mark-zuckerberg-facebookcontent-policy-guidelines-hate-free-speech

20 Statista. 'Most Popular Social Networks Worldwide as of October 201, Ranked by Number of Active Users (In Millions).' https://www.statista.com/statistics/272014/global-social-networks-ranked-by-number-of-users/

21 Skelly Belle (@literElly). 'when you just wanted to create a website that rates women as hot or not and degrades people on your college campus but you end up being grilled by the government years later about contributing to a worsening genocide in a foreign country and you can't handle it,' Twitter, April 10, 2018, 12:43 p.m., https://twitter.com/literElly/status/983792582508589056

22 Newton, C. 'It Took a Genocide for Facebook to Ban a Country's Military Leadership.' The Verge, August 28, 2018. https://www.theverge.com/2018/8/28/17789202/facebook-myanmar-ban-genocide-military-leadership

23 Wagner, K. 'Mark Zuckerberg Says He's "Fundamentally Uncomfortable" Making Content Decisions for Facebook.' Recode, March 22, 2018. https://www.recode.net/2018/3/22/17150772/mark-zuckerberg-facebookcontent-policy-guidelines-hate-free-speech

24 Associated Press. 'Zuckerberg on Refugee CrisisL "Hate Speech Has No Place on Facebook".' *The Guardian*, February 27, 2016. https://www.theguardian.com/technology/2016/feb/26/mark-zuckerberg-hate-speech-germany-facebook-refugee-crisis
Fiegerman, S, Rocha, V and Ries, B. 'Mark Zuckerberg Testifies Before European Parliament.' *CNN*, May 22, 2018. https://edition.cnn.com/europe/live-news/zuckerberg-testimony-european-parliament/index.html

25 Zuckerberg, M. 'Building Global Community.' Facebook, February 17, 2017. https://www.facebook.com/notes/mark-zuckerberg/building-globalcommunity/10154544292806634/

26 Inman Grant, J. 'Australia's Approach to Keeping its Citizens Safer Online – The Risks, Challenges & Opportunities.' Speech, Barton, ACT, October 3, 2018.

27 Rainie, L, Anderson J and Albright, J. *The Future of Free Speech, Trolls, Anonymity and Fake News Online.* Pew Research Center, March 2017, 11. http://assets.pewresearch.org/wp-content/uploads/sites/14/2017/03/28162208/PI_2017.03.29_Social-Climate_FINAL.pdf

28 Hinchliffe, E. 'Twitter's Jack Dorsey Promises Changes to Anti-Harassment Policies After #WomenBoycottTwitter.' Mashable Australia, October 15, 2017.https://mashable.com/2017/10/14/jack-dorsey-women-boycott-twitter/#Bn_5typ0nOqP

29 Facebook. *Submission to The Senate Legal and Constitutional Affairs Committee: Inquiry into the Adequacy of Existing Offences in the Commonwealth Criminal Code and of State and Territory Criminal Laws to Capture Cyberbullying.* October 18, 2017, 2–3. https://www.aph.gov.au/Parliamentary_Business/Committees/Senate/Legal_and_Constitutional_Affairs/Cyberbullying/Submissions

30 European Commission. 'Countering Illegal Hate Speech Online – Commission Initiative Shows Continued Improvement, Further Platforms Join.' January 19, 2018. http://europa.eu/rapid/press-release_IP-18-261_en.htm

31 Rohleder, B. 'Germany Set Out to Delete Hate Speech Online. Instead, It Made Things Worse.' *The Washington Post*, February 20, 2018. https://www.washingtonpost.com/news/theworldpost/wp/2018/02/20/netzdg/?noredirect=on&utm_term=.e3547a425d0a

32 Gadde, V. Twitter to Amnesty International. February 14, 2018. https://amnesty.app.box.com/s/0qnmsbzek0uj9jlz65zzjdmpodffdbcj

33 Amnesty International. 'Chapter 4 – The Reporting Process' in *Toxic Twitter – Women's Experiences of Violence and Abuse on Twitter.* https://www.amnesty.org/en/latest/research/2018/03/online-violence-against-women-chapter-4/#topanchor

34 Garlick, M. 'Facebook Submission to the Senate Constitutional and Legal Affairs References Committee', Appendix A, 6 March 2017 [sic], 3.

35 Rosen, G. 'Facebook Publishes Enforcement Numbers for the First Time.' Facebook Newsroom, May 15, 2018. https://newsroom.fb.com/news/2018/05/enforcement-numbers/

36 Picchi, A. 'Fake News: Twitter Still Flooded with Sham Accounts. *CBS News*, October 4, 2018. https://www.cbsnews.com/news/fake-news-twitter-still-flooded-with-sham-accounts/

37 Davis, A. 'Protecting People from Bullying and Harassment.' Facebook Newsroom, October 2, 2018. https://newsroom.fb.com/news/2018/10/protecting-people-from-bullying/

38 Schultz, A and Rosen, G. *Understanding the Facebook Community Standards Enforcement Report Q4 2017 – Q1 2018.* https://fbnewsroomus.files.wordpress.com/2018/05/understanding_the_community_standards_enforcement_report.pdf

39 Wray, D. 'The Companies Cleaning the Deepest, Darkest Parts of Social Media.' Vice, June 27, 2018. https://www.vice.com/en_us/article/ywe7gb/the-companies-cleaning-the-deepest-darkest-parts-of-social-media

40 Gorman, G. 'Life with an Imperforated Anus: "You Hate Your Body, You hate Yourself"'. News.com.au, February 18, 2017. https://www.news.com.au/lifestyle/health/health-problems/life-with-an-imperforated-anus-you-hate-your-body-you-hate-yourself/news-story/aeb09330209024ee858fc8601e2ab4ee

41 Silver, E. 'Hard Questions: Who Reviews Objectionable Content on Facebook – And Is the Company Doing Enough to Support Them.' Facebook Newsroom, July 26, 2018. https://newsroom.fb.com/news/2018/07/hard-questions-content-reviewers/

42 The Senate Legal and Constitutional Affairs References Committee. 'Recommendations' in *Adequacy of Existing Offences in the Commonwealth Criminal Code and of State and Territory Criminal Laws to Capture Cyberbullying*. March 2018. https://www.aph.gov.au/Parliamentary_Business/Committees/Senate/Legal_and_Constitutional_Affairs/Cyberbullying/Report/b01

43 'White House Drafts Order to Investigate Social Media Platforms.' *Financial, Review*, September 22, 2018. https://www.afr.com/news/politics/world/white-house-drafts-order-to-investigate-social-media-platforms-20180922-h15q67

44 Amnesty International. 'Chapter 1 – A Toxic Place for Women' in *Toxic Twitter – Women's Experiences of Violence and Abuse on Twitter*. https://www.amnesty.org/en/latest/research/2018/03/online-violence-against-women-chapter-1/

45 Picchi, A. 'Fake News: Twitter Still Flooded with Sham Accounts. *CBS News*, October 4, 2018. https://www.cbsnews.com/news/fake-news-twitter-still-flooded-with-sham-accounts/

46 Amnesty International. 'Chapter 7 – Human Rights Responsibilities' in *Toxic Twitter – Women's Experiences of Violence and Abuse on Twitter*. https://www.amnesty.org/en/latest/research/2018/03/online-violence-against-women-chapter-7/#topanchor

47 Amnesty International. 'Chapter 4 – The Reporting Process' in *Toxic Twitter – Women's Experiences of Violence and Abuse on Twitter*. https://www.amnesty.org/en/latest/research/2018/03/online-violence-againstwomen-chapter-4/#topanchor

48 Amnesty International. 'Chapter 7 – Human Rights Responsibilities' in *Toxic Twitter – Women's Experiences of Violence and Abuse on Twitter*. https://www.amnesty.org/en/latest/research/2018/03/online-violence-against-women-chapter-7/#topanchor

49 Inman Grant, J. 'Australia's Approach to Keeping its Citizens Safer Online – The Risks, Challenges & Opportunities.' Speech, Barton, ACT, October 3, 2018.

Notes in the margins: White women are cancer

1 Murphy, L. 'The Curious Case of the Jihadist who Started Out as a Hacktivist.' *Vanity Fair*, December 15, 2015. https://www.vanityfair.com/news/2015/12/isis-hacker-junaid-hussain

2 Manning, C. 'The Years Since I was Jailed for Releasing the "War Diaries" Have Been a Rollercoaster.' *The Guardian*, May 28, 2015. https://www.theguardian. com/commentisfree/2015/may/27/anniversary-chelsea-manning-arrest-war-diaries

3 Abramson, S. 'Listen Up, Progressives: Here's How to Deal with a 4Chan ("Alt-Right") Troll.' Medium, May 3, 2017. https://medium.com/@Seth_Abramson/ listen-up-progressives-heres-how-to-deal-with-a-4chan-alt-right-troll-48594f59a303

4 Raincoaster. 'Adrian Lamo, Hacker, Dead at 37.' The Crytosphere, March 16, 2018. https://thecryptosphere.com/2018/03/16/adrian-lamo-famed-hacker-is-dead/

PART 3: Troll hunting

12. Hunting a terrorist troll

1 Bornstein, J. 'White Supremacists Stole My Identity to Spew Hatred on the Times of Israel.' *The Guardian*, May 6, 2015. https://www.theguardian.com/ world/2015/may/05/identity-stolen-white-supremacists-times-of-israel

2 Bornstein, J. 'White Supremacists Stole My Identity to Spew Hatred on the Times of Israel.' *The Guardian*, May 6, 2015. https://www.theguardian.com/ world/2015/may/05/identity-stolen-white-supremacists-times-of-israel

3 Moon Metropolis (@MoonMetropolis). '@ASankin Did you see this demented Times of Israel blog post before it got taken down? https:// archive.today/6pzYT,' Twitter, April 9, 2015, 7:21 a.m. https://twitter.com/ MoonMetropolis/status/586171994950901760

4 Potaka, E and McMahon, L. 'FBI Says "Australian IS Jihadist" is Actually a Jewish American Troll Named Joshua Ryne Goldberg.' *The Sydney Morning Herald*, September 12, 2015. https://www.smh.com.au/national/australian-is-jihadist-is-actually-an-jewish-american-troll-20150911-gjk852.html

5 'Melbourne Man Posts Islamic State Guide.' *SBS News*, May 5, 2015. https:// www.sbs.com.au/news/melbourne-man-posts-islamic-state-guide

6 This Twitter user was a woman called Sylvia Posadas using the handle @Jinjirrie.

7 'United States District Court Criminal Complaint against Joshua Ryne Goldberg.' September 10, 2015. https://www.justice.gov/opa/file/769556/download

8 Citron, D. *Hate Crimes in Cyberspace*. Cambridge, Massachusetts: Harvard University Press, 2014, 26–27.

9 Franceschi-Bicchierai, L. 'Here are 14 Facebook and Instagram Ads that Russian Trolls Bought to Divide Americans.' Motherboard, November 2, 2017. https:// motherboard.vice.com/en_us/article/a377ej/facebook-instagram-russian-ads

10 Bessi, A and Ferrara, E. 'Social Bots Distort the 2016 U.S. Presidential Election Online Discussion.' *First Monday* 21, no. 11 (2016). http://firstmonday.org/ojs/ index.php/fm/article/view/7090/5653
Rainie, L, Anderson, J and Albright, J. 'The Future of Free Speech, Trolls, Anonymity and Fake News Online.' Pew Research Center Internet & Technology,

March 29, 2017. http://www.pewinternet.org/2017/03/29/the-future-of-free-speech-trolls-anonymity-and-fake-news-online/
Assessing Russian Activities and Intentions in Recent US Elections. January 2017. https://www.dni.gov/files/documents/ICA_2017_01.pdf

11 *Assessing Russian Activities and Intentions in Recent US Elections*. January 2017. https://www.dni.gov/files/documents/ICA_2017_01.pdf

12 Leathern, R and Rodgers, E. 'A New Level of Transperency for Ads and Pages.' Facebook Newsroom, June 28, 2018. https://newsroom.fb.com/news/2018/06/transparency-for-ads-and-pages/

13 Roth, Y and Harvey, D. ' How Twitter is Fighting Span and Malicious Automation.' Twitter blog, June 26, 2018. https://blog.twitter.com/official/en_us/topics/company/2018/how-twitter-is-fighting-spam-and-malicious-automation.html

14 Picchi, A. 'Fake News: Twitter Still Flooded with Sham Accounts. *CBS News*, October 4, 2018. https://www.cbsnews.com/news/fake-news-twitter-still-flooded-with-sham-accounts/

15 Rainie, L, Anderson, J and Albright, J. 'The Future of Free Speech, Trolls, Anonymity and Fake News Online.' Pew Research Center Internet & Technology, March 29, 2017. http://www.pewinternet.org/2017/03/29/the-future-of-free-speech-trolls-anonymity-and-fake-news-online/

16 O'Brien, L. 'The Making of an American Nazi.' *The Atlantic*, December 2017. https://www.theatlantic.com/magazine/archive/2017/12/the-making-of-an-american-nazi/544119/

17 Evidence of weev being connected to NAQDI is in this thread: '/pol/ - Politically Incorrect.' May 8, 2015. http://archive.is/jAHIP

18 Wood, M. 'Cop Shares Gunfight Lessons from ISIS-Inspired "Draw the Prophet" Terrorist Attack.' PoliceOne.com, September 16, 2017. https://www.policeone.com/active-shooter/articles/419451006-Cop-sharesgunfight-lessons-from-ISIS-inspired-Draw-the-Prophet-terrorist-attack/

19 SWT is also short for an Arabic phrase used to glorify God.

20 The United States Department of Justice. 'Florida Man Sentenced to 10 Years in Federal Prison on Bomb Charge.' June 25, 2018. https://www.justice.gov/opa/pr/florida-man-sentenced-10-years-federal-prison-bomb-charge

21 Potaka, E and McMahon, L. 'FBI Says "Australian IS Jihadist" is Actually a Jewish American Troll Named Joshua Ryne Goldberg.' *The Sydney Morning Herald*, September 12, 2015. https://www.smh.com.au/national/australian-is-jihadist-is-actually-an-jewish-american-troll-20150911-gjk852.html

22 Potaka, E and McMahon, L. 'FBI Says "Australian IS Jihadist" is Actually a Jewish American Troll Named Joshua Ryne Goldberg.' *The Sydney Morning Herald*, September 12, 2015. https://www.smh.com.au/national/australian-is-jihadist-is-actually-an-jewish-american-troll-20150911-gjk852.html

23 'United States District Court Criminal Complaint against Joshua Ryne Goldberg.' September 10, 2015, 31–33. https://www.justice.gov/opa/file/769556/download

24 The United States Department of Justice. 'Florida Man Sentenced to 10 Years in Federal Prison on Bomb Charge.' June 25, 2018. https://www.justice.gov/opa/pr/florida-man-sentenced-10-years-federal-prison-bomb-charge

25 'Golberg Gets 10 years.' YouTube Video, 2:43, posted by 'WJXT – News4Jax,' June 25, 2018. https://www.youtube.com/watch?v=MX0JMa5yP8Y

13. The internet was my parent

1 Turnbull, M. 'Remarks at the Safer Internet Day Event.' Speech, Parliament House, Canberra, ACT, 6 February 2018

2 United States of America v. Joshua Ryne Goldberg, Case no. 3:17-cr-249-BJD-JRK, 27 https://extremism.gwu.edu/sites/g/files/zaxdzs2191/f/Goldberg DefendantsSentencingMemorandum.pdf

3 Leigh, H. 'Man Accused in Terror Plot Found Not Competent.' News4Jax, December 14, 2015. https://www.news4jax.com/news/competency-hearing-for-man-accused-in-bomb-plot

4 Shorstein, P. 'Defendants Sentencing Memorandum, United States of America v. Joshua Ryne Goldberg.' 3, 14–15. https://extremism.gwu.edu/sites/g/files/zaxdzs2191/f/GoldbergDefendantsSentencingMemorandum.pdf

5 Shorstein, P. 'Defendants Sentencing Memorandum, United States of America v. Joshua Ryne Goldberg.' 6–7, 12. https://extremism.gwu.edu/sites/g/files/zaxdzs2191/f/GoldbergDefendantsSentencingMemorandum.pdf

6 Shorstein, P. 'Defendants Sentencing Memorandum, United States of America v. Joshua Ryne Goldberg.' 8, 20, 27. https://extremism.gwu.edu/sites/g/files/zaxdzs2191/f/GoldbergDefendantsSentencingMemorandum.pdf

7 Shorstein, P. 'Defendants Sentencing Memorandum, United States of America v. Joshua Ryne Goldberg.' 24, 25. https://extremism.gwu.edu/sites/g/files/zaxdzs2191/f/GoldbergDefendantsSentencingMemorandum.pdf

8 Autor, D and Wasserman, M. *Wayward Sons: The Emerging Gender Gap in Labor Markets and Education.* http://economics.mit.edu/files/8754 Peterson, J. 'Boys are Being Set Up to Fail.' *The Australian*, February 3, 2018. https://www.theaustralian.com.au/news/inquirer/decline-in-men-atuniversities-bad-for-both-sexes/news-story/eccc91aeb9d772c874feac873b7b4493

9 'Jordan Peterson: The War on Masculinity.' YouTube Video, 5:25, posted by 'Essential Truth', March 11, 2018. https://www.youtube.com/watch?v=kn1q6GRnxx0

10 Gadher, D. 'British Hacker is No 3 on Pentagon "kill list".' *The Times*, August 2, 2015. https://www.thetimes.co.uk/article/british-hacker-is-no-3-on-pentagon-kill-list-6g95bfqwfnz

11 De Freytas-Tamura, K. 'Junaid Hussain, ISIS Recruiter, Reported Killed in Airstrike.' *The New York Times*, August 27, 2015. https://www.nytimes.com/2015/08/28/world/middleeast/junaid-hussain-islamic-state-recruiter-killed.html

12 Murphy, L. ' The Curious Case of the Jihadist who Started Out as a Hacktivist.' *Vanity Fair*, December 15, 2015. https://www.vanityfair.com/news/2015/12/isis-hacker-junaid-hussain

13 Wikipedia. 'weev.' https://en.wikipedia.org/wiki/Weev

14. White men at the centre

1 O'Connor, B. 'Internet Trolls Vandalize Hillary and Bill Clinton's Wikipedia Pages in Extremely NSFW Way.' The Slot, October 13, 2016. https://theslot.jezebel.com/hillary-and-bill-clintons-pages-subject-toex-1787755920

2 Know Your Meme. 'Cuck.' https://knowyourmeme.com/memes/cuck

3 Phillips, W. *This Is Why We Can't Have Nice Things: Mapping the Relationship between Online Trolling and Mainstream Culture*. Cambridge, Massachusetts: The MIT Press, 2015, 5, 8, 39.

4 Watson, P. 'Shameless Looters Display Stolen Goods on Twitter.' October 31, 2012, https://web.archive.org/web/20130808235626/http://www.infowars.com/shameless-looters-display-stolen-goods-on-twitter/

5 Shergold, A. '"Even momma got outta house to loot new shirt": Looters brag on Twitter.' *Daily Mail Australia*, November 1, 2012. http://www.dailymail.co.uk/news/article-225663/Superstom-Sandy-lootersbrag-Twitter-Even-momma-got-outta-house-loot-new-shirt.html

6 Dillon, K. 'Less Looting, More Trolling: Daily Mail, Drudge Get Pwnd By Twitter Pranksters #SandyLootCrew.' *Observer*, November 2, 2012. http://observer.com/2012/11/less-looting-more-trolling-daily-mail-drudge-get-pwnd-by-twitter-pranksters/

7 Phillips, W. *This Is Why We Can't Have Nice Things: Mapping the Relationship between Online Trolling and Mainstream Culture*. Cambridge, Massachusetts: The MIT Press, 2015, 5, 8, 39.

8 Morris, K. 'Trolling Twitter to Expose The Media's Racial Biases.' The Daily Dot, November 6, 2012. https://www.dailydot.com/news/trolling-fake-hurricane-sandy-looting-tweets-media/

9 Phillips, W. *This Is Why We Can't Have Nice Things: Mapping the Relationship between Online Trolling and Mainstream Culture*. Cambridge, Massachusetts: The MIT Press, 2015, 5–6.

10 http://stoptonymeow.com

11 Back, A. 'Stopping "Stop Tony Meow": How Web Plug-In Caught the Department of Prime Minister's Attention.' *The Sydney Morning Herald*, April 22, 2014. http://www.smh.com.au/federal-politics/political-news/stopping-stop-tony-meow-how-web-plugin-caught-the-department-of-prime-ministers-attention-20140422-zqxuu.html

12 Terrorism Research & Analysis Consortium. 'Gay Nigger Association of America (GNAA). https://www.trackingterrorism.org/group/gay-nigger-association-america-gnaa

13 Eordogh, F. 'Whither the Old Anonymous? "Hackers" Rustle League Want to Be the Andy Kaufman of Trolling.' Motherboard, February 23, 2013. https://motherboard.vice.com/en_us/article/mggnbq/rustle-league-a-hackergroup-that-would-troll-anonymous

14 Skinner, A. 'The Slippery Slope of Dehumanizing Language.' The Conversation, June 4, 2018. https://theconversation.com/the-slippery-slope-of-dehumanizing-language-97512

15 '2018 JG Crawford Oration: Vinton G. Cerf, The Future of the Internet.'
    YouTube Video, 46:50, posted by 'ANU TV', June 26, 2018. https://www.
    youtube.com/watch?v=huUDdOpeYe8

16 Chandler, D. 'Technological or Media Determinism.' http://visual-memory.
    co.uk/daniel/Documents/tecdet/tdet08.html

17 David L. 'Online Disinhibition Effect (Suler).' *Learning Theories*, December 15,
    2015. https://www.learning-theories.com/online-disinhibition-effect-suler.html.

18 Whitney Phillips makes a similar point here: Morrison, P. 'Privilege Makes
    Them Do It – What a Study of Internet Trolls Reveals.' *Los Angeles Times*,
    July 1, 2015. http://www.latimes.com/opinion/op-ed/la-oe-morrison-phillips-
    20150701-column.html

19 Eordogh, F. 'Whither the Old Anonymous? "Hackers" Rustle League Want to
    Be the Andy Kaufman of Trolling.' Motherboard, February 23, 2013. https://
    motherboard.vice.com/en_us/article/mggnbq/rustle-league-a-hackergroup-
    that-would-troll-anonymous

20 Basko, S. 'Rustle League Attack.' Subliminal Ridge blog, Last updated
    February 24, 2013. http://subliminalridge.blogspot.com.au/2013/01/rustle-
    league-attack.html

21 Basko, S. 'Rustle League, Encyclopedia Dramatica, and Doxbin – their
    attacks against me, in a nutshell.' Subliminal Ridge blog, March, 2014. http://
    subliminalridge.blogspot.com.au/2014/03/rustle-league-doxbin-and-
    encyclopedia.html

22 'Trolls.' SBS. https://www.sbs.com.au/news/insight/tvepisode/trolls

23 Jaime Cochran: Memorial of a Psychedelic Hackress. Facebook page. https://
    www.facebook.com/events/2059984010901480

24 Amnesty International. 'Chapter 2 – Triggers of Violence and Abuse Against
    Women on Twitter' in *Toxic Twitter – Women's Experiences of Violence and
    Abuse on Twitter*. https://www.amnesty.org/en/latest/research/2018/03/online-
    violence-against-women-chapter-2/#topanchor

25 Squirrell, T. 'Opinion: Reddit's Advertising Strategies Still Hide Hate Speech.'
    Quartz, April 6, 2018. https://qz.com/1246087/opinion-reddits-advertising-
    strategies-still-hide-hatespeech/

26 'Made Me Say It!' 2013. https://www.reddit.com/r/WTF/comments/1t66sq/
    made_me_say_it/

27 Young, M. 'Carly Findlay Suffers Skin Condition, Wins Internet After Copping
    Abuse on Internet Site Reddit.' News.com.au, December 20, 2013. https://www.
    news.com.au/technology/online/carly-findlay-suffers-skin-condition-wins-
    internet-after-copping-abuse-on-internet-site-reddit/news-story/062a7d78b19
    7eacebfa2d38fef2bd041

28 Murphy, L. 'Media and Speaking.' https://raincoastermedia.com/media-and-
    public-speaking/
    Please note this was the link to the original article but most of the content is no
    longer live: Murphy, L. 'How Anonymous Helped Prevent a Teen's Suicide.' The
    Daily Dot, November 15, 2012. https://www.dailydot.com/news/anonymous-
    kylie-suicide-trollsbully/

29 The LODE RADIO HOUR is Creating Radio Shows Patreon page. https://www.patreon.com/l0de

30 PEN America. 'PEN America Position Statement: Online Harassment and Free Expression.' https://onlineharassmentfieldmanual.pen.org/about-this-field-manual/

31 Slay, M. 'Moslem Whore Mariam Veiszadeh Gets a Woman Arrested for Hurting Her Feelings Online – Stormer Troll Army, You Know What Must Be Done.' The Daily Stormer blog, February 20, 2015. https://archive.is/O4X4d#selection-571.0-571.29

32 Stephens, K. 'Ipswich Woman Charged Over Muslim Hate Attacks Online.' *Brisbane Times*, February 18, 2015. https://www.brisbanetimes.com.au/national/queensland/ipswich-woman-charged-over-muslim-hate-attacks-online-20150217-13hamf.html

33 Potaka, E and McMahon, L. 'Unmasking a Troll: Aussie "Jihadist" Australi Witness a 20-Year-Old American Nerd.' *The Sydney Morning Herald*, September 12, 2015. https://www.smh.com.au/national/unmasking-a-troll-aussie-jihadist-australiwitness-a-20yearold-american-nerd-20150909-gjil47.html
McMahon, L. 'Revealing the Secrets of One of Australia's Worst Online Trolls.' *The Sydney Morning Herald*, April 16, 2017/ https://www.smh.com.au/national/revealing-the-secrets-of-one-of-australias-worst-online-trolls-20170413-gvklv8.html

34 Phillips, W. *This Is Why We Can't Have Nice Things: Mapping the Relationship between Online Trolling and Mainstream Culture.* Cambridge, Massachusetts: The MIT Press, 2015, 133.

35 Solon, O. 'George Soros: Facebook and Google a Menace to Society.' *The Guardian*, January 26, 2018. https://www.theguardian.com/business/2018/jan/25/george-soros-facebook-and-google-are-a-menace-to-society#top

36 Conger, K. 'Harassment of Ghostbusters' Leslie Jones Shows Twitter Needs to Change.' Tech Crunch, July 19, 2016. https://techcrunch.com/2016/07/19/leslie-jones-twitter-harassment/

15. A professional racist

 1 Pasternack, A. 'No More Lulz: Should Weev, the World's Most Notorius Troll, Go to Jail for "Hacking"?' Motherboard, November 22, 2012. https://motherboard.vice.com/en_us/article/vvvvqa/no-more-lulz-shouldweev-the-world-s-most-notorious-troll-go-to-jail-for-hacking

 2 Schwartz, M. 'The Trolls Among Us.' *The New York Times Magazine*, August 3, 2008. http://www.nytimes.com/2008/08/03/magazine/03trolls-t.html?pagewanted=all

 3 Chen, A. 'The Internet's Best Terrible Person Goes to Jail: Can a Reviled Master Troll Become a Geek Hero?' Gawker blog, November 27, 2012. http://gawker.com/5962159/the-internets-best-terrible-person-goes-to-jailcan-a-reviled-master-troll-become-a-geek-hero

4 Chen, A. '"The Best Fucking Thing That Could Possibly Happen": Hacker Convict Weev Bids Farewell to Freedom.' Gawker blog, March 22, 2013. http://gawker.com/5991737/the-best-fucking-thing-that-could-possibly-happen-hacker-convict-weev-bids-farewell-to-freedom

5 Please note the website http://freeweev.info/, where this quote came from, is no longer live.
Pasternack, A. 'No More Lulz: Should Weev, the World's Most Notorious Troll, Go to Jail for "Hacking"?' Motherboard, November 22, 2012. https://motherboard.vice.com/en_us/article/vvvvqa/no-more-lulz-shouldweev-the-world-s-most-notorious-troll-go-to-jail-for-hacking

6 Sandoval, G. 'The End of Kindness: Weev and the Cult of The Angry Young Man.' The Verge, September 12, 2013. https://www.theverge.com/2013/9/12/4693710/the-end-of-kindness-weev-and-the-cult-of-the-angry-young-man

7 Ralle, D. '"weev" in Beirut: I Can't Go Home Until "Most of the Agents of the Federal Government are Dead."' Pando, November 21, 2014. https://pando.com/2014/11/21/troll-tales-catching-up-with-weev-in-beirut/

8 Southern Poverty Law Center. 'Andrew "Weev" Auernheimer.' https://www.splcenter.org/fighting-hate/extremist-files/individual/andrewweev-auernheimer

9 Chen, A. 'The Internet's Best Terrible Person Goes to Jail: Can a Reviled Master Troll Become a Geek Hero?' Gawker blog, November 27, 2012. http://gawker.com/5962159/the-internets-best-terrible-person-goes-to-jailcan-a-reviled-master-troll-become-a-geek-hero

10 'Race Ghost Roast to Roast 5 – Feel Good Hit of the Yuletide | Weev Podcast.' YouTube Video, 1:18:25, posted on December 21, 2017. https://www.youtube.com/watch?v=pq3Iy05iYAw

11 Auernheimer, A. 'Dear White People.' January 7, 2018. http://archive.is/zCofS

12 Hayden, ME. 'Neo-Nazi Who Calls for "Slaughter" of Jewish Children is of Jewish Descent, His Mom Says.' Newsweek, January 3, 2018. http://www.newsweek.com/neo-nazi-andrew-weev-auernheimer-dailystormer-jewish-descent-768805

13 Loomer, L (@LauraLoomer). '"Weev", the Admin for #DailyStormer & colleague of Nazis who rallied in #Charlottesville "I unequivocally support the killing of children,"' Twitter, August 16, 2017, 10:48 a.m., https://twitter.com/LauraLoomer/status/897877851839631360
Southern Poverty Law Center. 'Andrew "Weev" Auernheimer.' https://www.splcenter.org/fighting-hate/extremist-files/individual/andrewweev-auernheimer
https://www.splcenter.org/fighting-hate/extremist-files/individual/andrew-weev-auernheimer

14 Hayden, ME. 'Neo-Nazi Who Calls for "Slaughter" of Jewish Children is of Jewish Descent, His Mom Says.' Newsweek, January 3, 2018. http://www.newsweek.com/neo-nazi-andrew-weev-auernheimer-dailystormer-jewish-descent-768805

15 English Oxford Living Dictionaries. 'Shill.' https://en.oxforddictionaries.com/definition/shill

16 Cornell Law School. '18 U.S. Code § 875 – Interstate Communications.' https://www.law.cornell.edu/uscode/text/18/875

17 Cornell Law School. '47 U.S. Code § 230 – Protection for Private Blocking and Screening of Offensive Material.' https://www.law.cornell.edu/uscode/text/47/230

18 Wikipedia. 'Fighting Words.' https://en.wikipedia.org/wiki/Fighting_words

19 'Azzmador'. 'Charlottesville: Why You Must Attend and What to Bring and Not to Bring!' August 8, 2017. http://archive.is/Xuj6L#selection-411.0-411.9

20 Hauser, C. 'GoDaddy Severs Ties With Daily Stormer After Charlottesville Article.' *The New York Times*, August 14, 2017.https://www.nytimes.com/2017/08/14/us/godaddy-daily-stormer-whites-upremacists.html

21 Worley, W. 'Neo-Nazi Website Asks Readers to Target Funeral of Heather Heyer who Died in Charlottesville Violence.' *The Independent*, August 16, 2017. https://www.independent.co.uk/news/world/americas/america-top-neonazi-website-daily-stormer-orders-followers-harass-funeral-heather-heyervictim-a7895496.html

23 Loomer, L (@LauraLoomer). 'Screenshot of deleted tweet from #DailyStormer's System admin "Weev" who said he's sending Nazis to protest #HeatherHeyer funeral today,' Twitter, August 16, 2017, 9:16 a.m. https://twitter.com/LauraLoomer/status/897854499536211969

24 Hayden, ME (@MichaelEHayden). 'Not to be lost in this is just how violent weev's rhetoric about Jews has really become. He's explicitly calling for terrorism against children: http://www.newsweek.com/neo-nazi-andrew-weev-auernheimer-daily-stormer-jewish-descent-768805 ...' Twitter, January 3, 2018, 8:16 a.m. https://twitter.com/MichaelEHayden/status/948588788174946304

25 'Insight, Trolls.' https://www.sbs.com.au/news/sites/sbs.com.au.news/files/transcripts/363601_insight_trolls_transcript.html

26 Dawson, C and Thornely, J. *Air Kiss and Tell*. Australia: Allen & Unwin, 2012.

27 'Charlotte Dawson Speaks Out.' YouTube Video, 3:22, posted by 'Sunriseon7,' September 2012. https://www.youtube.com/watch?v=nrwnBGsyX8o

28 Penny, L. 'Who Does She Think She Is?' Longreads, March 2018. https://longreads.com/2018/03/28/who-does-she-think-she-is/

29 Smith, T. 'Non-Profit Reacts to Richmond Schools' Budget Controversy.' *ABC8 News*, March 17, 2017. http://wric.com/2017/03/17/non-profit-reacts-to-richmond-schools-budget-controversy/

30 Auernheimer, A. 'My Presentence Report, Where My Mom Helps the Feds Attack Me Again.' March 9, 2013. https://weev.livejournal.com/405118.html

31 Email Correspondence with Alyse Auernheimer. https://marc.info/?l=full-disclosure&m=125472104014875

32 Email Correspondence with Alyse Auernheimer. https://marc.info/?l=full-disclosure&m=125472104014875

33 Kushner, D. 'We All Got Trolled.' Medium, July 22, 2014. https://medium.com/matter/the-martyrdom-of-weev-9e72da8a133d